To Toi

Fairest Picture

Mark Twain at Lake Tahoe

David C. Antonucci

Copyright © 2012
David C. Antonucci
Edition 1.01
All rights reserved.
ISBN 978-1463765699
Library of Congress Control Number: 2011913475
For additional copies: Your local bookstore or
www.CreateSpace.com/3654392

Cover image: Sam Clemens and John Kinney drift over submerged boulders offshore of Stateline Point; from original pastel "Balloon Voyage" by Jenny Antonucci

**Art of Learning Publishing
Lake Tahoe, California**

For Jenny and Dominic

As it lay there with the shadows of the mountains brilliantly photographed upon its still surface, I thought it must surely be the fairest picture the whole earth affords.

> Mark Twain's recollection of his first sighting of Lake Tahoe from the trail high above Crystal Bay, as recounted in *Roughing It*

Contents

Lake Tahoe and Mark Twain 1
Mark Twain's Lake Tahoe of 1861-65 3
Interpreting the Writings of Mark Twain 79
A Wood Ranch or So and Become Wealthy 89
Restored at Lake Bigler 142
Up Among the Clouds 151
I Measure All Lakes by Tahoe 163
In the Footsteps of Mark Twain 182
Debunking the Mark Twain-Lake Tahoe Myths 201
Epilogue – A Final Farewell 243
Selections from the Literature of Mark Twain 247
Lake Tahoe Campsites Sequence and Identification 268
Sources 277
About the Author 287
Index 290

Introduction

Lake Tahoe and Mark Twain

The setting for this book is Lake Tahoe and the surrounding region. We see it through this book's central character, Mark Twain, and his unique viewpoint, influenced by his life and times in the West. We particularly focus on his personal experiences in and around Lake Tahoe. We see how they helped transform the man who would one day become one of America's greatest authors and humorists.

Fans of Lake Tahoe and Mark Twain will find this book adds new dimension and previously little-known information about both. For the first time, all of the known Mark Twain travels and experiences at Lake Tahoe appear in detail in one book. Of course, it was during this period and in this area that Samuel L. Clemens became Mark Twain and launched his writing and literary career. This book will introduce you to the Lake Tahoe that Mark Twain knew during his nearly three years of residence in the region. We see how Lake Tahoe is different and, in many ways, still the same as it was when Mark Twain prowled its shores. We learn about the first visits made by a young and opportunistic Sam Clemens and his struggle to establish a timber claim on the North Shore of Lake Tahoe. He returns less than two years later as Mark Twain, a popular news reporter for the Virginia City *Territorial Enterprise* and writes of his new experiences at lakeside resorts.

We follow Mark Twain's changing attitude about the name "Tahoe" and his view of the lake as a place of spiritual renewal, healthful restoration, and exceptional beauty, rivaled by no other lakes. For the first time, a comprehensive compendium of Mark Twain quotations about Lake Tahoe appears together with context and interpretation of his statements. This is counterbalanced by a thorough analysis and debunking of the Mark Twain-Lake Tahoe myths that have sprung up over the 150 years since his first visit.

Those interested in seeing and experiencing the same sites visited by Mark Twain will read about a number of locations described in this book together with directions on how to find them.

As you read this book, you will travel back in time. You will read about the same things that Mark Twain saw and experienced, and learn about the parallel history of Lake Tahoe during this period. Taken together, you will understand how Lake Tahoe influenced one of America's greatest writers and formed part of the foundation of his exceptional literary legacy.

For those only interested in Mark Twain's Lake Tahoe adventures, read Chapters 3 through 9. Mark Twain scholars will want to include Chapter 2 and Appendix II. If you are interested in some Lake Tahoe history in the time of Twain, also read Chapter 1. To get the full measure of Twain's Lake Tahoe writings, review Appendix I.

The author welcomes questions and comments about this book. Contact him at http://facebook.com/dcantonucci.

Chapter 1

Mark Twain's Lake Tahoe of 1861-65

The Lake Tahoe of today is not nearly the Lake Tahoe Samuel L. Clemens saw in 1861-65 or the Lake Tahoe Mark Twain would recall nostalgically in the early years of his literary career. What then, was Lake Tahoe like in those early days? How is Tahoe different, and yet still the same as when Clemens first laid eyes on it after emerging from the forest high above Crystal Bay?

On February 14, 1844, military explorer John Fremont and his Prussian-born cartographer, Henry Preuss, scrambled to the top of a distant mountain peak to take in the view. In a life-threatening predicament, they were in a desperate search for a clear path through the snowbound Sierra Nevada. Through a narrow fog-shrouded canyon, Fremont saw for the first time, *"a beautiful view of a mountain lake at our feet ..."* Back at camp, Fremont dutifully entered the event into his journal; he was the first Euro-American to record the sighting of Lake Tahoe.

Like many who came later, Fremont experienced the soothing beauty of Lake Tahoe and drew from it the emotional perseverance to confront the challenges ahead. In *Fremont: Explorations and Expeditions*, quoted in the Nevada Historical Society Papers of 1913-16, he recalled,

> For a long time we sat enjoying the view, for we had become fatigued with the mountains and the free expanse of moving waves was very grateful. It was like a gem in the mountains...

The two explorers saw a mountain paradise safely secluded from the outside world and in harmony with its Native American inhabitants. It was a pristine wilderness in the final days of its innocent splendor. A looming flood of land-seekers, miners, loggers, merchants and entrepreneurs would engulf Tahoe in a few short years, forever changing its environment and the lives of those who dwelled there.

In the early 1850s, Tahoe was just a rest stop on the trail to the California goldfields. Travelers were in a hurry to get to the Mother Lode and their dreams of unlimited opportunity. They had no time or economic incentive to linger in the spectacular beauty of the still unspoiled Tahoe Basin.

The discovery of silver in 1859 and the ensuing years of boom and bust in Virginia City, Nev., would seal the fate of Tahoe. The 1860s would be a time of jarring change that broke Tahoe out of its protective isolation. In the space of barely three decades, it descended from secluded mountain paradise to just another casualty of 19th century exploitation of the West.

Euro-American settlers would forcibly evict Native Americans from their long-established homelands and summering grounds. Its forests would fall to the woodsmen's ax. Multitudes of opportunity seekers would pass through on Gold Rush wagon roads and rest at a string of newly established way stations. Ranchers would seize the meadows to supply beef and dairy products. Water seekers would dam the outlet, capturing the free flowing waters for human uses. Commercial anglers would exploit and deplete abundant fisheries. Early hoteliers would cash in on the social, recreation, therapeutic values of the era by establishing luxury destination resorts and lodges.

In just a few decades after Fremont's sighting, the subjugation of Tahoe led to the exploitation of its rich and varied resources to support voracious mining activity and the larger development of the West. It was on the eve of this destruction in 1861 that a young and opportunistic Sam Clemens would amble into the Tahoe Basin and be inspired to write his emotive words celebrating the captivating beauty of the still pristine Lake Tahoe. Sadly, the depletion of the Tahoe forests, fisheries and wildlife, and the capture of its waters would be *fait accompli* by the dawn of the 20th century.

Lake Tahoe Basin Statistics and Facts

Maximum length	21.2 miles
Maximum width	11.9 miles
Maximum diagonal	21.8 miles
Shoreline perimeter	75.1 miles
Maximum depth	1,645 feet
Average depth	1,027 feet
Lake surface area	191 square miles
Tributary watershed area	312 square miles
Tributaries	63 streams
Volume	39,000,000,000,000 gallons
Annual recharge	212,000,000,000 gallons
Age	2,500,000-3,000,000 years
Water purity	99.994%

World lakes maximum depth rank 11th

World lakes volume rank 31st

World lakes size and elevation rank 2nd

World lakes oldest group rank 2nd

Another way to understand some of the basic characteristics of Lake Tahoe is to cast them in metaphorical terms. For maximum depth, consider that the bottom of the lake is still 107 feet below the elevation of Carson City, Nev.

Figure 1. A regional map shows the location of Lake Tahoe.

The volume of water stored in the lake could cover the entire state of California to a depth of 14½ inches. The total annual recharge of precipitation and runoff into the lake could provide annual water supply for a population of 5.8 million.

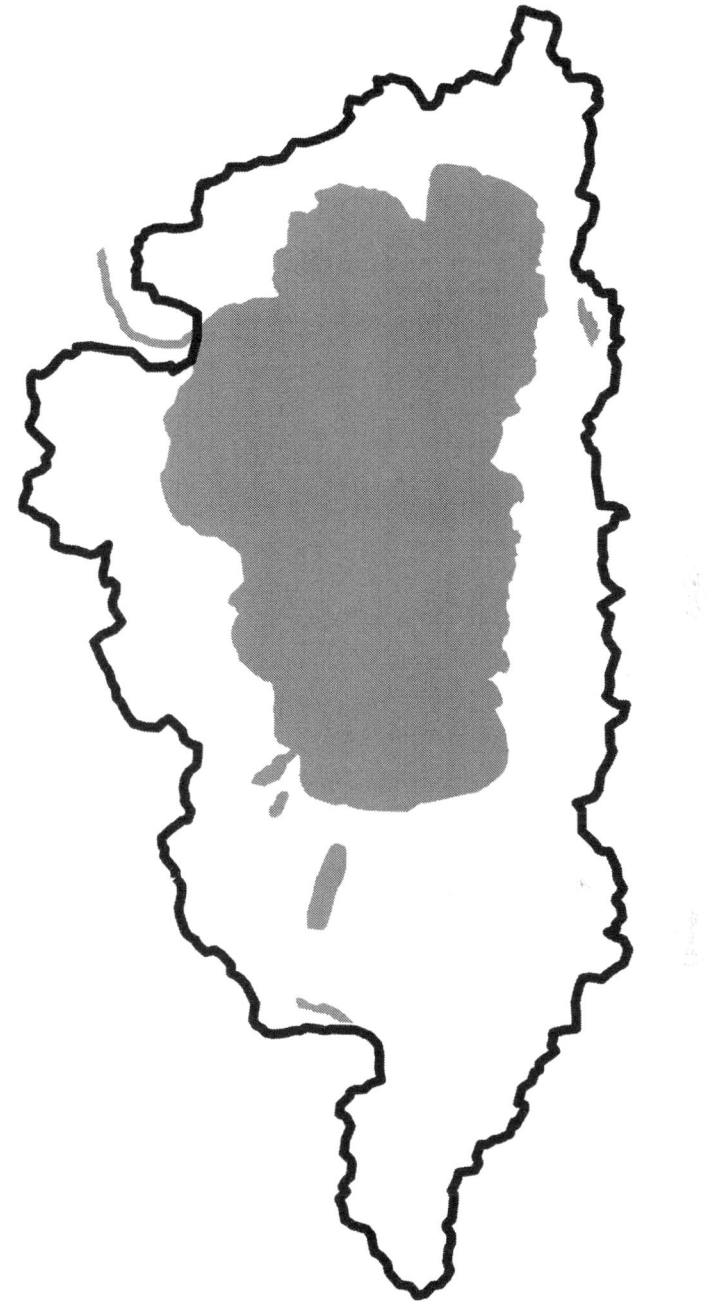

Figure 2. Lake Tahoe and its watershed boundary

The modern name of the lake, "Tahoe," is very likely derived from a mispronunciation of the first syllables Washoe Native American name for the lake, *da ow a ga*. In Chapter 4, "Mark Twain on Lake Tahoe," we explore in more depth the naming history and Twain's jaded view on the controversy.

Impressions of Early Visitors

In the wake of Fremont's 1844 brush with Lake Tahoe, a party of emigrants was ascending the Sierra Nevada from the Truckee River canyon. On November 14, 1844 and as a survival move, members of the Stephens-Townsend-Murphy Party split near the confluence of what are now Donner Creek and the Truckee River. A group of six horse-mounted pioneers followed the river to its source at Lake Tahoe and then over a pass on the West Shore to Sutter's Fort in the Sacramento Valley. The balance of the emigrant party camped briefly near a lake, later known as Donner Lake. They struggled westward over the pass beyond – a landmark that would ironically take its name from the Donner Party misfortune two years later. Eventually, all members of the Stephens-Townsend-Murphy Party would reunite safely at Sutter's Fort.

In a December 3, 1844 letter written by Angeline Morrison, one of the six in the equestrian party, she recounted the wonderment of their entry into the Lake Tahoe Basin on or about November 16, 1844. It was the first recorded visit to Lake Tahoe by Euro-Americans.

> *We ascended the southwards turning canyon [Truckee River] with no impediment caused by snow; ...we came out on the shores of a magnificent lake, verily an ocean, as blue as a sapphire in a setting of mountains. We could not see the end of it, but the water itself was as clear as glass. We crossed along the northern end of it, feeling such a medley of emotions as my pen is feeble to describe; such awe and wonder at this marvel...*

In 1855, civil engineer George H. Goddard passed through Tahoe as part of his work to locate a wagon route connecting California with points east. His detailed notes reflect the pristine condition and

Figure 3. An early illustration from Scenes of Wonder and Curiosity in California showed Lake Tahoe in 1855 from Johnson's Pass.

striking beauty of Lake Tahoe, officially called Lake Bigler, then.

> *A dense pine-forest extends from the water's edge to the summits of the surrounding mountains, except in some points where a peak of more than ordinary elevation rears its bald head above the waving forest. ...The deep blue of the waters indicates a considerable depth to the lake. The water is perfectly fresh. The lake well stocked with salmon and trout. ... There is no lake in California, which, for beauty and variety of scenery, is to be compared to Bigler Lake.*

Sketch artist Joseph Lamson visited the lake in the spring of 1861 and again in the summer of that year. With a local guide, he made a five-day circumnavigation of the lake in search of artistic scenes. While sketching the scenery, he made copious diary notes on his journey and his impressions of the scenery. He began with this overview from the vicinity of present-day Echo Summit,

> *I... pursued my journey on foot, and had at length the happiness to find myself at the summit [Johnson's Pass] of the Sierra Nevada mountains, and looking down upon a magnificent scene beyond them. Here I obtained a glimpse of Lake Tahoe through a mist, which veiled the distant landscape and I sketched the scene...*

Later, he surveyed a second panorama from an unnamed 7,750 ft. knob just south of present-day Meyers,

> *This morning I ascended a mountain ... and had a grand view of the valley below me with the mountains opposite, and Lake Tahoe gleaming in the sunlight at the northern extremity of the valley, with a faint and almost indistinguishable outline of the mountains beyond. ...Lake Tahoe has already acquired a great celebrity for the beauty and grandeur of its scenery; and in my opinion these have not been overestimated. Still it has been but seldom and but partially explored by persons competent to appreciate its peculiar beauties.*

About six weeks after Lamson departed from the lake, Sam Clemens made two back-to-back visits to the lake's North Shore along Agate Bay and Carnelian Bay. Years later as Mark Twain, he would recall in *Roughing It* his often-quoted impressions of Lake Tahoe. His descriptions are the most vivid and evocative of the extraordinary beauty of Lake Tahoe before the visible impact of humans.

We plodded on, two or three hours longer, and at last the Lake burst upon us--a noble sheet of blue water lifted six thousand three hundred feet above the level of the sea, and walled in by a rim of snow-clad mountain peaks that towered aloft a full three thousand feet higher still! It was a vast oval, and one would have to use up eighty or a hundred good miles in traveling around it. As it lay there with the shadows of the mountains brilliantly photographed upon its still surface I thought it must surely be the fairest picture the whole earth affords.

The forest about us was dense and cool, the sky above us was cloudless and brilliant with sunshine, the broad lake before us was glassy and clear, or rippled and breezy, or black and storm-tossed, according to Nature's mood; and its circling border of mountain domes, clothed with forests, scarred with land-slides, cloven by canons and valleys, and helmeted with glittering snow, fitly framed and finished the noble picture. The view was always fascinating, bewitching, entrancing. The eye was never tired of gazing, night or day, in calm or storm; it suffered but one grief, and that was that it could not look always, but must close sometimes in sleep.

College professor William H. Brewer was on a multi-year geological survey of California when he entered the Tahoe Basin in 1863. His comparison to European lakes emphasizes the absence of any apparent human impact at Lake Tahoe.

The purity of its waters, its great depth, its altitude, and the clear sky all combine to give the lake a bright but intensely blue color; it is bluer even than the Mediterranean, and nearly as picturesque as Lake Geneva in Switzerland. Its beautiful waters and the rugged mountains rising around it, spotted with snow which has perhaps lain for centuries, form an enchanting picture. It lacks many of the elements of beauty of the Swiss lakes; it lacks the grassy, green, sloping hills, the white-walled towns, the castles with their stories and histories, the chalets of the herders—in fact, it lacks all the elements that give their peculiar charm to the Swiss scenery—its beauty is its own, is truly Californian.

Figure 4. An illustration circa 1869 from California Scrap-book possibly showed Glenbrook Bay and Walton's Landing with the Edith Batty in the foreground and an early steamer underway in the background.

Visualizing the increasing popularity of Lake Tahoe in 1865, J. Ross Browne in his book *Washoe Revisited* extolled the potential of Tahoe as a resort.

> Within the past two years the people of California and Washoe have begun to discover the beauties of this charming region, and its rare advantages as a place of summer resort. Situated in the bosom of the Sierra Nevada mountains, 6000 feet above the level of the sea, with an atmosphere of wonderful purity; abounding in game; convenient of access, and possessing all the attractions of retirement from the busy world, amidst scenery unrivaled for its romantic beauties, there can be no doubt it will soon become the grand central

point of pleasure and recreation for the people of the Pacific Coast.

At that time, the term "Washoe" denoted the geographical area encompassing the fabulous Comstock Lode and western Nevada mining camps. While Browne's dreams about the coming tourism economy were prescient, he could not let himself imagine the coming nightmarish plunder of Tahoe's natural assets at the hands of Comstock timber barons, ranchers, water seekers and market hunters.

Climatic Conditions

In the mid-1800s, the regional climate was coming out of what climatologists characterized as the Little Ice Age. Climatic conditions were cooler, perhaps 2° F colder on average than the early 21st century climate. Severe drought had plagued the region since the 1700s and caused Lake Tahoe to dip below its natural rim for extended periods. Forests withdrew to the moister high elevations and wildfires were more prevalent. Trees became rooted in the exposed shoreline as the water held back for long periods.

The colder temperature maintained a perennial snowcap on the peaks of the Sierra Nevada. In *Roughing It*, Mark Twain recalled seeing Lake Tahoe "walled in by a rim of snow-clad mountain peaks" in mid-September 1861 during his first visits to Lake Tahoe. In 1865, government surveyors noted barren snow-covered mountaintops on their public land survey plats.

The mid-19th century saw a gradual return to wetter conditions and the beginning of natural warming of the climate. Lake Tahoe recovered and flow in the Truckee River increased. The Tahoe climate entered a wet cycle in the latter 1800s that lasted until the early 20th century. As the climate warmed, more precipitation fell as rain compared to snow, precipitation was more intense and the spring runoff occurred earlier. The perennial snowfields on the mountain peaks that Mark Twain and government land surveyors recalled seeing in late summer no longer existed.

Atmospheric Conditions

Recalling his early visits to Lake Tahoe, Mark Twain remarked that the Tahoe air was, "very pure and fine, bracing and delicious." This was perhaps a dual reference to clarity of the atmosphere and the perceived health restoring benefits of breathing clean mountain air. During this period, heating and cooking fires, wildfires, and natural dust all exerted an effect on atmospheric visibility. The well-developed forests also contributed to reduced visibility with organic emissions and seasonal pollen.

Natural wildfires, the most significant source of visibility obstructing pollutants, accounted for "spotty but persistent smoke in relatively low concentrations around the basin" according to scientific estimates for that period. An unrelenting thermal inversion acted like a lid to hold the smoke close to the ground surface. The condition subsided when prevailing winds and daytime surface heating dissipated the inversion and dispersed the low-lying haze. Traveling sketch artist Joseph Lamson, standing from a vantage point near Flagpole Peak in August 1861, noted the curtailed visibility. He wrote in his journal that the smoke he characterized as "vapors" initially obscured the view of Lake Tahoe some 15 miles distant until skies cleared later in the day.

If any smoldering wildfires existed, the view across the lake through the morning atmosphere would have appeared quite hazy from Sam Clemens' location on the North Shore, near present-day Tahoe Vista. Potentially, it could have temporarily obscured the opposite shore and mountain peaks looking southward. However, the haze condition cleared quickly as the inversion dissipated.

Native American Presence and Use

For the 1,300 years before the mid-19th century, the Washoe Tribe of Native Americans was in residence during summer and the milder months surrounding this season. Archeological investigations indicated that their prehistoric ancestors regularly entered the Tahoe Basin 8,000 to 9,000 years ago. The development of this seasonal migration practice followed the melt of glaciers and snowfields at lower elevations in the Tahoe Basin and the drying of the climate in Great Basin in general.

The traditional core territory of the Washoe was the Eastern Sierra drainage from Honey Lake, southward to include the upper reaches of the watersheds of the Truckee, Carson and Walker Rivers, and the entire Lake Tahoe watershed. Tribal activity periodically extended

Figure 5. Native American Washoe tribal members at Lake Tahoe circa 1870 illustrated the transition from traditional dress to western garments. (Wikimedia Commons)

beyond their established territory for plant gathering. One group would travel across the Sierra to gather acorns and trade with other tribes.

Each year, Washoe progressively relocated extended family groups into the Tahoe Basin beginning in the warmer months and following retreat of snow cover. When fully established for the season, they occupied campsites oriented to the major tributaries flowing into Lake Tahoe and Squaw Valley. Activities focused on food gathering and acquisition of resource materials. Tribal members collected plants and invertebrates, fished, or hunted, depending on the unique assets of their campsite. Before the onset of winter conditions, the tribe would relocate to the lower elevation areas of Honey Lake to the north, Carson Valley to the east and Diamond Valley to the south.

Before sustained contact with Euro-Americans in 1848, the tribal population peaked at perhaps 3,000. An 1859 population estimate placed the number of members at 900. By 1866, their numbers had dwindled to 500 individuals.

The majority of the campsites were concentrated in the southern half of the lake with the remaining several dispersed along significant stream outlets on the North and East Shores. The Upper Truckee River marsh was most important among all summering grounds. Campsites along the South and West Shores were notable for abundant fish and plentiful plants. Tribal members constructed seasonal shelters from locally available plant materials.

The range of foods spanned from fish, small and large mammals, insects and worms to roots, berries and seeds. The streams ran full with spawning Lahontan cutthroat trout that constituted a primary protein source in the Washoe diet. Washoe oral history describes Lahontan cutthroat trout large enough to pull a Washoe man into the water. In the fall, Washoe relocated to the Pine Nut Range on the east side of the Carson Valley to harvest pine nuts from pinion pines.

Washoe culture connected the availability of food resources with a spiritual requirement to maintain harmony with the sources of their sustenance. Harvesting entailed rituals and practices that ensured sustainability of the resource.

The Washoe was a passive tribe and persistently avoided contact during early incursions by Euro-Americans. It would be possible for a Tahoe visitor to conclude the Washoe were not in residence by construing their lack of visibility as an absence.

Lake Tahoe served another role in Washoe culture as the tribe's spiritual center and an annual gathering place that reinforced tribal unity. Washoe had a rich and complex relationship with the spiritual values imparted by the pure waters of the lake and the divine influence of physical features such as Cave Rock. The lake was a giver of life and spirit to people, land and animals.

Washoe mythology evoked supernatural creatures, some of which inhabited the lake. These legends constituted tribal oral history that explained important events and passed on cultural values and behavioral norms. The Ong monster-bird nested deep in the lake and could kidnap a person if they were inattentive to their surroundings. Water babies inhabited the lake and could seize a hapless Washoe, who ventured too far out into the water or could create havoc elsewhere in the Washoe world if they became agitated.

The tribe believed Cave Rock on the East Shore held supernatural power and was a sacred site approached by only a select few spiritual leaders. Tribal shamans would consult with spirits at the rock. They would make respectful offerings and in return, be infused with special powers from the rock.

As Euro-American encroachment on Washoe lands progressed, more interaction occurred, resulting in erosion of their culture and dependency on the local economy. In 1859, a government Indian agent sought to put the Washoe on two reservations, including one reservation shared with their long-time rivals, the Pyramid Lake Tribe of Paiutes. Washoe tribal leaders requested without success separate reservations on their traditional homelands.

By 1865, no tracts of sufficient size remained to accommodate the surviving tribal members on a sustainable basis. The following year, Indian agents determined that the tribe was in such a rapid decline

Figure 6. This 1875 view showed the south aspect of Cave Rock, the Washoe spiritual site. (Wikimedia Commons)

that the need for a reservation ceased to exist. With no other options and as a matter of survival, the Washoe began to adapt to the overwhelming presence of Euro-American settlers while they continued to practice what was left of their traditional life and culture.

Today, about 1,000 Washoe reside on five federal allotment sites spread throughout Carson City and Carson Valley in Nevada and Diamond Valley in California. The tribe remains largely exiled from its Tahoe Basin summering grounds, but still controls several allotments and land leases around the lake. The most notable are the Meeks Bay Resort and a parcel dedicated for tribal ceremonial purposes on the East Shore. United States Forest Service officials designated Cave Rock as a Washoe spiritual site and imposed public access restrictions, even though they continued the pair of highway tunnel bores penetrating the rock.

Forests and Logging

The mid-19th century or pre-contact (with Euro-Americans) forest was mature old growth and late successional stands. Late successional forest consisted of trees nearing maturity in size, density and species diversity, compared to the mature stands that had already stabilized in that condition. Forested land covered 94,740 acres or about 47% of the tributary watershed.

Massively large trees – up to three feet in diameter on the East Shore and up to five feet on the North and West Shores – populated the forest. The oldest trees were 200-300 years old. It was a mixed conifer forest, about one-third white fir. The balance of the forest spread its growth evenly among Jeffrey pines, sugar pines and other species grouped into incense cedars, Douglas firs and lodgepole pines. Trees were well spaced with about 45 percent tree cover and 900 trees per acre. Because of shading by the dense canopy, the understory was a sparse 20 percent of cover. Low intensity natural and Native American ignited fires burned through at 20 to 30-year intervals and burned the equivalent of 30 acres per day. These kept understory and sapling growth down but did little damage to the larger trees that were well adapted to periodic fires.

Period descriptions of the pre-contact forest, while rare, are vivid and expressive. A memorable quote by an early explorer painted a vibrant and dynamic image of a virgin forest, "dominated by giant pine trees with so much room on the forest floor that riders could travel at full gallop without losing their hats."

One 1859 awe-struck government expedition official gushed with a description normally reserved for national parks.

> Lake Valley [South Lake Tahoe] is like a beautiful park, studded with large, stately pines. The glades between the trees are beautifully green... The pines of various kinds are very large, and attain a height of probably from 100 to 150 feet. Their diameter is not infrequently as much as 8 feet, and they sometimes attain the dimension of 10 feet.

Mark Twain recalled the soaring forest rising on the North Shore above Agate Bay during his first visit to Lake Tahoe in 1861, "It was yellow-pine timberland—a dense forest of trees a hundred feet high and from one to five feet through at the butt." Even Twain's contemporary at the Virginia City *Territorial Enterprise*, Dan DeQuille, wistfully described its virgin state as sugar pines "... five, six, and some even eight feet in diameter; all are very tall and straight."

Before 1861, the logging industry was in its infancy with two small water-powered mills on the south end of the lake providing lumber for local settlements. Pixley's Mill and Woodburn's Mill took advantage of year-round flow in Trout Creek, and the latter produced 6,000 to 10,000 board feet per day. Owners sited the mills for proximity to local markets, readily accessible timber stands and perennial flowing streams for waterpower. Logging methods were a primitive combination of hand labor and draft animals. Men felled the trees, and limbed and bucked the trunks. Teams of oxen and horses dragged the logs to the mill.

Western Nevada mines and communities needed timber for industrial and commercial buildings, housing, mine shoring, and fuel. To meet the insatiable demand for timber products, steam and water-powered sawmills sprang up on the east facing forested slopes of the Carson Range. Sawmills were located on lower Clear Creek, Spooner Summit, Mill Creek (Ash Canyon) and Little Valley, just above the Washoe Valley. Wagon roads leading to Carson City and Virginia City serviced the mills.

Figure 7. This view of the East Shore showed the typical boulder-lined shoreline and pre-contact forest during the time Mark Twain made visits to Lake Tahoe. (Wikimedia Commons)

Two water-powered sawmills and a shingle mill were located in the upper part of Little Valley just outside the Tahoe Basin. These mills could haul lumber products to market using the Washoe Trail that passed through Little Valley and connected with other roads to markets in Western Nevada. Sam Clemens passed by these mills on his earliest trips to Lake Tahoe.

As timberlands were quickly exhausted or claimed for future cutting, and in the face of mushrooming demand, lumbermen targeted the rich stands in the Lake Tahoe watershed. Due to its close proximity to timber resources and major markets, the Spooner Summit-Glenbrook area on Tahoe's East Shore became the ignition point for the massive logging that was to come during the balance of the 19th century.

On the East Shore, Augustus Pray and partners settled at Glenbrook in 1860 and established the Lake Bigler Lumber Co. The following year they erected the first Tahoe Basin sawmill dedicated to production of lumber for the Western Nevada mining industry and communities. Using primitive logging methods with a crew of 15 and relying on waterpower from Glenbrook Creek, the Lake Bigler Lumber Co. mill produced a maximum of 10,000 board feet per day beginning in 1862. Wagons hauled finished lumber over Spooner Summit to markets in Carson City, Virginia City and outlying areas.

At Spooner Summit, Michele Spooner and partners engaged in small-scale logging and milling in 1861 and added a shingle mill to the mix two years later. By 1863, new sawmills had sprung up elsewhere around the lake. North of Sugar Pine Point, Casnell operated a mill and wharf for barging lumber to Glenbrook. At the mouth of Ward Creek, Augustus Saxton operated a water powered sawmill and cut timber along a haul road into Ward Valley.

Speculators made their moves to file claims on timberlands within the Tahoe Basin portion of newly created Nevada Territory. Individuals could preempt (the term for claiming government land

and converting it to private ownership under the Tyler Preemption Act of 1841) up to 160 acres if they established a structure on the property and met other requirements. It was a land rush to match the silver rush already underway.

A group of sycophantic followers associated with Nevada Territorial Governor James Nye established a timber claim at Lake Tahoe. Sam Clemens heard their talk about the claim, the literally "dirt cheap"

Figure 8. View of the Woodburn Mill in Lake Valley circa 1860 (Library of Congress)

land for the taking and the intoxicating beauty of Lake Tahoe. Clemens' penchant for get-rich-quick schemes and the allure of Lake Tahoe was too much to resist. Accompanied by a newfound friend, the two trekked to Lake Tahoe to try their hand at preempting timberland. Their ensuing adventures became the staple of two imaginative chapters in Mark Twain's 1872 creative nonfiction memoir, *Roughing It*.

The accelerated mining frenzy of the Comstock Lode in the early 1860s quickly depleted accessible stands on the east slope of the Carson Range. Lumber firms then focused almost exclusively on the virgin stands in the Tahoe Basin. A brief respite occurred in the latter 1860s as mining activity declined due to expected exhaustion of known ore deposits. The burgeoning demand from the transcontinental railroad construction and operation in the latter 1860s and the discovery of the Big Bonanza ore body in 1873 renewed and intensified lumbering activity.

The fate of the Tahoe forest is a stark example of the inevitable outcome of the libertarian attitudes prevalent in the 19th century west. Fueled by greed and avarice and absent any self-restraint or government oversight, timber barons consumed the forest with rapacious disregard. The last three decades of the 19th century witnessed the annihilation of Tahoe's forests on an unprecedented scale even as the mining activity was collapsing toward the end of the century. With the final act of logging in the surviving stands mainly for pulpwood, the voracious consumption of available timber resources had left a shocking expanse of devastation over the watershed.

The wholesale removal of timber stripped the watershed of its protective forest canopy. Runoff increased in volume and occurred sooner. Sediment-laden streams in destabilized channels oozed into the lake, creating visible plumes of polluted water. Nearly a century after workers dragged the last logs from the forest, scientists obtained sediment cores from the lake bottom. The cores showed significantly increased rates of sedimentation and accumulation of organic debris during and shortly after the intense 19th century logging.

Lest we be too harsh on the 19th century timber industry, understand the most people believed that a standing forest was a waste of a valuable resource or that the forests of the West were inexhaustible. Others simply saw the destruction as a regrettable but necessary cost of progress. The conservation ethic had yet to find its voice.

Over 100 years later, University of California – Davis Professor Michael G. Barbour in a research paper summed it up with a dismal assessment of the extent of resource depletion.

> ... [Almost] 60% of the... forest [was] clear-cut or partially harvested (the percent of trees taken ranging from 10 to 100%). At low elevations and on slopes easy to access, the harvest was much greater than 60%; at high elevations and on steep slopes, the harvest was less than 60%....
>
> [There are] fewer than 40 old-growth stands. They averaged [62 acres] in size, were seldom near one another, and [lay] scattered throughout the basin. The combined area of the old-growth stands comprises only 3% of forested land in the basin. This value is much lower than the 13% old-growth area for all the national forests in California and the 55% old-growth area for all the national parks in the Sierra Nevada.

Tahoe continues to feel the grip of the long absent axe-wielding hand of the industrial logging. Under a number of government-funded programs, its watershed is undergoing remediation and recovery measures that will extend well into the 21st century.

Fisheries and Subsistence and Commercial Fishing
The early 1860s Lake Tahoe fishing was legendary. Tales abounded of fish size and enormous catches.

Passing through the South Shore area in August 1863, William H. Brewer of the California State Geological Survey was impressed with the size and abundance of the native trout.

> *The lake abounds in the largest trout in the world, a species of speckled trout that often weighs over twenty pounds and sometimes as much as thirty pounds. Smaller trout are abundant in the streams. An Indian brought some into camp [near the Trout Creek outlet] and I gave him fifty cents for two, and they made us two good meals and were excellent fish.*

Coincidently, Brewer was camped near Lake House, on the edge of the meadow bordering Trout Creek, on August 21-24, 1863; exactly four days after Mark Twain sojourned at Lake House.

The dominant fish species and top aquatic predator was the Lahontan cutthroat trout. The cutthroat strain was unique to the Lake Tahoe-Truckee River-Pyramid Lake watershed and four other western river systems. At Lake Tahoe, the fish moved into tributaries for a February-July spawn. Based on observations made by Fremont's expedition of 1843-44, experts concluded the fish species occurred in 11 lakes and 3,600 miles of streams throughout their range.

Secondary to the cutthroat population was the mountain whitefish that also resided year-round in Lake Tahoe, swimming in small schools in deep water. Spawning occurred in the fall in lake tributaries. Six other species of lesser fish inhabited Lake Tahoe, including chubs, dace and suckers.

Fishing was essential to Washoe food gathering at Tahoe and their main campsites were located around stream outlets noted for reliable runs of spawning fish. Washoe took fish using traps, spears and nets and were careful to leave females to preserve the annual spawn. To increase the success of the spawn, they removed suckers who preyed on fish eggs.

In 1854, Washoe took large numbers of cutthroat trout at their fishing camps along the South Shore and attempted to stop settlers from fishing. In 1859, commercial fishing began near the mouth of the Upper Truckee River. In 1860, William W. Lapham established "Fish Market Landing" near Stateline, Nev.

Lahontan cutthroat trout eventually descended into extinction in Lake Tahoe caused by destruction of spawning habitat and government introduction of non-native aquatic invertebrates (crayfish and Mysis shrimp) and non-native fish species (rainbow trout and lake trout). Lahontan cutthroat still occur in five lakes and 482 miles of streams within their original habitat area. Ongoing efforts by fishery biologists aim at expanding the pure strain.

Figure 9. Lake Tahoe Lahontan cutthroat trout circa 1860-70 weighed 10-20 lb. Mark Twain praised this species of trout as one of his favorite dishes. (Library of Congress)

Wildlife and Hunting

In its undisturbed state, the Tahoe Basin was densely populated with diverse and numerous wildlife species, comparable to our modern-day national parks and wildlife refuges.

In the old growth forest and open hillsides, close to 100 bird species fed and nested. Smaller species included wrens, chickadees, woodpeckers, bluebirds, nuthatches, sparrows, Steller's jays and tanagers. Larger birds would have encompassed ravens, crows, doves, band-tail pigeons, quail, sage grouse and Sierra grouse.

Soaring above during the day were birds of prey that varied from eagles, hawks, ospreys, falcons and kestrels. At night, great horned and spotted owls patrolled the skies.

Along the lakeshore or near a marsh, and depending on the season, were geese, ducks, swans, loons, terns, mergansers, pelicans and California gulls. At the shoreline, one might have seen shorebirds such as herons and sandpipers and along a stream, dippers.

North American river otters and muskrats plied the near shore waters, stream outlets and marshes. The American beaver was probably present, although biologists consider it an introduced species. In upland areas, small mammals abounded such as rabbits, squirrels, chipmunks, ermines, mink, martens, fishers, skunks, mountain beaver (not to be confused with the American beaver), and badgers. Small mammals such as pikas and marmots inhabited the higher elevation locations.

Large mammals such as mule deer, wolverines, mountain sheep, black bears, grizzly bears, coyotes, mountain lions, bobcats, raccoons, and porcupines roamed the forests and meadows in the warmer months. During winter, they migrated or hibernated, or simply endured the winter conditions. In his *Roughing It* lectures, Mark Twain mentioned seeing mountain sheep, the Sierra Nevada big horn sheep. Twain mostly frequented the area next to the lake and from that vantage point, the best habitat to encounter Sierra

Nevada big horn sheep was the grazing terrain near Mt. Baldy on the North Shore.

The Washoe hunted extensively, and from their oral histories, we get an inventory of some of the more abundant edible species. They took small mammals such as rabbits and squirrels, waterfowl and large game, including deer and sheep. Their ethic of hunting in the fall and intent to take only the males and females without offspring ensured a natural balance and plentiful conditions for the future.

Traveling emigrants probably hunted large and small game to supplement their provisions as they passed through. Trappers concentrated on mink, river otters and weasels in the riparian zone along the lake and streams. At the higher elevation, they trapped badgers, marmots and marten. Market hunters concentrated on upland birds, waterfowl and deer to supply local way stations and hotels. Ranchers and shepherds killed predators such as coyotes, eagles, bobcats, grizzly bears and mountain lions to prevent depredation of their herds. All this activity intensified as mining activity and support industries drove population growth and new settlements in the Northern Nevada Territory.

During the heavy impact of the resource exploitation era of 1860-1900, species abundance dropped sharply but rebounded in its wake during the post-exploitation era of 1901-1960. Conversely, some species were unable to regain a foothold. Mountain sheep, grizzly bear, red fox, wolverine, peregrine falcon, sage grouse and seven other lesser wildlife species were extirpated (rendered extinct) from the Tahoe Basin by the early 20th century. The red fox and peregrine falcon are not gone as there have been occasional sightings reported recently.

Water Resources and Shorezone
In the early 1860s, engineer and entrepreneur Alexis von Schmidt was prowling around Tahoe imagining a grandiose scheme to dam the lake and divert its water. In 1865, he ignited vehement

opposition by floating the first of two doomed diversion proposals. He offered to pump water over Spooner Summit to Virginia City and later, through a tunnel in Squaw Valley to San Francisco. While nothing came of these plans, he succeeded in constructing the first dam on Lake Tahoe's outlet in 1870. This dam and subsequent dams forever changed the delicate natural balance of water resources at Lake Tahoe.

Before any damming and in an average year, the lake dropped below its natural rim (6,223.0 ft. L.T.D.[1]) in late October and all flow into the Truckee River ceased. Intermittent snowmelt and direct precipitation stimulated a slow rise of about six inches from November through March. Beginning in April, rapidly increasing snowmelt lifted the lake surface by 15 inches to its normal seasonal high of 6224.9 ft. L.T.D. in late May. Declining snowpack and continued losses through outlet flow and evaporation drew the lake down at four to six inches per month, causing the lake to fall back to its natural rim by late October.

The pre-dam two feet or so of normal variation in the level of Lake Tahoe over the millennia created a shoreline that was stable with beaches and supported a thick band of riparian vegetation dominated by willows, alders and grasses. The vegetation band was so thick, that it would be difficult to tramp along much of the shoreline without getting wet feet, unless the lake was unusually low.

Because of the narrow fluctuation in water level and the low amounts of sediment replenishment, most sandy beaches were thin, maybe just a few yards wide. In some locations around the lake, exceptionally wide beaches developed that could accommodate two men sleeping in the sand, as Mark Twain recounted in *Roughing It*.

---

[1] Lake Tahoe Datum, a reference to sea level and unique only to Lake Tahoe

The wider beaches were on the south-facing shores of Crystal Bay, Agate Bay and Carnelian Bay and the north facing shores along the South Shore. In these cases, the availability of sand replenishment from nearby streams, littoral drift (the movement of sediment parallel to the shore), a shallow offshore shelf, and significantly higher waves contributed to wide beach development. The wide beach at Sand Harbor is the result of an underwater canyon head that blocks littoral drift, resulting in the anomaly of a wide beach

Figure 10. This 1908 photograph of the Hurricane Bay shoreline showed typical dense vegetation that rising waters submerged after construction of the third Tahoe Dam. (Library of Congress)

compared to the area immediately south of Sand Harbor. Here, there was no beach development due to lack of sediment input from streams and no contribution from backshore erosion in the pre-dam era. Figure 11 shows development of beaches in the pre-dam era, e.g. 1861.

Precipitation records in Sacramento for 1860-61, indicate that 12-month period was well below average. Sacramento measured its yearly precipitation beginning on July 1 of each year. However, the winter of 1861-62 was extreme and major flooding occurred throughout California and the Northern Nevada Territory. In *Roughing It*, Mark Twain wrote of eight days stranded at a way station surrounded by the flooded Carson River. The following summer probably saw the level of Lake Tahoe temporarily rise well over five feet above its natural rim.

Construction of the first dam in 1870 dramatically altered the fluctuation of water levels in Lake Tahoe and affected the shoreline. Because the outflow was restricted, water impounded in Lake Tahoe increased. This lifted the average water level 2.5 ft. over the pre-dam condition. The operation of the dam caused the lake to reach its peak 1-2 months later than normal and kept water levels higher for longer periods. The result was an unstable shoreline that continued to erode and recede in response to the artificially high water level. The band of riparian vegetation could not withstand the extended inundation and gradually died back. The root systems remained, though dormant. Emergent shoots appeared during drought periods and resembled the pre-dam water level conditions.

The exceptional water clarity was stunning to many visitors and Mark Twain was no exception when he marveled at the extraordinary clarity of water in *Roughing It*.

> So singularly clear was the water, that where it was only twenty or thirty feet deep the bottom was so perfectly distinct that the boat seemed floating in the air! Yes, where it was even eighty feet deep. Every little pebble was distinct, every speckled trout, every hand's-breadth of sand.
>
> Down through the transparency of these great depths, the water was not merely transparent, but dazzlingly, brilliantly so. All objects seen through it had a bright, strong vividness,

Figure 11. Map showing sandy beaches on Lake Tahoe under pre-dam conditions. Boulders lined most of the shoreline and there were few sandy beaches except for the northern and southern ends.

not only of outline, but of every minute detail, which they would not have had when seen simply through the same depth of atmosphere.

In 1867, an editor for *Spirit of the Times* newspaper actually measured a maximum depth of 81 ft. for visibility of submerged boulders on the North Shore.

Notwithstanding Mark Twain's superlative description of lake water clarity, the first recorded scientific measurement of clarity did not occur until September 1873. Professor John LeConte submerged a white dinner plate and observed it to a depth of 108 ft. Depending on the time of the year of measurement and the previous seasonal runoff volume, maximum clarity could have approached 125 ft. in the 1860s. This value was comparable to other similar world lakes that escaped the ravages of resource exploitation and urban development. Some 150 years later and as the result of pollution from land development and vehicle emissions, clarity had declined to perhaps an average of 70 ft. in a good year.

Engaging in lake bottom sightseeing while adrift in a boat on the North Shore, Mark Twain recollected colorful detail. "There, the rocks on the bottom are sometimes gray, sometimes white." It was possible in the 1860s and for most of the ensuing 100 years to discern with the naked eye the color of submerged boulders. In the mid-20th century, this changed for the worse. Degraded water quality conditions stimulated the excessive growth of attached algae on offshore rocks around the lake. Called periphyton, this thick coating of the slippery fur-like algae obscured the rock surface. Since then, it has not been possible to see the exceptional rock coloring Mark Twain glimpsed while leaning over the gunwales of his drifting rowboat.

Mark Twain recalled in *Roughing It* the September 1861 lake water temperature as "rather chilly" for his occasional bathing. Although people no longer bathe in the lake, many swimmers would still concur with Mark Twain. The water retains its stiffening chill, despite having warmed somewhat since the early 1970s due to global climate change. Considering the mid-19th century climate on average was cooler than today, average water temperature at the surface could have been colder by perhaps 3°-4° F. While on average, this is hardly noticeable by human senses, the extreme at any one time might have been even colder on the surface for comparable times of the year.

In another aspect of lake water temperature, mid-19th century Lake Tahoe would have had a body of 40° F water from a depth about 950 ft. to the bottom. Again, because of global climate change, this body of water now has an increased average temperature closer to 41° F.

Watershed disturbance in the early 1860s was a relatively minor environmental factor, resulting in extremely low rates of soil erosion. Narrow wagon roads in 1861-65 conformed to the terrain rather than altered the terrain like modern highways. Clear-cut logging affected only a small amount of acreage. Eventually, significant logging depleted 97 percent of the total forested area. The balance of the early 1860s watershed had sparse and well-dispersed settlement development, and grazing was less intensive on the open range.

Because of relatively stable watershed of the early 1860s, annual sediment flow into the lake was still at the natural background level of 3,400 tons, compared to the massive peak of 30,000 tons estimated in 1998. The spring runoff in the early 1860s did not create expansive muddy plumes in the lake, a characteristic of a heavily disturbed watershed. These plumes most likely occurred during the late 19th century logging era, abated as the watershed repaired itself, but resumed during the post-1960 urbanization era.

Meadowlands and Agriculture
In its native setting, nature endowed the Tahoe Basin with 24,700 acres of meadowlands or about 12 percent of the watershed area. Many of these meadows were actually flood plains next to

waterways. During spring, runoff spread over the meadow allowing natural treatment processes to remove the small amount of sediment and other pollutants carried in the runoff before it drained into the lake. This was a critical step to maintaining the exceptional water clarity.

The beginning of the massive westward movement of emigrants and freight wagons through the south end of the Tahoe Basin in the mid-1850s pressed the meadowlands into service. The demand for locally raised meat, dairy products and animal feed spawned a seasonal agricultural industry largely based on the pristine open meadows richly stocked with grasses. When the direction of travel reversed to service the Comstock, the demand intensified in the 1860s. The ample meadows of Tahoe provided the rich pasture and crops of natural grasses needed to supply feed to the multitudes of animal-drawn wagons, pack trains, and cattle herds.

Enterprising farmers preempted unclaimed meadowlands adjoining the lake, and cut hay and timothy grass. They hauled their crop by wagon or shipped it by sailboat to the south end where traffic was concentrated. Harvesting operations were active in Tahoe City, Burton Creek, Griff Creek, Glenbrook, Marla Bay, Lake Valley, Meeks Bay and McKinney Creek.

Dairies found productive pasture at McKinney Creek, Griff Creek and Lake Valley and ready markets at the way stations and hotels along the main road.

New logging and mining activities simply added to the demand already exerted by way stations, stressing the renewable resource to near exhaustion. Despite this, Tahoe agriculture would survive long after the collapse of these industries to make the shift to serving the nascent tourism business. The overgrazing denuded the meadowland landscape, increasing runoff and triggering severe stream channel erosion.

The urbanization era would see agriculture eventually die out and much of the meadowland near urban areas converted to subdivisions, shopping centers, parking lots and golf courses.

Maritime Activities

The earliest settlers built watercrafts from native materials or hauled them over wagon roads, in whole or in part for assembly onsite. The initial collection included personal sized dinghies rigged for rowing or sailing, repurposed whaleboats, dugouts, barges and larger wind-powered vessels. Later, the first steamer on the lake joined the modest fleet.

One of the earliest recorded maritime adventures involved pioneer settler Asa Hawley and a rowboat he constructed. Hawley, John "Snowshoe" Thompson and a third man in 1856 or 1857 became the first persons to circumnavigate Lake Tahoe. Their voyage was primarily an exploration in search of the lake's outlet and a rudimentary survey to estimate the circumference of the lake.

In *Roughing It*, Mark Twain recalled his participation in early Tahoe maritime history. He crossed "a deep bend of the lake" (Crystal Bay) in a rowed skiff in 1861. In a letter to his mother and sister, he told of commandeering a (Carnelian Bay) cabin owner's dugout canoe to paddle the six miles back to his campsite and supply cache at Stateline Point.

Several sail-powered vessels plied the waters of Lake Tahoe in the early 1860s. Built at Glenbrook in the 1850s, the seven-ton displacement *Edith Batty* was a sloop fitted with extended oars for rowing in the event of calm conditions. She carried cargo and sightseers, taking a week to circle the lake. Several other sailing crafts from 19-30 feet owned by lakefront properties and resorts served pleasure boating needs.

The workhorse of the 1860s fleet was the 60-foot long twin-mast schooner *Iron Duke*. Built near the Truckee River outlet in 1860, the *Iron Duke* was a 125-ton capacity cargo ship operated by Fish and

Ferguson. The partnership cultivated wild hay in Squaw Valley and the meadows surrounding the Truckee River outlet and operated a lakefront building on the South Shore to receive shipments. Mostly, *Iron Duke* carried fodder for the teams pulling freight wagons passing through Lake Tahoe. Her regular stops were at the Truckee River outlet (eventually, Tahoe City), several wharfs on the South Shore, and Glenbrook. Beginning in 1861, the ship frequently transported freight across the lake from the Georgetown-Lake Bigler pack trail at McKinney Station to Walton's Landing at Glenbrook.

The nostalgic steamboat era was born with the 1863 launching of the steamer *Governor Blasdel*. History records the vessel name honored the first governor of the new State of Nevada, though the election of Governor Henry G. Blasdel did not occur until 1864, the same year Nevada achieved statehood.

Augustus Pray built the 42 ft. long *Blasdel* from lumber produced at his Glenbrook sawmill. He had the steam plant brought up from San Francisco in oxen-drawn freight wagons. Throughout the 1860s, the *Governor Blasdel* towed booms (bundles) of floating logs, carried sightseers when time was available, and hosted excursions for its namesake.

Transportation Routes
The initial distinction of Lake Tahoe was not as a destination itself, but as a passage to destinations in California. Beginning in the 1850s, the Tahoe Basin was a major physical feature on one principal and two lesser routes. Figures 12 and 13 show regional maps of the Lake Tahoe area and depict the through-transportation routes in use during 1861-65.

Known variously as the Georgetown to Lake Bigler Road or Georgetown to McKinney Station Road, this route followed an ancient Native American trail. The route connected the Gold Rush town of Georgetown in the Sierra foothills by following the Rubicon River canyon, then over the summit of the Sierra Nevada and down

McKinney Creek to McKinney Station on Lake Tahoe. Pack trains and travelers on foot were all that could negotiate the narrow and rough trace.

At McKinney Station, cargo and passengers destined for the mines and settlements in northern Nevada were loaded onto sailboats for transport eastward across the lake to the overwater terminal, Walton's Landing, at Glenbrook Bay on the East Shore. In 1860, Rufus Walton constructed a wharf and house to serve his waterborne shipping operation. Arriving travelers and supplies were loaded onto wagons and transported from Glenbrook over Spooner Summit and down Clear Creek on a toll road owned by Walton. From there, roads connected to Carson City, Virginia City and other destinations in northern Nevada.

Pioneered in 1852 and known originally as Scott's Road and later, the Washoe Trail, this route connected Washoe Valley, Nevada Terr. with Yankee Jim's in the Central Mother Lode of California. Starting at Franktown in the Washoe Valley, the trail followed Franktown Creek southward through Little Valley. At the head of Little Valley, it turned west to surmount the Carson Range and descended Tunnel Creek to Lake Tahoe. It traversed the northerly extent of Lake Tahoe to the Truckee River outlet. Following the Truckee River, it headed west at the confluence with Squaw Creek, through Squaw Valley and over the summit of the Sierra Nevada near Granite Chief Peak. From the summit, it negotiated the ridges and the canyon of the Middle Fork of the American River to the Gold Rush town of Yankee Jim's in the Sierra Nevada foothills.

In August 1856, Placer County Surveyor Thomas A. Young traveled the route on horseback all the way to Washoe Valley, Utah Terr. to evaluate its potential as a trans-Sierra route. He proposed government-funded trail improvements to upgrade it to a full width wagon road. Optimistically renamed the Placer County Emigrant Road, it never secured the sought after government funding and continued on as a little used, but still locally known trail to and from Lake Tahoe. A second unsuccessful attempt to make it a full-fledged road occurred in July 1860. M.S. Stangroom surveyed the trail from Auburn, Calif. to Washoe Valley, Nev. Terr. and submitted his proposal to the Placer County and Washoe Wagon Road Company.

In November and December of 1857, R.M Bucke and Ethan Allan Grosh traveled across the route from their claims near present day Virginia City to the Sierra Foothills. Bucke and Grosh carried the samples of ore that proved the silver deposits from which the Comstock Lode would arise three years later. Bucke's description of the route in a magazine article 25 years later characterized it as not much more than a wide pathway,

> It will be proper in this place to give some description of the Washoe trail, by which we were now about to attempt the passage of the mountains; it was used by Indians and by occasional travelers on foot or horseback, but was not practicable for wheeled vehicles.

Because of its confusing status, some cartographers and surveyors overlooked it as an inconsequential footpath while others showed it as a well-defined trail or road. The opening of passable routes elsewhere in the Tahoe Basin eclipsed its potential as a major trans-Sierra route, but it was reborn as a local transportation route as settlement of the North Shore progressed in the 1860s. Sam Clemens would walk parts of this route in his search for a timber claim in 1861. Today, Highway 28 in California and Nevada approximately follows parts of this historic route.

The central and most heavily traveled west-to-east corridor connected Placerville, California and Carson City, Nevada Territory and passed through the south end of Lake Tahoe. Known by several monikers, but most commonly, Lake Tahoe Wagon Road, it largely consisted of a series of interconnected toll roads and way stations. With the mining activity accelerating in the Nevada Territory, the

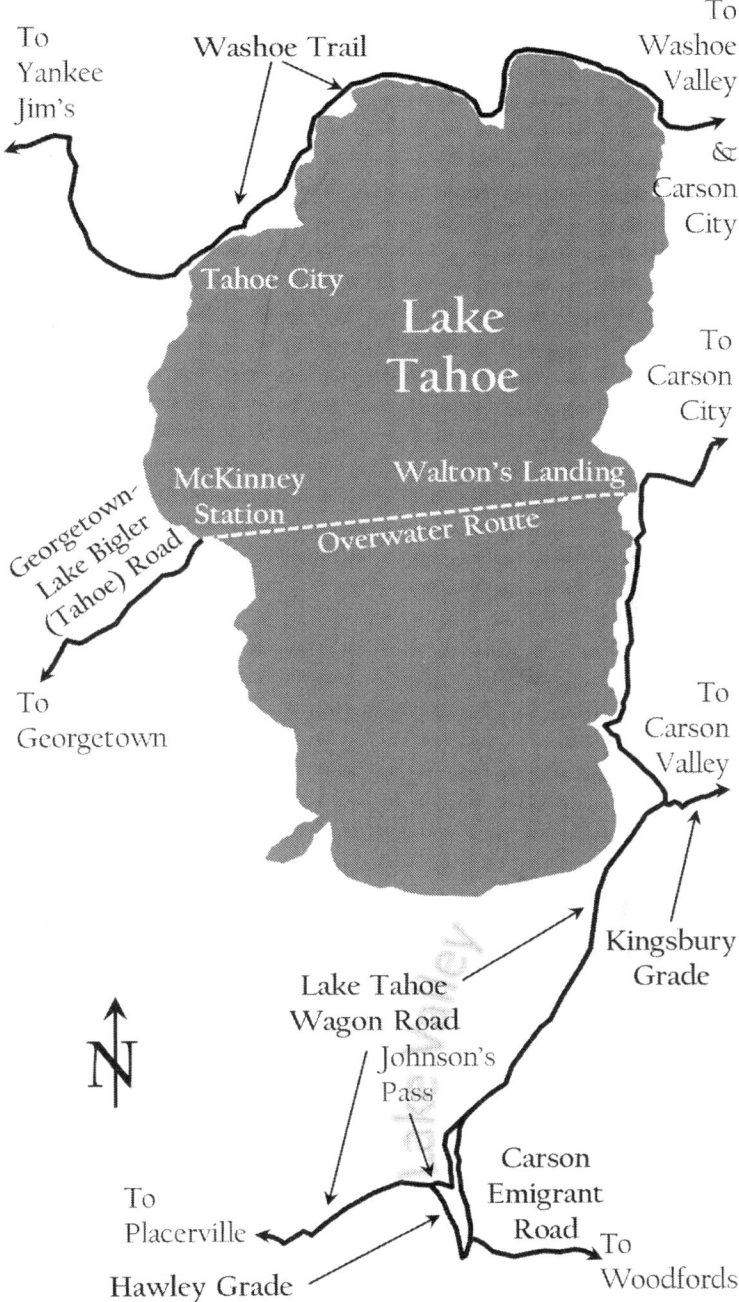

Figure 12. Major transportation routes of 1861-65

bulk of the direction of travel in the 1860s was eastward from supply points in California.

Using Placerville on the west slope of the Sierra Nevada as a starting point for describing its early 1860s alignment, it negotiated the canyon of the South Fork of the American River toward its westerly summit on the edge of the Tahoe Basin. The road then surmounted the Sierra Nevada at Johnson's Pass, near present-day Echo Summit, and descended the narrow Hawley Grade into Upper Lake Valley, now known popularly as Christmas Valley.

Once on the valley floor, the main road in 1860 turned southward to surmount Luther Pass followed by a descent into Hope Valley, Carson Valley and then into Carson City and the Comstock. Today, State Routes 89 and 88 approximately follow this alignment into Nevada.

Beginning in 1861, the road more directly descended into Lake Valley, eliminating the need to negotiate the Hawley Grade. The newer alignment followed the Upper Truckee River northward toward Lake Tahoe. Near present-day Meyers, it forded the river and turned northeastward to avoid the soft ground of the meadows and marsh created by the delta of Upper Truckee River. It clung to the higher and drier ground on the foothills below Freel Peak to cross the California state line near present-day Stateline, Nevada. Modern-day Johnson Pass Road, Upper Truckee Road, Highway 50 and Pioneer Trail generally follow parts of this historic corridor from Echo Summit to South Lake Tahoe.

Just past the state line, the road alignment sharply turned eastward to ascend the newly opened Kingsbury Grade. The Kingsbury Grade topped the Carson Range at Daggett Pass and descended toward Genoa in the Carson Valley. From there, the road followed the valley northward to Carson City and points beyond. Nevada Route 207 traces roughly this historic wagon road.

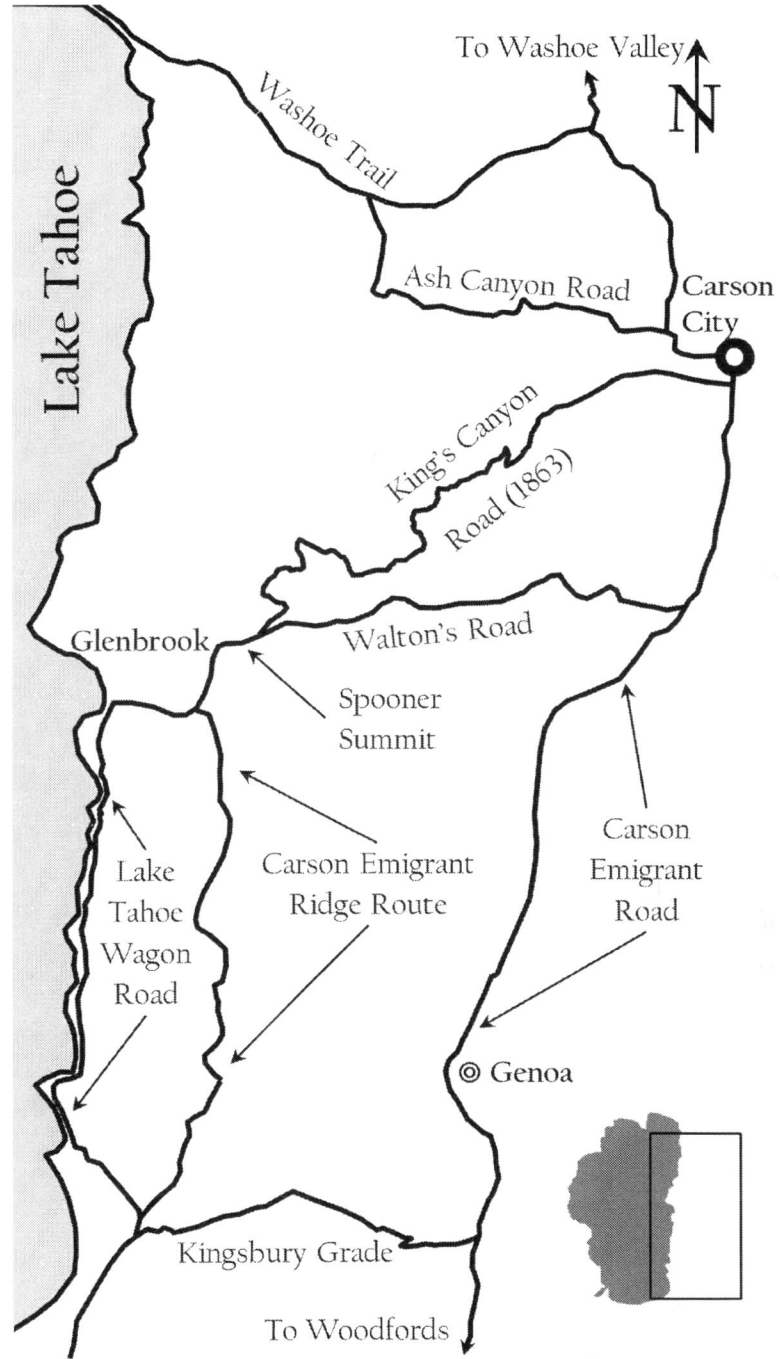

Figure 13. East Shore roads connected to Carson City.

Mark Twain's Lake Tahoe 43

In 1862, the competing Rufus Walton Toll Road opened as a more usable route and diverted traffic along the East Shore of Lake Tahoe to Spooner Summit. Walton's road descended Spooner Summit along Clear Creek to emerge from the Carson Range well south of Carson City.

The improved East Shore road hugged the shoreline and probably followed an old Washoe trail. The roadway initially ascended steeply over the inland shoulder of Cave Rock. Rubble masonry retaining walls and a wooden trestle around the lake-facing precipice side of

Figure 14. This circa 1866 scene from the Lake Tahoe Wagon Road along the East Shore showed where Mark Twain passed through while traveling to and from Lake Tahoe and San Francisco. (Library of Congress)

the rock replaced this section in 1863. All along its length, the East Shore roadway afforded magnificent and commanding views of Lake Tahoe that surely impressed those who came that way.

The following year, the Kings Canyon Road opened and became the preferred route over the Carson Range. Kings Canyon was the major east-west route over the Carson Range until new highway construction in 1927-28 resurrected the old Clear Creek alignment and became the precursor to Highway 50.

Mark Twain was very familiar with the Kings Canyon Road and traveled across it as many as 12 times, including passage through Glenbrook each way. In 1863, he mentioned it specifically in his letter of December 12 to the Virginia City *Territorial Enterprise*. He cited the convenient 15 miles over the new Kings Canyon Road from Carson City to reach an early resort hotel that was the primary subject of his report.

Movement of People, Goods and Information
Once word was out about the Comstock discovery, a steady stream of fortune-seekers normally headed west through Tahoe to the California Mother Lode had reversed itself by 1860. New throngs headed eastward to Washoe, the term for what was then the Utah Territory and the Comstock mining region. Even the road took on a new nickname, Bonanza Road, in deference to the hype and tales of quick fortunes easily made in the mines of Washoe. All means of locomotion came into play where movement of goods, people and information were concerned. This wave of humanity met in the early years a countercurrent stream of silver ore shipments headed to smelters in California that reduced the ore to silver metal.

At one station over a three-month period in 1864, an observer kept a tally of the total movement through Tahoe. Though the volume would not peak until years later, it served to give a captivating statistical view of the early traffic volume by mode of transportation.

Perhaps because of economics or expediency, many were on foot carrying just a pack or pushing a cart or wheelbarrow filled with their worldly possessions. Traveling writer J. Ross Browne aptly described the appearance of the procession in 1860.

> An almost continuous string of Washoeites [Comstock-bound travelers] stretched "like a great snake dragging its slow length along" as far as the eye could reach. In the course of this day's tramp we passed parties of every description and color: Irishmen, wheeling their blankets, provisions, and mining implements on wheelbarrows; American, French, and

Figure 15. Mule teams pulled Washoe wagons past Cave Rock circa 1866 on the new section of the road that bypassed the climb over the rock. Mark Twain passed this point while traveling on the Lake Tahoe Wagon Road. (Wikimedia Commons)

German foot-passengers, leading heavily-laden horses, or carrying their packs on their backs, and their picks and shovels slung across their shoulders…

In this category was the largest volume of travelers at 6,667 persons, according to the 1864 tally.

Figure 16. Long lines of freight wagons bound for the Comstock passed through Swift's Station on the King's Canyon Road circa 1865. Mark Twain passed through this point while traveling to and from Lake Tahoe and San Francisco. (Wikimedia Commons)

Next in volume came the 3,164 stagecoach passengers. The Concord coach was the luxury liner of the era, carrying nine passengers plus mail and monetary valuables behind a team of six handpicked horses. Atop was the flamboyant driver, the elite among teamsters, and a "shotgun messenger" or armed guard to escort valuable private shipments and ensure security over dangerous terrain.

Lake Tahoe lay on the Central Overland Route serviced by a chain of express companies that held mail contracts and handled packages and passengers. The way stations along the Lake Tahoe Wagon

Figure 17. An 1861 illustration from the book Peep at Washoe showed Washoe-bound travelers on foot (Wikimedia Commons)

Road provided convenient respite and refreshment for passengers and livery service for the teams. The 24-hour operational Wells Fargo stage typically covered the distance between San Francisco and Virginia City in as little as 24 hours.

Mark Twain rode the stage lines many times beginning with his initial journey to the Nevada Territory in 1861. In *Roughing It*, Twain described their overland stagecoach for the trip out West as,

> a great swinging and swaying stage, of the most sumptuous description – an imposing cradle on wheels. It was drawn by six handsome horses, and by the side of the driver sat the "conductor," [shotgun messenger] the legitimate captain of the craft; for it was his business to take charge and care of the mails, baggage, express matter, and passengers.

Figure 18. A stagecoach prepares to leave Virginia City, Nevada Territory circa 1870s. The stagecoach was similar to the models Mark Twain rode in during his time in the West. (Library of Congress)

Twain followed his epic transcontinental journey with many local stagecoach trips in the region and completed 13 trans-Sierra trips to San Francisco.

Eventually, Wells Fargo acquired other stage companies, setting themselves up in monopoly over the long-haul route until the completion of the transcontinental railroad in 1869. Local stagecoach service continued where rail lines were absent.

If not on foot or traveling in the aristocratic comfort of a stagecoach, horse or mule-mounted travel was next favored. The three-month tally observers counted 883 mounted travelers in 1864.

Transport of freight and livestock was another major component of wagon road traffic. The three-month census pegged the parade at 4,649 head of cattle, 5,000 pack train animals and 2,564 teams with wagons. Total annual tonnage of freight varied between 45,000 and 70,000 tons and road tolls climbed as high as $12,000,000 in 1863, making the point that the real money lay not in the mines, but in servicing the mining industry.

The need to transport with expediency large amounts of freight over long distance to the Nevada mines created the need for a super freight wagon. Known as the Washoe Wagon, it was the 19th century animal-powered equivalent to a modern-day semi-trailer truck. Typically, the Washoe Wagon would be made of three large, high-sided wagons and possibly, a small trailer, all pulled by a team of 16 sturdy mules. It could haul an arduous load of 25 tons up steep grades and over 7000 ft. summits.

Professor Brewer summarized the enormity of the movement of people and goods when he wrote in his journal,

> It is stated that five thousand teams are steadily employed in the Washoe trade and other commerce east of the Sierra—not little teams of two horses, but generally of six horses or

mules, often as many as eight or ten, carrying loads of three to eight tons, on huge cumbrous wagons.

The storied and legendary Pony Express, a relay of horse mounted riders carrying express mail, passed through Lake Tahoe on its 2,000-mile, 10-day route from St. Joseph, Mo. to Sacramento, Calif. From April 1860 to October 1861, riders raced on the Carson

Figure 19. Washoe wagons posed for a photo as they moved through Slippery Ford west of Johnson's Pass. Mark Twain passed through this point while traveling to and from San Francisco. (Wikimedia Commons)

Emigrant Road over Luther Pass and beginning in May 1860, over Kingsbury Grade and the new section of Lake Tahoe Wagon Road. In the Lake Tahoe region, home (relay) stations were at Carson City, Genoa and Friday's Station in the Nevada Territory and Lake Valley House (until May 1860) and Yank's Station (beginning in May 1860) in California. The completion of the transcontinental telegraph and crippling financial losses ended the Pony Express on October 24, 1863.

Mark Twain recalled in *Roughing It* a much-anticipated encounter with a Pony Express rider on his 1861 journey westward. The excerpt begins with the stagecoach driver shouting to the thrilled passengers,

"HERE HE COMES!"

Every neck is stretched further, and every eye strained wider. Away across the endless dead level of the prairie a black speck appears against the sky, and it is plain that it moves. Well, I should think so! In a second or two it becomes a horse and rider, rising and falling, rising and falling-- sweeping toward us nearer and nearer--growing more and more distinct, more and more sharply defined-- nearer and still nearer, and the flutter of the hoofs comes faintly to the ear—another instant a whoop and a hurrah from our upper deck, a wave of the rider's hand, but no reply, and man and horse burst past our excited faces, and go winging away like a belated fragment of a storm!

So sudden is it all, and so like a flash of unreal fancy, that but for the flake of white foam left quivering and perishing on a mail-sack after the vision had flashed by and disappeared, we might have doubted whether we had seen any actual horse and man at all, maybe.

Figure 20. This Pony Express rider with packhorse in 1861 was similar to the single-horse rider described in Mark Twain's Roughing It. (US National Archives & Records Administration)

During the heavy Sierra winter, keeping the road free of snow was dicey at best. Teams of horses pulled scrapers and chains to keep the road open as long as possible. Figure 21 shows a wagon passing on the road, confined on each side by snow banks equal in height to the loaded freight wagons.

With roads clogged with snow, a special kind of person challenged the forbidding conditions to carry through mail and small packages. During a 20-year period beginning in January 1856, John A. "Snowshoe" Thompson, made the twice-monthly trip on hand-carved skis, called snowshoes then. Thompson, a Norwegian immigrant, carried 40-60 pounds of mail in a pack on his back over Kingsbury Grade and the Lake Tahoe Wagon Road, starting in the Carson Valley and ending in Placerville. Although Thompson was

Figure 21. Teams passed over the western summit on the Lake Tahoe Wagon Road in early spring circa 1865. The road was kept open as much as possible year-round. Mark Twain passed through this point while traveling to and from San Francisco. (Wikimedia Commons)

not the first to carry mail on skis over the Sierra Nevada, his superior endurance and bravery became a classic in the annals of western ski history.

Settlements, Resorts and Washoe Tribal Campsites

We begin our look at the pioneer settlements of the era, as though we were circumnavigating Tahoe by water and land in a clockwise direction beginning about five miles downstream of the origin of the Truckee River at the Lake Tahoe outlet. Most settlements were along the shore to take advantage of a prime waterfront location that enabled ease of travel by watercraft or lateral movement along the exposed parts of the shoreline when water levels were very low. Other settlements established themselves along the transportation routes with the larger and more prosperous operations located along the Lake Tahoe Wagon Road.

The accompanying maps represent the measurements, findings, and interpretations made by Government Land Office surveyors as they laid out plats for the U.S. Public Land Survey. The plats were part of a system that inventoried, located, and identified federal government lands. These plats are the basis for the maps in this book. The Public Land Survey covered Tahoe Basin portions of the Nevada Territory in 1861 (with the exception of one township) and the Tahoe Basin portion of the State of California in 1865.

The maps represent the Tahoe Basin and adjacent areas within the Nevada Territory and the State of California as of 1865. The author added points of interest if there was sufficient credible documentation to show such a point existed in 1861-65. This is because government land surveyors either ignored or overlooked the point of interest, as was the case with the Washoe tribal campsites. In the case of the Nevada Territorial plats, the author added a point of interest if it appeared within four years after the initial 1861 survey.

The Tahoe Basin never experienced a mining boom but various

speculative strikes erupted in the early 1860s just beyond the North Shore. Knoxville and Claraville were small boomtowns that sprang up in the summer of 1863 along the Truckee River near Squaw Valley. They exploded with feverish mining activity fueled mainly by the hype of the Comstock discovery. Town lots were for sale at outrageous prices, and an assortment of ramshackle shops, hotels and saloons catered to the needs of over-optimistic miners. Like many boomtowns, reality settled in after the bluster died out, and by May 1865, visiting General Land Office surveyors classified the towns as abandoned.

Even as these towns imploded after a short intense life, they spread the seeds of early settlement. Their main contribution to the region was the many disappointed miners who migrated to North Lake Tahoe in pursuit of occupations that were more reliable. They founded the first town site, established agricultural enterprises, built tourist and traveler accommodations and engaged in early lumbering. Their surnames still resound as geographical monikers in the region – Ward, Ellis, Blackwood and Madden.

Fish and Ferguson harvested natural hay in Squaw Valley and the meadow abutting the Truckee River outlet. They maintained the small cabin called Outlet Station visited by sketch artist Joseph Lamson in August 1861, and they assembled their schooner *Iron Duke* here. A toll road connected the Truckee River-Donner Summit route through the Truckee River canyon to the outlet area in 1860 and followed the segment of the Placer County Emigrant Road from Squaw Valley to the Lake Tahoe outlet.

Following the collapse of the boomtowns along the Truckee River, miners moved upriver to its headwater at Lake Tahoe. Here, they laid out a town site and engaged in other town improvements. They called the place "Tahoe," and the "City" surname did not attach until years later. One former miner, William Pomin, was the first to set up in Tahoe City in 1864. He later opened the Tahoe House hotel in

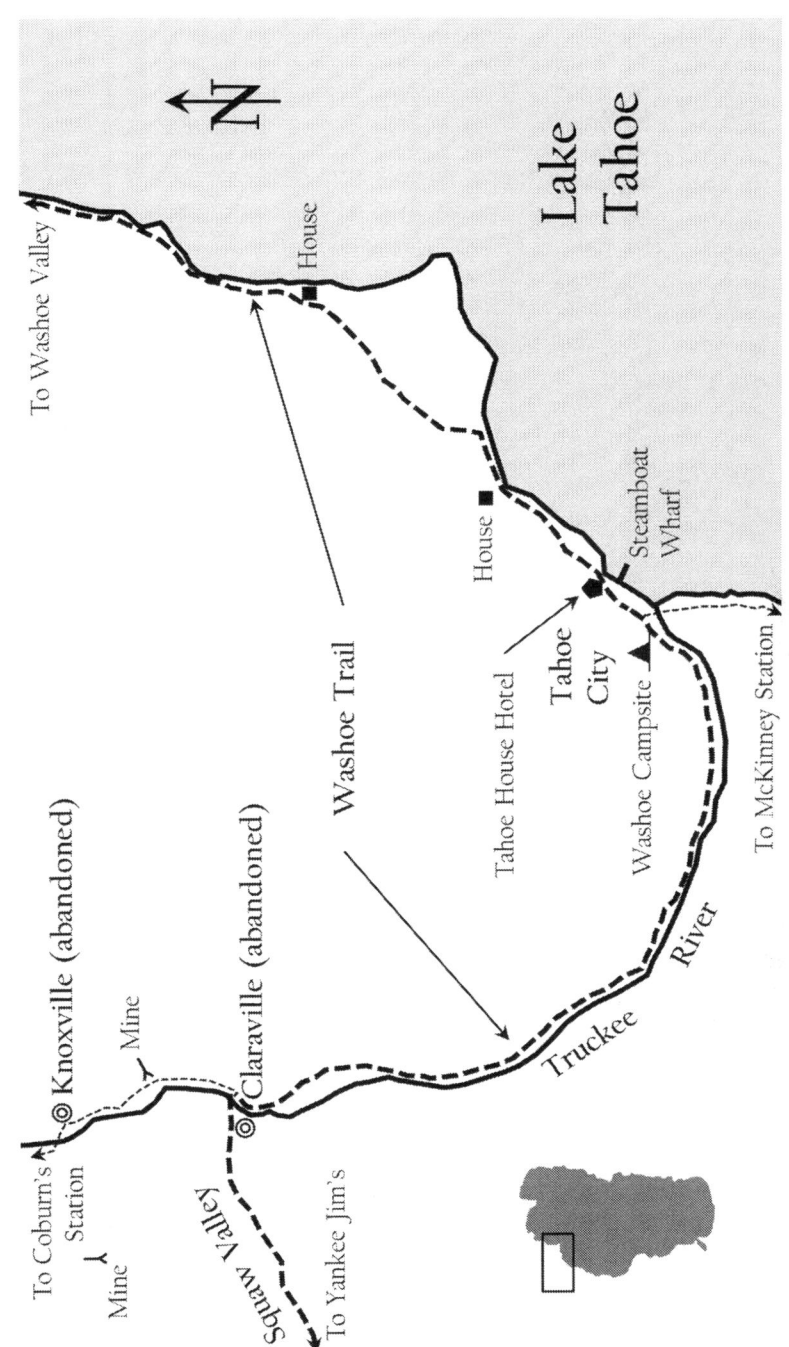

Figure 22. Map showing North Shore and Truckee River

1868, and became the patriarch of a line of descendants who enmeshed themselves in Tahoe history for the next 150 years. By 1865, Tahoe City had 15 residents and a "steamboat wharf." A year later, the place had suddenly achieved regional popularity with 50 houses, 2 hotels and a small fleet of fishing and pleasure boats moored offshore from its public commons.

On a hill overlooking the Truckee River outlet, was a seasonal Washoe village, *da ba dor da wet*, primarily devoted to fishing and collecting of grasshoppers. Tribal members collected swallow eggs from nests on the overhanging rock formation that abutted what is now Commons Beach.

Traveling generally eastward from Tahoe City toward Carnelian Bay, a string of rustic cabins appeared along the shoreline. Even though the government did not survey the land plats in this area until 1865, officials opened unmapped government land in the 1850s under the Preemption Act of 1841. These cabins were part of the land improvements required by the Preemption Act for settlers to complete the ownership process. One of these cabins would play a role in Sam Clemens' first visit in September 1861.

Closer to Stateline Point, D. H. Wright built a large log cabin in 1865 along the Washoe Trail and near the shore. Called Pine Grove Station, it was a wood camp for gathering of cordwood, first for the Comstock and later in 1869 for the community of Truckee.

Between the Truckee River outlet and Crystal Bay were seasonal Washoe tribal camps strategically located on outlets of these major streams: Burton, Watson, Griff and Incline creeks. The campsites took advantage of fish migration and the rich diversity of plants and edible creatures along the riparian zone. Upstream from the Watson Creek campsite was a quarry where Washoe mined basalt for tools and trading with other tribes.

Figure 23. An 1865 view of Agate Bay from a point just west of the state line showed Dollar Point in the background. Sam Clemens and friend John Kinney passed through this location on foot and by boat in 1861 (Wikimedia Commons)

From Stateline Point and around the shoreline of Crystal Bay there were no settlements or signs of any permanent Euro-American habitation for at least 12 miles. The first sign of civilized habitation was the James Nye & Co. cabin close to the shoreline and near the mouth of Bliss Creek as shown on Figure 25. This was the site of the timber claim filed by Territorial Governor James Nye and his partners.

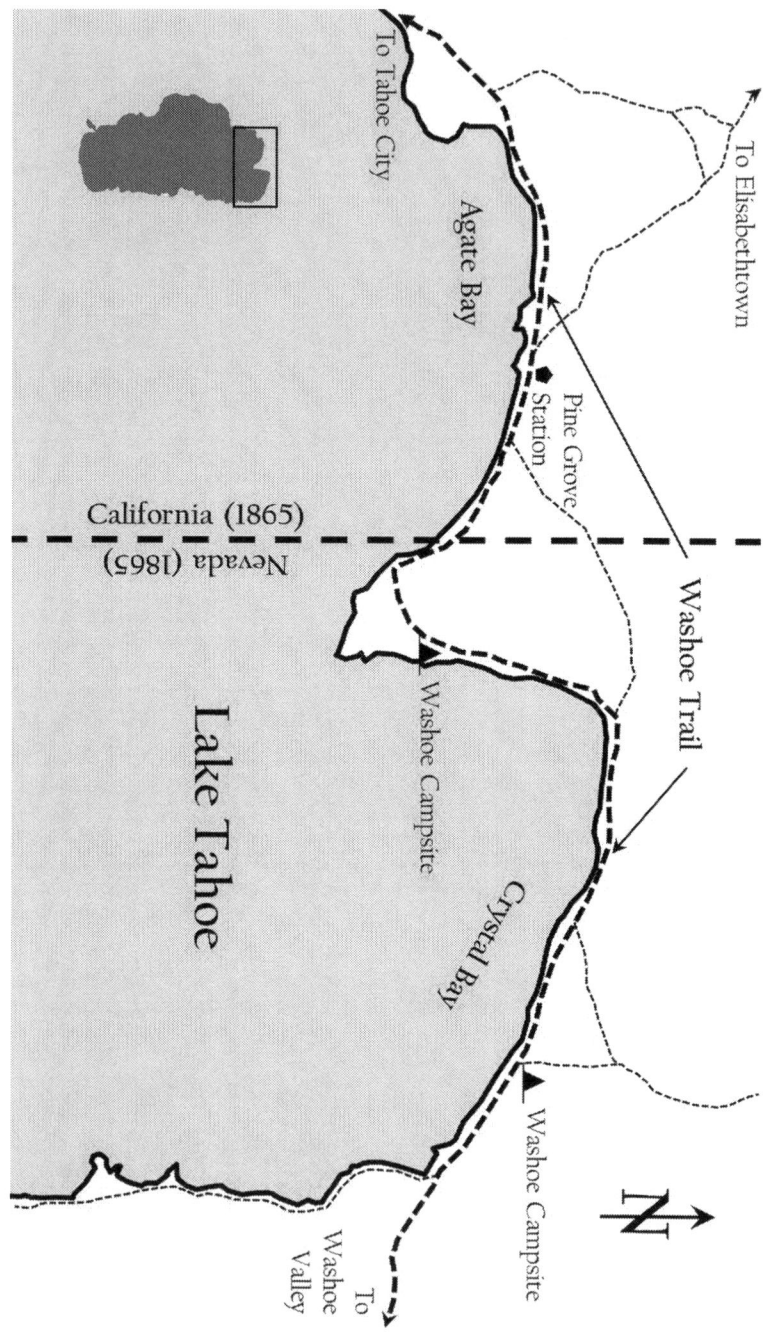

Figure 24. Map showing North Shore near Agate Bay

Two miles south of the Nye cabin, another log cabin was nestled on the shoreline. This likely existed for the same reason as the Nye cabin: to complete the ownership requirements by demonstrating improvement of the land. It was notable for its adjacent wharf that would be an inviting East Shore landing for small craft in search of a safe harbor. Glenbrook was a center of intense maritime activity and nascent lumber and agricultural production. Here, Rufus Walton, a former Maine lumberman, operated Walton's Landing while living in a nearby cabin on the south end of Glenbrook Bay, known briefly as Walton's Bay in 1860. Walton received over-water shipments from Casnell's Wharf, later known as McKinney's Landing or McKinney Station, which was 11 miles across the lake. Workers transferred the cargo to large freight wagons for delivery to the Comstock and other emerging communities over the Walton Toll Road.

On May 27, 1861, sketch artist and fellow Mainer Joseph Lamson, stayed overnight with Walton, his wife and daughter while walking to Carson City. Lamson noted Walton's cabin was made of roughhewn logs with wide gaps and furnished with equally rough, sparse pieces. Lamson found amusements in the squirrels that came and went at-will, snatching small food scraps from his table. While circumnavigating the lake by boat, Lamson paid a repeat visit to his host on August 2.

Just steps away from Walton's cabin, the Lake Bigler Lumber Co. sawmill, founded by Augustus Pray and partners, was under construction in 1861. Water diverted from Glenbrook Creek powered the mill. In a normal year, flow in Glenbrook Creek becomes negligible by late-July and insufficient to power a sawmill. The mill was under construction in 1861 and could not have been in production in September of 1861 since the winter of 1860-61 was 75 percent of average. The mill remained idle until the spring of 1862 when flow resumed in Glenbrook Creek. Because of the exceptionally short seasonal flow even in normal years, Pray

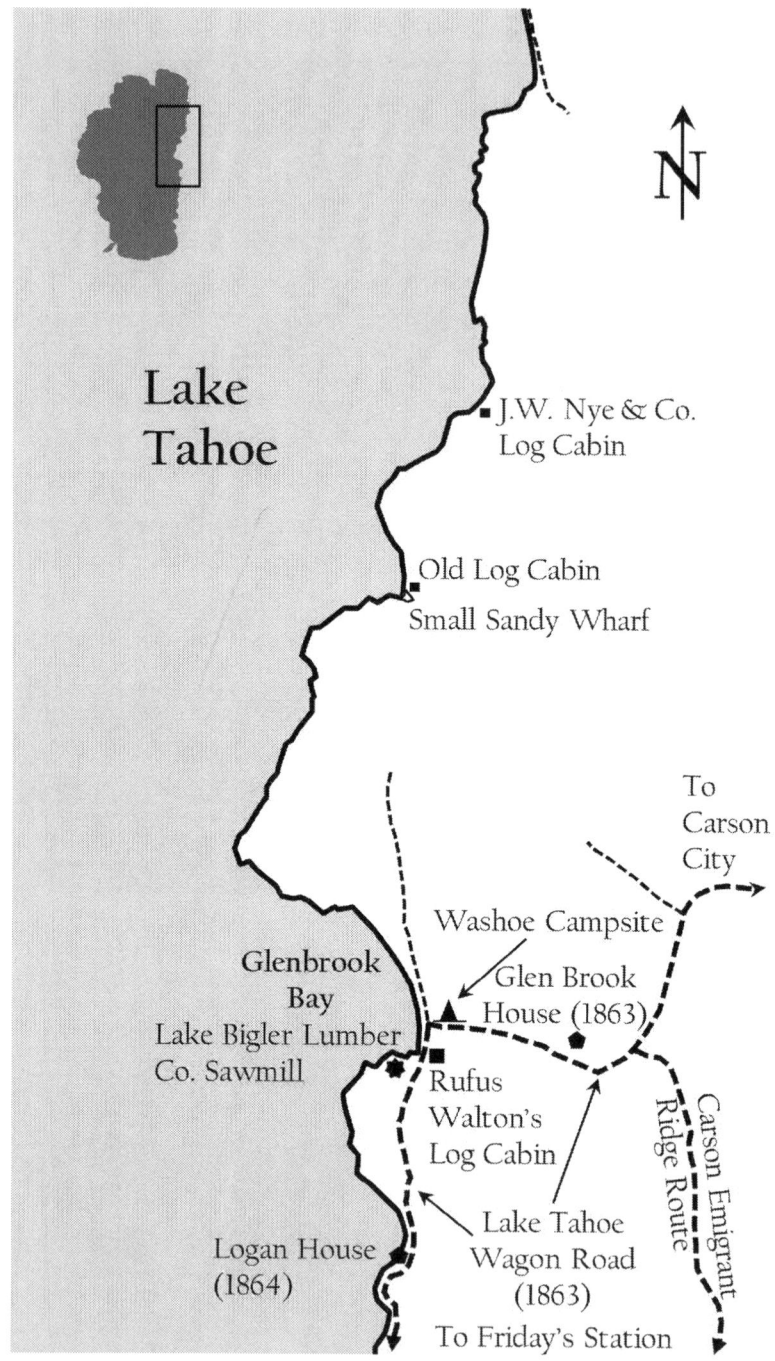

Figure 25. Map showing East Shore near Glenbrook Bay

converted the mill to steam power two years later. Farther up the canyon, French-Canadian Michele Spooner and partners cut timber and operated a steam-powered mill located on the Walton Toll Road.

In the meadow and south of Glenbrook Creek was a major Washoe camp, *da ek wa dop push*. The Native Americans fished in nearby streams and gathered berries at the south end of the bay. The camp persisted despite the Euro-American settlement and agricultural activity.

The 1863 opening of the Kings Canyon Road brought increased traffic through Glenbrook. Responding to the windfall business opportunity, one of Pray's former partners and another person opened a luxury hotel on the new road that same year. Glen Brook House sat on five acres on the edge of the upper meadow, about a one-half mile from the lake. Among the early resorts, it was among the finest in terms of furnishings and appointments.

Two miles along the shoreline and south of Glenbrook, Robert Logan founded Logan House, a.k.a. Logan Hotel, in 1863. Logan and partner Wellington Stewart ran the two-story hotel aimed at low-budget travelers along the Lake Tahoe Wagon Road with rates less than the luxury Glen Brook House just up the road. Mark Twain stayed at this hotel in 1863 and wrote a particularly adorning piece about his visit in the *Territorial Enterprise*.

Proceeding farther south along the East Shore was the most prominent natural landmark on the Lake Tahoe shoreline, Cave Rock. Known to the Washoe as *da ek wa dop push*, it was the spiritual centerpiece of the tribe. Geologically speaking, the formation was the remaining visible vestige of the solidified throat of a long extinct volcano. Just south of Cave Rock and bordering on a scenic bay of the same name, Zephyr Cove House was another lakeside hostelry for travelers and freight haulers on the Lake Tahoe Wagon Road.

Departing from the shoreline about a half-mile inland and close to the California-Nevada border was the junction of three key roads: Lake Tahoe Wagon Road (1863), Kingsbury Grade (1860), and a third local road (*circa* 1861 or earlier) that more or less ran parallel to the shoreline and reconnected to the main road farther west. At this strategic junction was Friday's Station, which was initially a log cabin and later, a substantive structure with accommodations, blacksmith shop and livery services. Just west of Friday's was Lapham's Hotel with its saloon and dining room. Lapham engaged

Figure 26. This circa 1865 photo showed the view to the north from the site of Logan Hotel. No known images of the Logan Hotel structure exist. Mark Twain saw this same view during his stay at Logan Hotel in 1863. (Library of Congress)

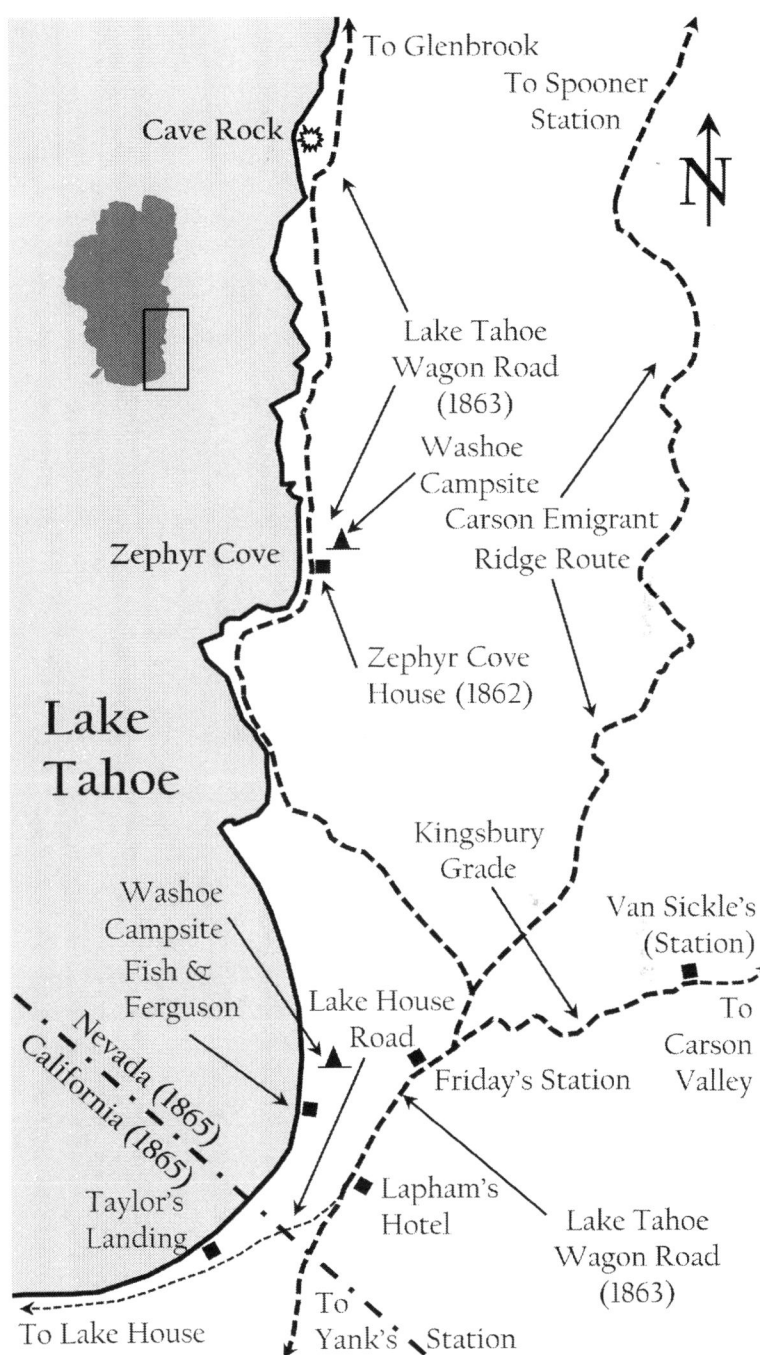

Figure 27. Map showing East Shore near Zephyr Cove

Figure 28. Cave Rock was visible through the trees from the Lake Tahoe Wagon Road in this 1866 photo. Mark Twain saw the same view from his stagecoach as he traveled through Lake Tahoe. (Library of Congress)

in commercial fishing and operated a fish market, known as Lapham's Fish Market and Landing, possibly at Fish & Ferguson's site on the waterfront. Washoe anglers who were not subject to fishing regulations supplied the market with fish along with the commercial fishing enterprise of Burke and Company.

Beginning with Friday's Station, and stretching along 16 miles the Lake Tahoe Wagon Road toward the summit of the Sierra, was a series of roadhouses that provided varied services to travelers and teamsters. Heading southwest from Friday's, one would have encountered Lapham's Hotel, The bawdy roadhouse serving the masses on their way to the Comstock. Travelogue writer J. Ross

Figure 29. This photo showed Zephyr Cove House as it appeared in 1866. Logan House may have been a similar looking structure. (Library of Congress)

Browne described the Cabin, Sierra House, Pine Grove House, Yank's Station and Asa Hawley's Lake Valley House before confronting the steep climbs up the Hawley Grade or Johnson's Cutoff to Johnson's Pass. After the completion of the railroad over the Sierra Nevada, many of the roadhouses and inns went into decline but found renewed use as headquarters for logging operations in the 1870s and 1880s.

In 1851, Martin Smith originally founded the predecessor to Yank's Station as the first trading post in the Tahoe Basin. He later sold it to

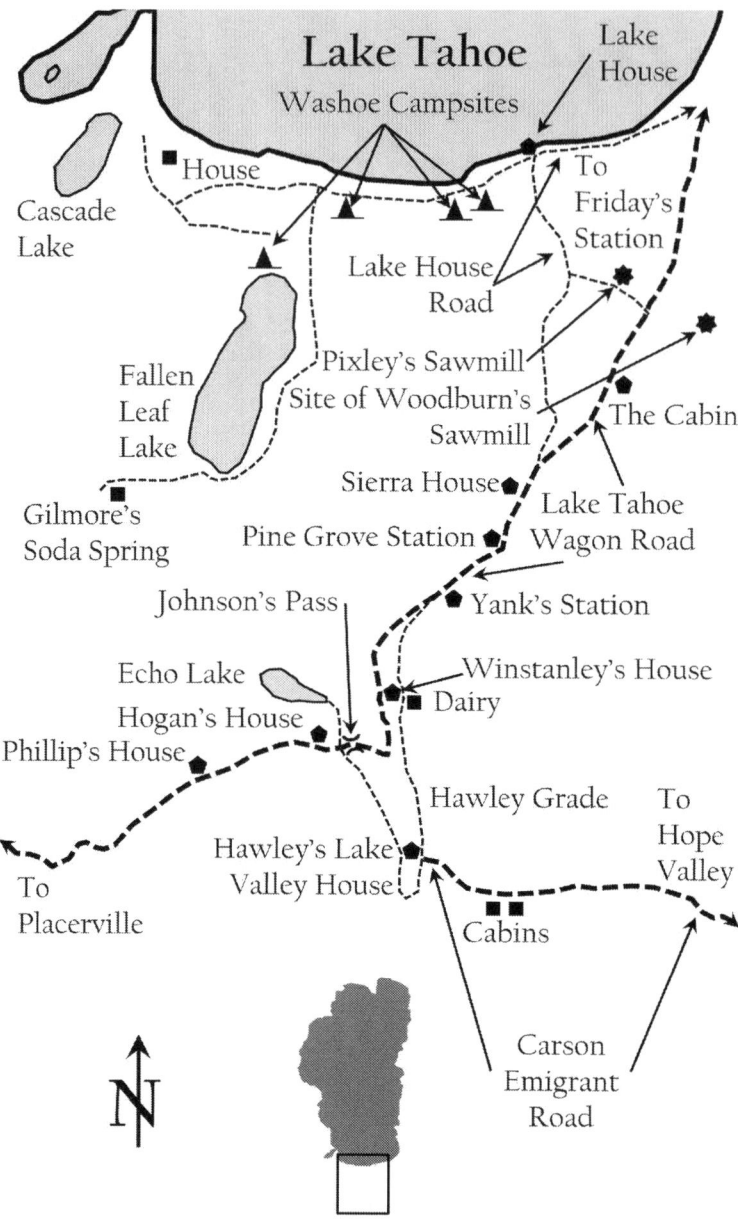

Figure 30. Map showing the South Shore and Lake Valley

Figure 31. This photo showed Friday's Station circa 1866. Mark Twain passed through this station while traveling to and from San Francisco. (Library of Congress)

Ephraim "Yank" Clement, who lent his nickname to the property.

Lake Valley House held a well-earned reputation as raucous, squalid and overcrowded. In Browne's brief March 1860 visit at Lake Valley House, he characterized the structure as a "tolerably good-sized shanty at the foot of the [Hawley] grade." Here, he found 100-300 stranded Comstock fortune seekers waiting out a late winter snowstorm along with a much-harried proprietor. The inn had little to eat and only offered a vile form of whisky to drink.

Returning to the lakeshore near Friday's Station, the substantial Washoe campsite *lam watah* occupied the large spring-fed meadow that led to the shore. Notable for its concentration of bedrock mortars, the Washoe favored this campsite for its nearby fishing in

Edgewood Creek and plentiful berries, roots and grass seeds. The Lake Tahoe Wagon Road, traveled by Mark Twain, passed between the meadow encampment and the lake.

Continuing with the circumnavigation of the shoreline and moving about three miles west into California was the storied Lake House. Completed in the fall of 1859, Lake House was the first commercial

Figure 32. This photo showed Yank's Station as it appeared in 1866. Mark Twain passed through this station on the stage line and might have stepped off for a rest while traveling to and from San Francisco. (Library of Congress)

lakeside retreat at Lake Tahoe. Initially known as Lake Bigler House, the owners abridged the name to Lake House in response to the anti-Governor Bigler political movement (See Chapter 4). Mark Twain stayed here in the summer of 1863 in search of an elusive cure for a persistent upper respiratory illness.

Following the destruction of the first building by fire in 1866, new owners rebuilt it into a more sophisticated way station in 1868 and christened the new construction Rowland's Lake House and Station. Between the Upper Truckee outlet by Lake House, along the shoreline, and all the way to the Taylor Creek outlet from Fallen

Figure 33. The Lake House, formerly Lake Bigler House, as it appeared in this 1866 photo. Mark Twain stayed here in 1863. (Library of Congress)

Leaf Lake, the Washoe occupied the largest concentration of significant campsites. All these campsites were largely devoted to fishing the plentiful waters of nearby streams. Washoe camped near, but not next to, water to avoid flood damage from unusually large summer storms. The Washoe tribal members were quite protective of their streamside fishing locations and actively discouraged Euro-Americans from taking fish.

About seven miles from the shore and above Fallen Leaf Lake was Gilmore's Mineral Spring at Glen Alpine. While on a pleasure hike in the 1850s, Nathan Gilmore discovered a spring seep and pool of naturally carbonated mineral water. By 1865, he had erected a cabin and tent platforms to cater to tourists interested in the perceived health benefits of mountain air, sleeping outdoors and imbibing in the naturally carbonated spring water for supposed medicinal purposes.

Farther up along the West Shore at the head of Emerald Bay was the seasonal residence of Ben Holladay, Jr. known as "The Cottage," and completed in 1863. It was the first home built for pleasure purposes at Lake Tahoe. Holladay's cabin, wharf and boathouse occupied the northwest corner of the bay. He shared the location with other long-term seasonal residents, the Washoe, who camped at the outlet of Eagle Creek. In the past, the Washoe had fought here with trespassers from the California tribes in the Sierra foothills.

A visitor to the Holladay's villa would have encountered his colorful caretaker, Captain Dick Barter, known as the "Hermit of Emerald Bay." He was most notable for the tomb he constructed for himself near the top of Fannette Island. The tomb was a final resting place he never occupied; Barter was lost in a boating accident in 1873.

Six shoreline miles northward along the West Shore was a cabin facing Meek Bay. The cabin probably housed herders and workers for Meeks and Company, who grazed at the meadow and cut wild hay. The Washoe camp m*agulu watah* was here, and provided good fishing and plentiful rhubarb, strawberries and raspberries.

Another two miles along the shore and just north of the outlet of General Creek was the cabin of the pioneer settler General William Phipps, the first recorded pioneer on this part of the lake in 1860. Phipps constructed a cabin in 1862-63, and added a wharf, boathouse, and sailboat to his reclusive domain by 1865. Setting

Figure 34. This photo showed the island in Emerald Bay circa 1866 and the surrounding pre-contact forest on the shoreline. (Wikimedia Commons)

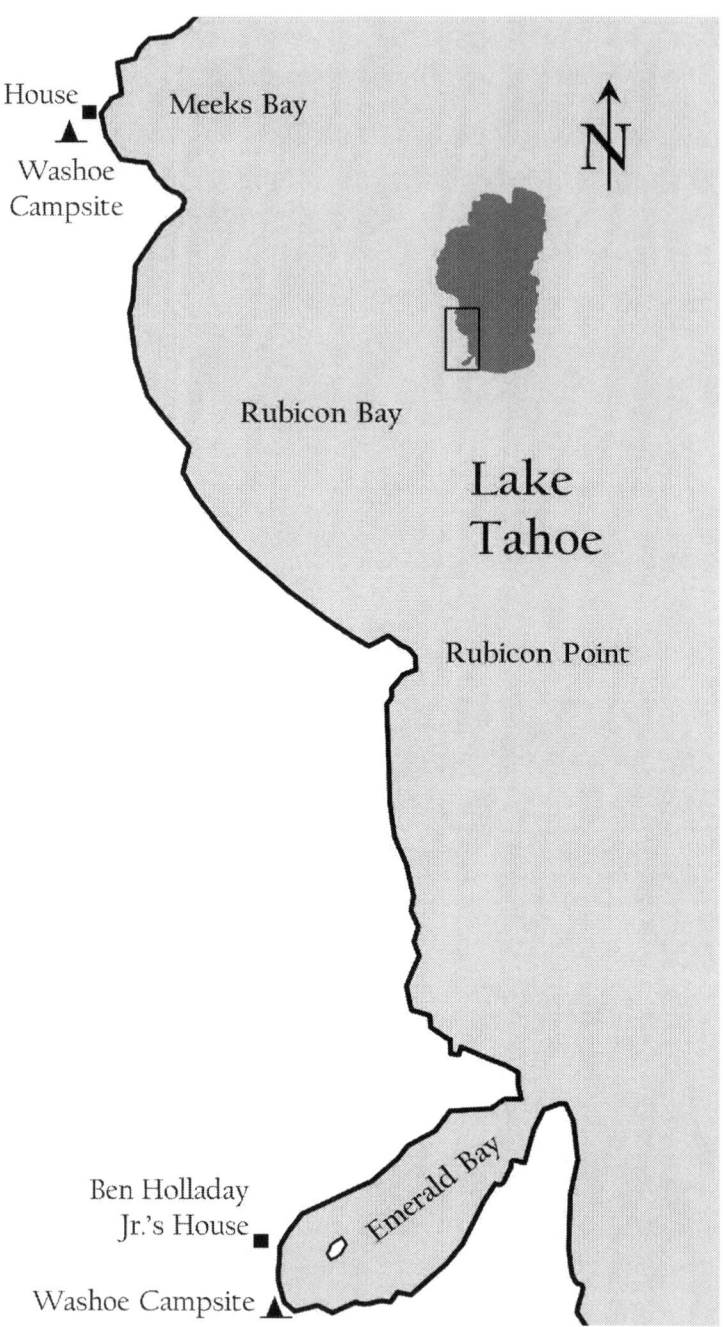

Figure 35. Map showing Emerald Bay and West Shore areas

Figure 36. In this view of Emerald Bay taken in 1866, Ben Holladay Jr.'s summerhouse, "The Cottage" was visible in the background along the shoreline. (Library of Congress)

back from the shore and along the same stream was the Washoe camp, *mayala watah*, favored for its production of fish and rare medicinal plants. Two miles north of Sugar Pine Point, at the point where the Georgetown-Lake Bigler pack trail ended at the Lake Tahoe shoreline was Casnell's cabin, sawmill, and wharf. Later known as McKinney Station, it was the point of transfer for goods and passengers from pack trains to waterborne transit across the lake to Walton's Landing at Glenbrook.

About one mile farther north was the Washoe camp *shoo we tuc watah* situated at Madden Creek and set back from the shore. Tribal

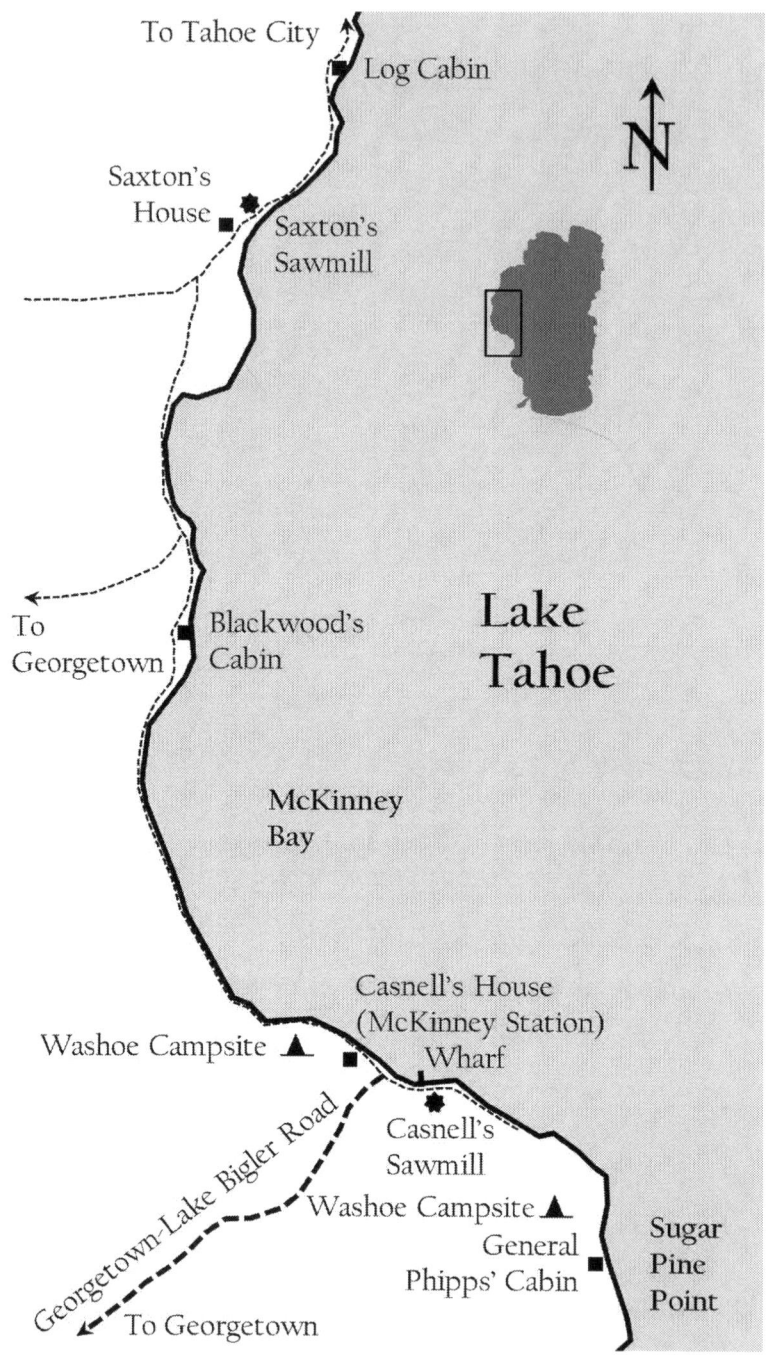

Figure 37. Map showing West Shore and McKinney Bay

members fished here and in nearby McKinney Creek and harvested abundant berries, tiger lily seeds, and sunflower seeds.

About one mile north of the Washoe camp was the 1863 cabin of a former Squaw Valley silver miner-turned-rancher, Hampton Blackwood. Blackwood's cabin was on the lakefront and just south of the mouth of his namesake, Blackwood Creek. Blackwood became notorious in the 1860s for shooting to death a Washoe, who set a fish trap in Blackwood Creek.

Farther north along the shoreline and north of the Ward Creek outlet were a water-powered sawmill and house built by Augustus H. Saxton in 1863. Saxton serviced markets associated with the Central Pacific Railroad construction over Donner Summit and the Con-Virginia Mine in Virginia City.

Our 1861-65 circumnavigation ends at a commonplace log cabin a few steps from the shore of Lake Tahoe and one mile south of Tahoe City.

In Mark Twain's time, Lake Tahoe was a place of astounding beauty, pristine scenery, and rich untapped resources. Far from the uninhabited wilderness that Mark Twain portrayed in *Roughing It*, the South and East Shores were teeming with travelers and freight wagons headed east to opportunity waiting in the burgeoning mining industry in the Nevada Territory. Strung along this road to opportunity were crowded way stations and ranches that served the massive movement of humanity, animals and goods. Camped in its scenic meadows and still pristine forest were Washoe families living out their final days of aboriginal innocence. The forests, meadows and marshes hosted a dense and diverse population of wildlife. Spawning fish filled its streams bank to bank and immense schools of fish swam its depths. Nevertheless, Tahoe was on the brink of sweeping change. Mark Twain saw it in its final pristine form and wrote eloquently about its virtues without ever acknowledging its eventual fate at the hands of timber barons, water seekers, ranchers and landowners.

Chapter 2

Interpreting the Writings of Mark Twain

Understanding and interpreting the clues within the relevant writings of Mark Twain require a multidisciplinary approach. Simple knowledge of the very limited instant facts is not enough, nor is broader knowledge of the works of Mark Twain alone sufficient. A thorough analysis views the relevant literature through the lenses of geology, limnology, physics, geography, astronomy, biology, semantics, deductive reasoning, and, of course, the natural and cultural histories of Lake Tahoe. For example, to reconstruct accurately the timber claim adventure, one must think in terms of the conditions as they existed in 1861, and not as they appear today.

Roughing It presents the biggest challenge since it contains information that may be true, exaggerated, deliberately untrue, or inadvertently wrong. *Innocents Abroad* contains some exaggerated accounts. The news articles and creative pieces concerning Lake Tahoe can contain exaggerations or just plain wrong information, whether deliberate or careless. In one case, Twain mistakes Cisco, the Central Pacific Railroad temporary terminus on the west slope of the Sierra Nevada, for Donner Summit on the crest of the Sierra.

The reader may wish to read or review the relevant sections of *Roughing It* contained in Appendix I before continuing with this chapter.

Mark Twain or Samuel L. Clemens?

In this book, we follow the convention observed by many scholars and identify the central character as Sam Clemens or Mark Twain, depending on which persona is the source. For example, in the passages concerning Lake Tahoe in Roughing It and Innocents Abroad, it is Mark Twain recounting and interpreting the observations and recollections of Sam Clemens. In personal letters of the period of 1861-65, it is Sam Clemens, as he signed them.

Multiple Sources Compared and Contrasted to Interpret *Roughing It*

Chapters 22 and 23 in *Roughing It* are one of three core sources, but *Roughing It* is largely a work of creative nonfiction. The two chapters contain inaccuracies, omissions, misremembered events and humorous exaggerations. Prominent Mark Twain scholar R. Kent Rasmussen advises *Roughing It* readers, "… many of its descriptions of incidents and people are either embellishments or wholesale inventions." One must exercise critical thinking, engage in circumspection, and fully use knowledge of the book's settings to evaluate the veracity of any of its passages.

To get a better fix on the reality of the Lake Tahoe timber claim adventure, we bring into the mix 1861 letters written by Clemens to relatives that covered the same subject and relevant remarks by Mark Twain during 1870s lectures promoting the publication of *Roughing It*.

As a first step, we reconcile the conflicting and vague information using the letters, lectures and book text. *Roughing It* provides the only account of the route from Carson City to Lake Tahoe. The letters generally provide the documentation for the activities and events at Tahoe during the 1861 visits with any gaps filled in by *Roughing It* material, where appropriate. Where there is a conflict, the letters take precedence as the most credible source, followed by the narrative in *Roughing It*, amplified by the reported lecture remarks. In Appendix II, we use this hierarchy to determine the time line and sequence of campsites. In one case, we rely on statements of Mark Twain interviewer and biographical writer George Wharton James to corroborate the location.

Roughing It Was Creative Nonfiction with Inaccuracies

Chapters 22 and 23 of *Roughing It* covered Mark Twain's time at Lake Tahoe as Sam Clemens. These chapters told the story as though it was a single trip but were actually a composite of two visits to the lake in 1861. To these events, we had the passage of time (about 9-10 years) on his recollection of events, the order in which he presented them and even which factual and fabricated aspects he chose to include. Overlaid on all of this was Mark Twain's penchant for humor and exaggeration. The result was a work of creative nonfiction where the author took a factual base and used the techniques of a novelist and humorist to produce an economically viable literary piece. Others have characterized the book as a memoir, travelogue or historical novel. It is perhaps a composite of all these forms with an overlay of humorous exaggeration, tall tales and invented elements and characters.

We know there were a number of major and minor inaccuracies in the Lake Tahoe account that were not obvious humorous exaggerations. Here, we list, and correct some of Twain's misremembered events and features, errors in narrative, erroneous imagery, and over dramatization. Elsewhere in this book, we deal with other inaccuracies in line with the relevant portion of the story.

Twain stated it was the "end of August" and recalled the length of time spent as, "two or three weeks." Both the date and length of time

Figure 38. Portrait of Mark Twain circa 1871 during the time of writing of *Roughing It* (Wikimedia Commons)

spent at the lake are erroneous. From Clemens' letters written in September and October of 1861, we identify two trips to Tahoe for staking a timber claim. The first occurred in the date range of September 14-19 and served as one part of the primary storyline for the *Roughing It* version.

According to the intent expressed in the September letter, he made a second trip a day or two after the first visit, beginning no earlier than September 21 and ending no later than September 30, since Clemens began paid work for his brother Orion on October 1. This appears to be primarily a trip to complete work on a timber claim and may account for much of the recreation activity described in the book text. In an October 25, 1861 letter to his sister, Clemens responded to his sister's earlier inquiry, reassuring her that work was complete on the timber claim naming her husband and others as principals.

Insofar as the *Roughing It* timber claim tale is a composite of two trips, we are able to reason out the conflicting and consistent parts of the accounts contained in the book and two letters. The process of our reasoned analysis appears in Appendix II, "Lake Tahoe Campsite Sequence and Identification" and the results form the basis of the narrative in Chapter 3, "A Wood Ranch or So and Become Wealthy" As Twain recalled sighting the lake for the first time and although he could not see the entire lake in one view, he nonetheless estimated, "... one would have to use up eighty or a hundred good miles in traveling around it." An accurate measurement of the Tahoe shoreline was unknown until the completion of the 1865 General Land Office survey on the California side. With this information in hand, the surveys determined the lake shoreline length was 75.1 miles.

In *Roughing It*, Twain estimated the population of the Tahoe Basin at not more than, "fifteen other human beings." We know from 1861 Tahoe history (see Chapter 1) that the south and southeast areas of the lake were overrun with hundreds of persons headed for the

Comstock and surrounding area. This underestimated population is another clue to Twain's location on the lake. If he had passed through Glenbrook, as some speculate, he would have observed the passage of freight and travelers at Walton's Landing. Since he was on the sparsely populated North Shore, Twain derived his estimate from this slender view of Tahoe without the benefit of knowing about the massive movement of goods and people through Glenbrook or the mass of humanity and freight moving through Lake Valley.

A second issue with the low population estimate is the oversight of the hundreds of Washoe tribal members in residence. Here, we suspect that Clemens never saw any tribal members because of their cultural proclivity of not revealing themselves to strangers. An alternative explanation is that Clemens was aware of the Washoe presence, but did not consider them consequential because of Mark Twain's prejudicial attitude toward Native Americans.

Twain erred slightly in his report on the depth of Lake Tahoe, "By official measurement the lake in its centre is one thousand five hundred and twenty-five feet deep!" The maximum depth of Lake Tahoe was not accurately determined until 1875 when a newspaper editor, C. F. McGlashan, and an astronomy enthusiast, Charles Burkhalter, used a weighted Champagne bottle to plumb its maximum depth of 1,645 feet. The first U.S. Coast and Geodetic bathymetric survey of Lake Tahoe confirmed the measurement in 1923.

In constructing the solitude of the timber claim setting, Twain wrote that the quietude and soothing sounds were punctuated by "the far-off thunder of an avalanche." Though the highest mountain peaks of the Sierra Nevada held year-round snow in 1861, the possibility of late summer avalanches was nil. Even less likely events, recurring rockslides, sometimes characterized as avalanches, could not have occurred in close proximity to the timber claim.

Twain vividly exaggerated the description of the wildfire conflagration and concluded with the destruction of the valuable timber within the claim. The wildfire did not reach the intensity he described and did not destroy the timber. More analysis and information on the wildfire episode is in Chapter 3, "A Wood Ranch of So and Become Wealthy"

The *Roughing It* storyline inserts a working sawmill into the Lake Tahoe setting for the timber claim. At first blush, this might appear to be the Lake Bigler Lumber Company mill at Glenbrook but is actually a misrembered feature. The mill was under construction in 1861, could not have been in production in September 1861 when Clemens was on the North Shore, and did not produce lumber until 1862. Clemens even wrote his mother in 1861 about the need for a lumberman to bring a sawmill to Lake Tahoe.

The mill was a water-powered sawmill that diverted the flow of Glenbrook Creek through a millrace, a type of water flume, to the waterwheel. Water flow in Glenbrook Creek is mainly from snowmelt, peaks in normal years in mid-May, and falls below one cubic foot per second by mid-July.

The Lake Bigler Lumber Company mill used an overshot waterwheel where water flows to the top of the wheel. This type of waterwheel requires a minimum of one cubic foot per second of water flow for activation and much more to develop enough power to saw timber into lumber. The winter of 1860-61 was 75% of average, so water flow would have dropped well below the minimum requirement by the end of May, even if the mill had been completed that quickly.

Clemens did not enter Lake Tahoe until the latter part of September of 1861. Compare this date to the end of May when flow in Glenbrook Creek was too low to be useful. The inescapable conclusion is that the mill was not operational and workers would not have been present when Clemens appeared at Tahoe. The workers and sawmill to which he referred could not have been the Lake Bigler Lumber Company mill.

As many as a dozen illustrators prepared the illustrations in *Roughing It*. In general, one should not read too much into the illustrations since the publisher commissioned them. They represented the artist's interpretation of Twain's descriptions or instructions directly from the publisher. Many were illustrations prepared for other unrelated books. Only one of the six illustrations spread within the two Lake Tahoe chapters has the identifiable monogram of True Williams, who illustrated Twain's first book, *Innocents Abroad*.

Many aspects of the illustrations in the Lake Tahoe chapters appeared to have accurate aspects corroborated by other information. The scene "At Business" (Figure 69) showed the two men drifting among boulders that protruded above the water. This appears to be accurate for the area around Stateline Point. The scene "I Steered" (Figure 51) showed the two rowing across Crystal Bay. It seems plausible except for the extreme topography in the distance. The scene of the wildfire, "Fire at Lake Tahoe" (Figure 64) showed the fire immediately burning to the water's edge, suggested they had to watch the fire burn from the boat, and depicted a very tall sheet of flame. The description in one of the letters discredited all of these. The distant mountain peak and the nearby mountainside roughly depicted in a compressed view the ridgeline along the North Shore near the timber claim and the west-facing slope of Stateline Point, respectively. The image of the brush house, "Our House" (Figure 62) is plausible and fits the relatively flat terrain of the North Shore timber claim. The remaining illustrations are so general that they offer no clues or other specifics.

The conclusion of the Lake Tahoe chapters in *Roughing It*, has Twain making "many trips to the lake" after the initial timber claim adventure and enduring "many a hair-breadth escape and blood-curdling adventure." Twain did make two or three more destination trips to Lake Tahoe and about 12 through trips along the South Shore on his way to San Francisco but never incurred the "many a hair-breath escape and blood-curdling adventure" he supposes.

The news reports of the *Roughing It* promotional lectures portray Twain as pretty much sticking to fact, at least as he knew it then, with a generous dose of relevant humor. Twain spoke of the unique characteristics and magnificent beauty of Lake Tahoe. For these he had no need to exaggerate the natural aspects of the lake; they were impressive enough at face value.

Innocents Abroad Contained Creative Nonfiction and Inaccuracies

Twain's first book was *Innocents Abroad*, the 1869 travelogue on Twain's experiences and impressions of Europe, the Holy Land and North Africa. Insofar as Lake Tahoe was concerned, he used it for comparative purposes mostly. The book contained a few inaccuracies and the beginnings of Twain's penchant to insert tall tales into otherwise nonfiction books for humor or darker purposes. One example had Twain claiming he could count the microscopic-sized scales on a trout at 180 feet depth in Lake Tahoe. In another passage, he told readers the Native American-derived word "Tahoe" meant grasshopper soup. Neither was true. The former was a successful attempt at humorous exaggeration, but the latter was an ethnically motivated criticism of Native American culture.

News Articles Were Generally Accurate

Early in his reporting career, Twain enraged news editors when he wrote a hoax news story that was dutifully reprinted as legitimate news in western papers. In the case of the news stories used as sources for this book, we generally found them accurate with a few minor exceptions such as the confusion between Cisco and Donner Summit. As was Twain's style, he laced his news reporting with personal opinion, such as an article on new fishing laws that diverged into a tirade about the Bigler to Tahoe name change. In these cases, the appearance of opinion over fact was obvious and taken into account.

Chapter 3

A Wood Ranch or So and Become Wealthy

Prologue
Responsibility fell to newly inaugurated President Abraham Lincoln to implement the formation of the Nevada Territory that was carved out of the larger Utah Territory by federal law in 1861. The action came after the discovery of a significant silver ore deposit at Virginia City. Residents wanted local control in the mining area, then known as Washoe. In the tense political environment leading up to the Civil War, federal officials saw the opportunity to strengthen the balance of power by creating a new state free of slavery.

Separate reasons brought Sam Clemens and his older brother Orion to the newly formed Nevada Territory. Owing to his political connections, Orion obtained an appointment from President Lincoln to the office of Secretary of the Nevada Territory. Sam was a riverboat pilot, but lost his job when Civil War hostilities closed down traffic on reaches of the Mississippi River. With little to keep him near home, Sam decided to accompany his brother to his new life in the West. Orion promised to make Sam his assistant, "secretary to the secretary," as Sam put it, in exchange for Sam paying Orion's fare.

The two brothers traveled six days by riverboat to St. Joseph, Missouri where they embarked on the Overland Mail company stagecoach for a tortuous 20-day crossing to Carson City, the newly

Figure 39. Samuel L. Clemens (Mark Twain) in 1863 (Wikimedia Commons)

selected seat of the Nevada Territory. The brothers arrived in Carson City on or about August 14, 1861. Abe Curry and William Ormsby founded Carson City in 1858 on the land of its predecessor, Eagle Ranch. Curry and Ormsby envisioned the new town as the capital of a new territory. The founders laid out 30 ft. x 80 ft. town lots with waffle iron precision. They dedicated about 10 acres in the center as a plaza for a future capitol building. Commercial structures lined up on the west side of the main north-south running thoroughfare, Carson Street. Cross streets led to a scattering of outlying dwellings. In the vacant plaza, horse traders set up auctions, the public gathered for Civil War rallies, and travelers rested their stock while camping there.

Figure 40. Illustration of Carson City in 1861 from A Peep at Washoe (Wikimedia Commons)

Situated on a flat plain called Eagle Valley, Carson City was at the transition from Great Basin desert to the foothills of the Carson

Range. Visitors in 1860 described Carson City as a "thriving settlement" with perhaps 150 buildings made of brick, wood and stretched canvas. Depending on the influx of travelers, the population varied between 1,000 and 1,500 persons. The city's name honors Christopher "Kit" Carson, a mountain man and member of the Fremont 1844-45 expedition in the West.

In a letter to his mother, Sam expressed his opinion of Carson City and showed the early vestiges of the literary talent and humorous style that would propel him through his life.

> ... [W]e are situated in a flat, sandy desert – true. And surrounded on all sides by such prodigious mountains, that when you gaze at them awhile, – and begin to conceive of their grandeur – and next to feel their vastness expanding your soul – and ultimately find yourself growing and swelling and spreading into a giant – I say when this point is reached, you look disdainfully down upon the insignificant village of Carson, and in that instant you are seized with a burning desire to stretch forth your hand, put the city in your pocket, and walk off with it.

> ... Now, although we are surrounded by sand, the greatest part of the town is built upon what was once a very pretty grassy spot; and the streams of pure water that used to poke about it in rural sloth and solitude, now pass through on dusty streets and gladden the hearts of men by reminding them that there is at least something here that hath its prototype among the homes they left behind them. And up "King's Canon," (please pronounce canyon, after the manner of the natives,) there are "ranches," or farms, where they say hay grows, and grass, and beets and onions, and turnips, and other "truck" which is suitable for cows – yes, and even Irish potatoes; also, cabbage, peas and beans.

The houses are mostly frame, unplastered, but "papered" inside with flour-sacks sewed together, and the handsomer the "brand" upon the sacks is, the neater the house looks. Occasionally, you stumble on a stone house. On account of the dryness of the country, the shingles on the houses warp till they look like short joints of stove pipe split lengthwise.

[Remainder of the letter is missing.]

Figure 41. Carson City in the early 1860s looking south along Carson Street from the plaza (Library of Congress)

Facing the vacant Carson City plaza area was the Ormsby House, a hotel that was both sleeping quarters for Sam and Orion at night and an interim office for Orion during the day. Later, Sam moved upstairs to room with 14 other men he came to call the Irish Brigade. Both men had their meals at Mrs. Bridget Murphy's boardinghouse.

Figure 42. In the overview of Carson City in the mid-1860s, evident is its expansion from its early 1860s "outpost" size (Wikimedia Commons)

In *Roughing It*, Twain recalled or creatively wrote about living and eating at Bridget O'Flannigan's boardinghouse, but scholars believe he actually roomed at the Ormsby House while eating at Murphy's boardinghouse.

After settling into their accommodation, Orion and Sam got down to work making arrangements for the inaugural meeting of the territorial legislature. As Sam quickly found out, there was not enough work to keep him gainfully employed. The $800 stake he carried from Missouri kept a roof over his head and food on the table during this period. Eventually, Sam was able to earn eight dollars per day assisting Orion between October 1 and November 29. Between his mid-August arrival in Carson City and the onset of temporary gainful employment in October, Sam turned his attention to other endeavors in hope of providing a source of income.

While killing time in Carson City, Sam met up with another recent arrival, John Kinney, from Cincinnati, Ohio. Kinney had traveled on the overland stage with two justices for the territorial court, arriving the second week of September. He was active in real estate dealings and mining speculation and remained in the Nevada Territory until March 1862.

A World of Talk
Several lumber mills were operating on the east slopes of the Carson Range. Lumbermen had already cut available stands of trees, and speculators controlled the remaining uncut stands. Clearly, future timber supplies would have to come from the Tahoe Basin once the limited stands on the east slope of the Carson Range were exhausted.

In the dormitory at Ormsby House and around Mrs. Murphy's dining table, Sam heard "a world of talk" about the wonders of Lake Tahoe, called Lake Bigler in 1861. Members of the Irish Brigade had been there and established a timber claim in anticipation of a lumbering boom. Sam's curiosity and newly kindled desire to stake a similar claim motivated him to visit the lake. The Irish Brigade offered the use of their rowboat beached at the northeast corner of lake and access to their food and supplies cache on the North Shore.

A Mountain a Thousand Miles High
Sam and John Kinney agreed to hike to Lake Tahoe together and form a partnership on a timber claim. As Mark Twain wrote in *Roughing It*, both men were intrigued and consumed with the goal, "… to take up a wood ranch or so ourselves and become wealthy."

From the date of arrival of Kinney in Carson City, we know that Sam actually set out for Lake Tahoe about September 14, or a day or two later, and not the end of August as he recounted in *Roughing It*.

Not owning horses, the two men necessarily set out on foot and traveled lightly with only blankets and axes. Given their destination as the North Shore, they chose the shortest established route between Carson City and Lake Tahoe. Apparently, members of the Brigade told them the distance was 11 miles, although the actual distance was closer to 11.7 miles. The difference was probably due to inaccuracies in distance measurements during that era of poor mapping of the region. For all the exaggeration and disgust over the difficulty of the hike expressed in the *Roughing It* account, Mark Twain later recalled the distance as 10 miles twice in lectures.

They followed a wagon road that served lumber and ore processing mills in Ash Canyon, called Mill Creek in 1861. This road led to the Washoe Trail that would bring them to the northeast shore of Lake Tahoe. The overall route appears on Figure 43, and the route profile appears on Figure 44, both annotated with quotes from *Roughing It*.

Leaving the valley, Clemens and Kinney followed the wagon road that began its steep climb through Ash Canyon. They passed sagebrush-covered hills with few trees other than cottonwoods, alders and willows growing along watercourses.

As they continued climbing up the canyon, they passed another settler's house and two quartz stamp mills. The water-powered stamp mills used heavy iron columns that acted like hammers to crush the quartz rock into powder.

Once in a powder form, chemical leaching could extract the mineral values, principally gold. The eastern slopes of the Carson Range around Carson City held gold-bearing quartz veins of limited value.

At about the 5,400 ft. elevation, the two entered the remains of the conifer forest that would surround them for most of their journey. It

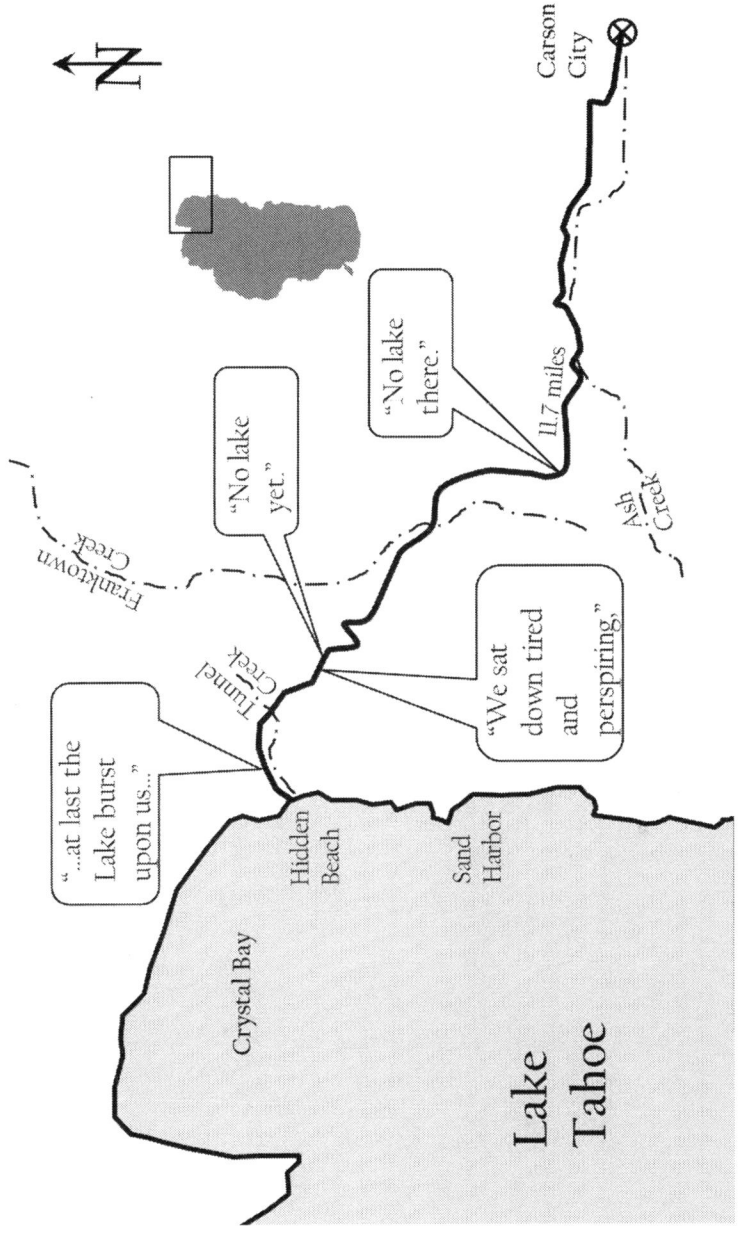

Figure 43. Map showing the route Sam Clemens and John Kinney followed from Carson City to Lake Tahoe.

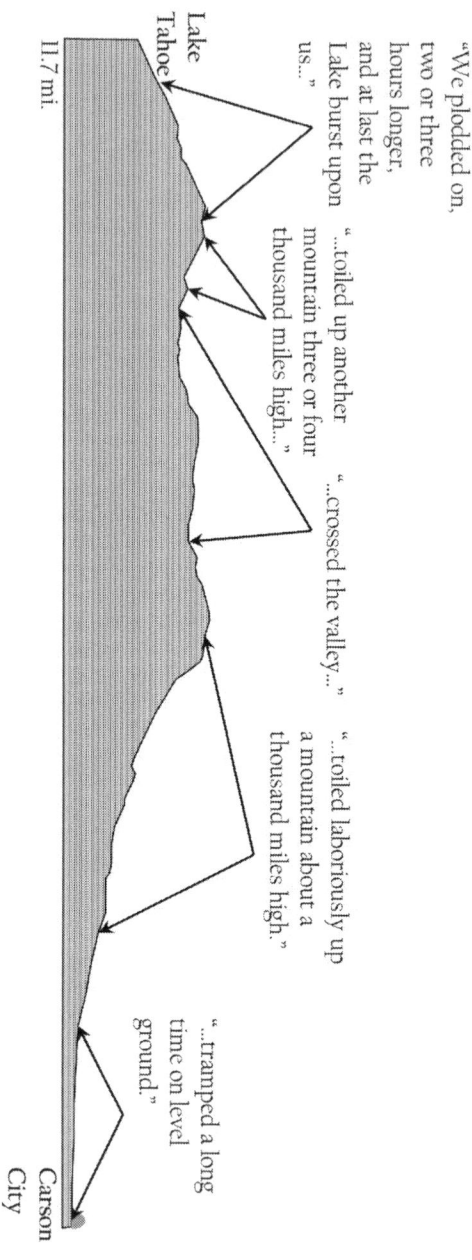

Figure 44. Profile of the route followed by Sam Clemens and John Kinney from Carson City to Lake Tahoe (2x elevation display)

98 A Wood Ranch or So

Figure 45. Modern-day Ash Canyon Road, starting in the lower right of the photo, winds its way into the Carson Range

is almost certain that loggers had already clear-cut the lower elevation forest, leaving vast stump fields on either side of the canyon as they struggled to ascend the Carson Range. At four miles from Carson City, Clemens and Kinney passed near the Alexander Ashe sawmill and the namesake for Ash Canyon. One mile further north, they encountered the sawmill of Treadwell and Thompson.

Mark Twain recalled ten years later as he was writing *Roughing It*, the hike was physically demanding and they "toiled laboriously up a mountain about a thousand miles high." They had reached the first summit at just under five miles having steadily climbed nearly 3,100 ft. from Carson City. As Mark Twain recalled, they looked over the summit, "No lake there." Indeed, topography makes the sighting of Lake Tahoe from this ridge impossible.

From the first summit, the men turned northward looking for the connection to the Washoe Trail. They descended the slope to follow Franktown Creek, or a trail paralleling the creek, downstream to the

Figure 46. A modern-day view shows the approach to Ash Canyon. The lower part of the canyon suffered a wildfire in 2004.

ford of the Washoe Trail. In *Roughing It*, "We descended on the other side, crossed the valley…"

Once at the Washoe Trail crossing of Franktown Creek, the two men turn westward to scale the next ridge, or as Twain recalled, they "…toiled up another mountain three or four thousand miles high, apparently, and looked over again."

Now at about nine miles into their journey, they looked westward again but, "No lake yet." The terrain and old growth forest still obscured any possible sighting of Lake Tahoe.

According to the *Roughing It* account, just past the summit, they sat down for a long rest and encountered Chinese workers. They paid them to curse the Brigade members who "beguiled" them to undertake this adventure. Was this Twain's creative imagination coming into play, or could such an encounter have actually occurred? The truth is, perhaps, somewhere in between. Chinese found employment as lumber workers and wood scavengers and reasonably could have been in the area to supply sawmills lower down in the Franktown Creek watershed. Did Clemens pay them to

Figure 47. View towards Lake Tahoe on the Ash Canyon Road from the first summit

curse the Brigade, or is this the humor of Mark Twain showing itself? It is doubtful that money changed hands and Twain never mentioned the encounter or the supposed payment in any of his reported lectures.

After a good long rest, the two men pushed forward over a level area on the summit and past two ephemeral lakes, now known as Twin Lakes. They continued to follow the Washoe Trail toward Lake Tahoe, passing through virgin old growth forest that still obscured any distant views. The trail turned north to follow the contour of the dividing ridge as it began its descent into the Lake Tahoe watershed. At a bend in the road and about three miles from their last rest stop, the two men finally emerged from the forest.

Figure 48. Modern-day road in the general area of the Washoe Trail as it climbs toward the second summit.

Figure 49. Modern-day level terrain along the Washoe Trail at the top of the second summit in the Carson Range

Fairest Picture

Exhausted from the strenuous hike, the view that suddenly appeared as they emerged from the forest was both stunning and emotional. It is here that Clemens for the first time saw Lake Tahoe. At an altitude of almost 1,000 feet above the lake, the men had a commanding view of Lake Tahoe. Through the wide canyon, they saw the curvature of the North Shore, an encircling ring of snowcapped mountains of the Sierra Nevada, and because the lake was calm on that day, the image of the snowcapped mountains in a flat-water reflection. The view was so awe-inspiring and breathtaking that it indelibly etched Clemens' imagination and memory with its vividness and emotion. Ten years later, he recalled the magical moment in *Roughing It*,

> ...at last the lake burst upon us, a noble sheet of blue water lifted six thousand three hundred feet above the level of the sea, and walled in by a rim of snow-clad mountain peaks that towered aloft full three thousand feet higher still! It was a vast oval, and one would have to use up eighty or a hundred good miles in traveling around it. As it lay there with the shadows of the mountains brilliantly photographed upon its still surface I thought it must surely be the fairest picture the whole earth affords.

Given this description and particularly, the brilliantly reflected image, one must consider the position of the sun and the effect of afternoon winds on the water surface. The sun must be high enough in the sky to shed enough light on the Sierra Nevada to generate a vivid reflection and the lake surface flat enough to yield a reflection. This suggests that the two men arrived in this location within a few hours after noon. However, it would be unlikely for the men to have covered the 10 miles and the 4,400 feet of climbing to that point if they had started their journey at daylight from Carson City. At a grade this steep and with brilliant sun bearing down, it is likely their average walking speed would have been less than half their normal speed, further decreased by their extended rest periods. It seems highly probable that they started in the predawn hours and walked by moonlight to avoid the blistering Nevada sun.

A historical astronomical projection revealed that the moon was 85% or more illuminated beginning on September 14 as it approached its full phase on September 19, 1861. This suggests that walking by moonlight was feasible, though there is no mention of it. We do know that in September 1862 Clemens walked the 90 miles from a Nevada mining camp, most of it at night by moonlight, to report for work at the *Territorial Enterprise* in Virginia City.

After pausing to take in the view, the two men followed the trail and stream (Tunnel Creek) to a sandy beach on the shore of Lake Tahoe.

We Were on the North Shore
At the Lake Tahoe shore in a location now known as Hidden Beach, they found the Brigade's skiff, as Twain called it. A skiff is a shallow, flat-bottomed open boat with sharp bow and square stern. However, the illustration in *Roughing It* seemed to contradict this. The boat in the illustration appeared to have a square bow with benches, more like a johnboat. Keep in mind that Twain did not draw the book illustrations himself, they were drawn by artists based on his description and the publisher's direction, so either type is a possibility. Like other Lake Tahoe boats of the era, the owners fabricated it there or hauled it to the lake.

From the beach, the two men "set out across a deep bend of the lake toward the landmarks that signified the locality of the camp[,]" according to *Roughing It*. The deep bend of the lake is Crystal Bay and the landmarks that signified the location of camp were the highly distinctive ridge of Stateline Point and the small beach on the tip of the point. Kinney handled the oars while Clemens sat on the stern and operated the rudder while facing toward the direction of travel. In *Roughing It*, Twain claimed he chose to steer because

Figure 50. The modern-day view of Lake Tahoe form the location where Sam Clemens first sighted Lake Tahoe in 1861

Figure 51. The modern-day view of Hidden Beach where Clemens and Kinney found a boat.

riding backwards while rowing made him sick and not because he was trying to avoid the exertion of rowing.

Why did Twain use the phrase "deep bend of the lake" instead of the word "bay," a term he later used to describe other parts of the shoreline? Twain was a trained riverboat pilot and knew that the term "bay" did not fit such a wide and open feature. Instead, he likely drew on his memories of deep sweeping bends of the banks of the Mississippi River, similar to the wide curvature of the Crystal Bay shoreline, as the inspiration for his descriptive phrase. Indeed, the word "bend" appears frequently in his book, *Life on the Mississippi*, where Mark Twain is describing the wide curvature of the Mississippi River.

Though Twain recalled in *Roughing It* a "three-mile pull" across the water, it was actually 3.4 miles from Hidden Beach to their destination on Stateline Point. The two men arrived at the first night's campsite at dusk, perhaps before 7:00 p.m. In his letter, Clemens named this campsite "upper camp." Use of the term "upper" was Clemens way of associating the name of the campsite

Figure 52. An illustration from *Roughing It* depicted Clemens steering while Kinney rowed.

with the adjacent terrain – the steep and relatively high topography of Stateline Point. He described the timber claim campsite as "lower camp," a reference to the low and wide valley that spilled out to his campsite there. Appendix II contains the detailed reasoning on use of the terms "upper" and "lower" and how to associate the campsites with their locations.

Figure 53. Overview of modern-day Crystal Bay showing the obvious "deep bend of the lake" cited by Mark Twain.

At the first campsite, they found the Irish Brigade's food and supplies cache in the rocks on the hillside. Kinney was still doing the drudgery; he gathered the wood, started a fire and cooked a dinner of bacon, hot bread, and coffee. Given that the men carried no fresh food with them, the bacon was probably salt cured for preservation. The hot bread was likely hardtack, a type of hard and thick bread-like cracker, fried in the bacon grease to soften it.

In *Roughing It*, Twain made two observations about his location: a lake-wide population of less than 15 persons and workers at a sawmill three miles away. We know from Chapter 1, that since he was on the desolate North Shore he would have seen few other Euro-American people. On the latter, there is no historical record of any sawmill with workers within three miles of Stateline Point. Here,

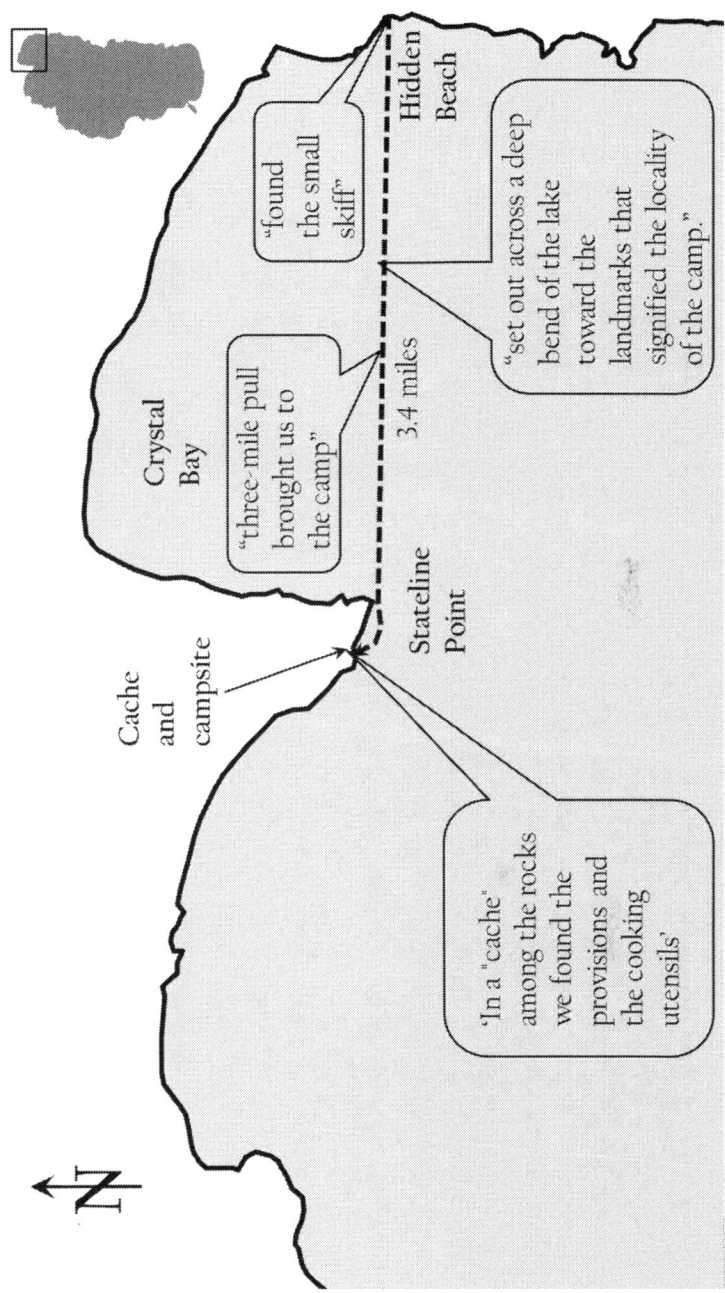

Figure 54. Map showing probable course of the skiff across Crystal Bay to first night's campsite on Stateline Point

Twain is simply making an incorrect recall since the sawmill had no role in the storyline and no humorous exaggeration associated with it. See also, the discussion in the subsection "Consider that Claim Better than Bank Stock" regarding Clemens' desire to encourage a Mr. Jones to erect a sawmill near his timber claim, because no nearby sawmill existed.

Twain wrote of absorbing the spectacular scenery and then drifting off to sleep, following his "delicious" dinner.

> As the darkness closed down and the stars came out and spangled the great mirror with jewels, we smoked meditatively in the solemn hush and forgot our troubles and our pains. In due time we spread our blankets in the warm sand between two large boulders and soon feel asleep, careless of the procession of ants that passed in through rents in our clothing and explored our persons. Nothing could disturb the sleep that fettered us, for it had been fairly earned, and if our consciences had any sins on them they had to adjourn court for that night, anyway. The wind rose just as we were losing consciousness, and we were lulled to sleep by the beating of the surf upon the shore.

The beach at Stateline Point, now known as Speedboat Beach, was the only significant sandy beach on the point in 1861. As it is now, large granite boulders, many of them with flat surfaces, studded the beach in 1861. Twain wrote they slept among these protecting boulders while ants prowled over the two men. Current photos of the general area of the campsite appear in Figures 55-56.

On the morning of the second day, the two men set off on foot to scout for timber. Ideally, they were looking for an unclaimed forest of large ponderosa, Jeffrey or sugar pines, flat terrain and a sandy beach to land logs for water transport to a sawmill.

Figure 55. View from offshore showing part of beach at first night's campsite on Stateline Point with water now covering the area where Clemens and Kinney camped.

Figure 56. View of shoreline and beach at first night's campsite

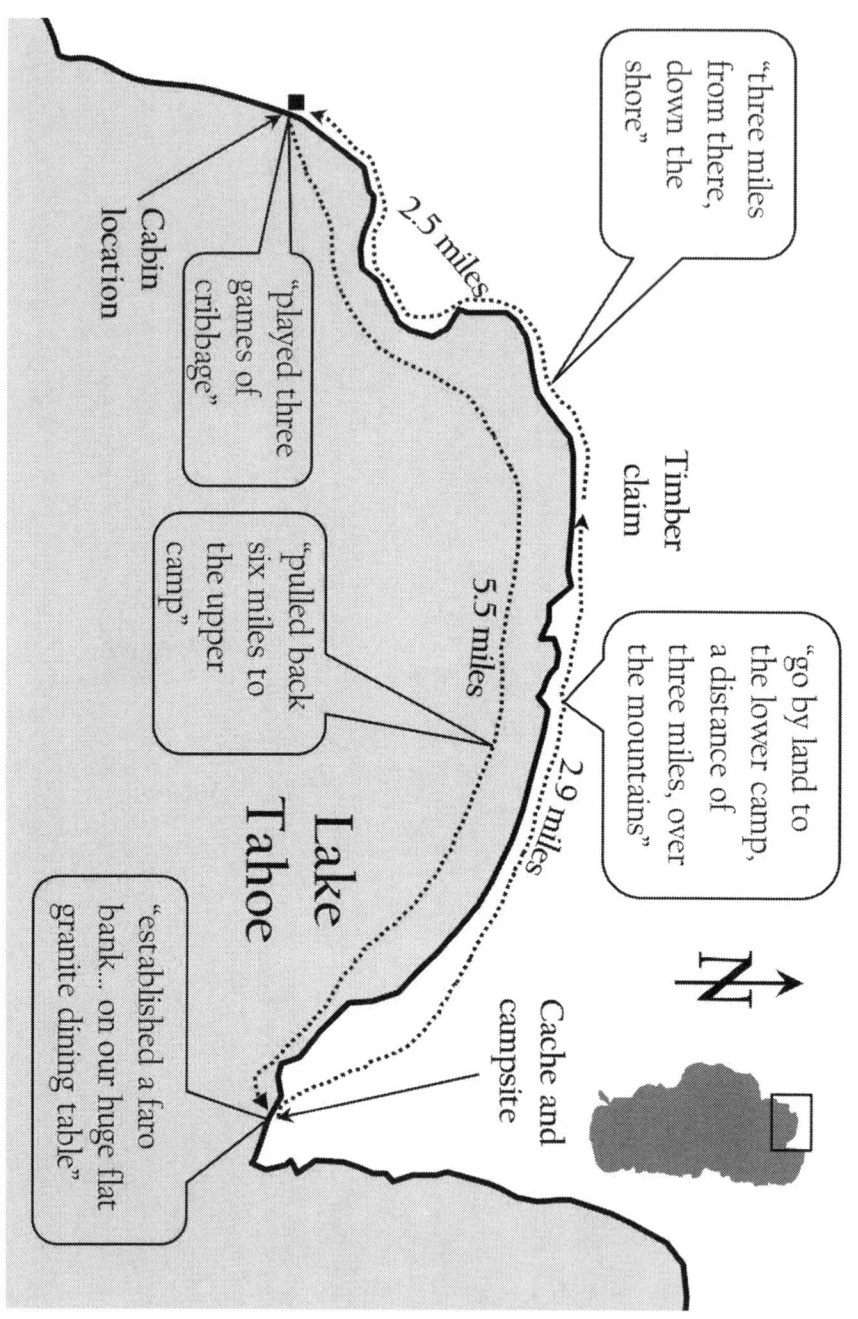

Figure 57. Map showing land and water routes followed by Clemens and Kinney on the second day.

The two started out over the steep and rough terrain on the west slope of Stateline Point, each carrying an ax in anticipation of cutting trees for a log cabin and fence enclosure. Clemens wrote to his mother afterward that it was, "the steepest, rockiest and most dangerous piece of country in the world." Clemens bemoaned that Kinney hiked in bursts of activity, stopping frequently to assess his precarious position, and then carefully moving onward, only to pause again and ponder. After struggling for three miles over four hours, they reached a site that seemed suitable as a timber claim. In his letter, Clemens dubs this site "lower camp" because it is next to the relatively flat ground of a wide valley that spills out to the lake. For clarity, the author uses "timber claim site" for lower camp and "cache site" for upper camp.

In *Roughing It*, Twain recalled the timber claim site as, "… yellow pine timber land [most likely, ponderosa and Jeffrey pines] – a dense

Figure 58. A modern-day view of the west slope of Stateline Point showing the steep and rough terrain

forest of trees a hundred feet high and from one to five feet through at the butt." This clearly fits the description of the mature forest on the North Shore based on scientific analysis of stump fields left after the intense 19th century logging period and the size of surviving trees found there today. Archeologists found evidence the trees were up to 5.5 ft. in diameter. The 5.1 ft. base diameter of several existing trees that escaped the logging onslaught confirms these findings.

Using Clemens' three miles distance estimate in his letter and the location of an 1861 sandy beach that distance from Stateline Point, places the campsite near modern-day Tahoe Vista. Figure 57 is a map showing this location and Figure 59 is a photo of the general area as it looks today. Erosion caused by unnaturally higher lake levels and pier and jetty construction have heavily modified the shoreline from its 1861 condition. Builders frequently relocated the large rocks in the water to protect their shoreline developments and

Figure 59. Modern-day view of highly impacted shoreline area at the Clemens-Kinney timber claim site

any of these may have been the protective boulders that Twain recalled sleeping between in *Roughing It*.

At the timber claim site, they realized they had not brought provisions along and considered how to get back to the food cache. Because they had just covered difficult terrain, Kinney refused to go back the way they came. Instead, the two mounted floating logs and attempted to paddle back to the cache site. However, the typically rough afternoon water on that part of the lake thwarted them, and they gave up on that idea.

Clemens and Kinney decided to continue and hiked another three miles beyond, even though the steep rocky terrain became challenging again. Clemens wrote in his letter, *"... they set out for the only cabin on this side of the lake,"* suggesting that they seemed to know of the existence of the cabin. In a December 14, 1871 lecture, Twain spoke of observing mountain sheep at Tahoe through a "spyglass," an archaic term for a handheld telescope. It may be that Clemens or Kinney had a telescope and could see the cabin across the water from east of the timber claim site.

The two men hiked the difficult three miles to the unoccupied cabin, reaching it just before dark, and played three games of cribbage. They probably intended to spend the night at the cabin, but found no food there. They instead discovered the owner's dugout canoe and decided to appropriate the canoe for an evening return trip to camp. Since they reached the cabin just before dark, they played the card games as a way to kill time until the moon was high enough above the ridge of the Carson Range, at about 8:00 p.m. Aided by the bright light of the waxing gibbous moon, they paddled back to camp. Once back at the food cache at the Stateline Point campsite, they wasted no time preparing and eating their dinner. The fate of the borrowed dugout canoe remains unknown.

As Clemens wrote in his letter,

> *After supper we got out our pipes – built a rousing camp fire in the open air – established a faro bank (an institution of this country,) on our huge flat granite dining table, and bet white beans till one o'clock, when John went to bed.*

The mention of the "flat granite dining table" referred to the flat surface granite boulders that are common on Stateline Point. They occur elsewhere along the shoreline of Lake Tahoe where exposed granite rock occurs on the adjacent land surface. Figure 60 shows examples of flat surface boulders on the beach at Stateline Point, any of which could have been the "flat granite dining table" Clemens wrote about.

On the third day at the lake (Figure 61), the two rose early, caught a Lahontan cutthroat trout and ate their catch for breakfast. Clemens' ineptitude at cooking or just simple carelessness caused him to add more tea to the simmering coffee pot and more coffee to the boiling tea. The results, he wrote his mother, were *"villainous mixtures."*

With Clemens superintending again and Kinney on the oars, the two men skirted the shoreline three miles west to the timber claim site. They claimed 300 acres by posting notices on trees and proceeded to construct the requisite fence to define the property boundaries. The two began to fall trees in a pattern that would create a loosely fenced enclosure. However, after dropping three trees each, the work became too hard, and they decided to make their case solely on what little fence construction they had accomplished. Twain later opined in *Roughing It* that they did not worry about the land running away and so what, if it did. The two returned by boat to the cache site that night.

On the fourth day (Figure 62), both men again traveled by boat to the timber claim site with the goal of building a cabin that would qualify as a dwelling. They cut and prepared the first tree for a log cabin but then concluded a log structure was too much work. They elected to build a lesser structure of saplings, but backed away from that after

Figure 60. Examples of flat granite rocks at the cache location campsite

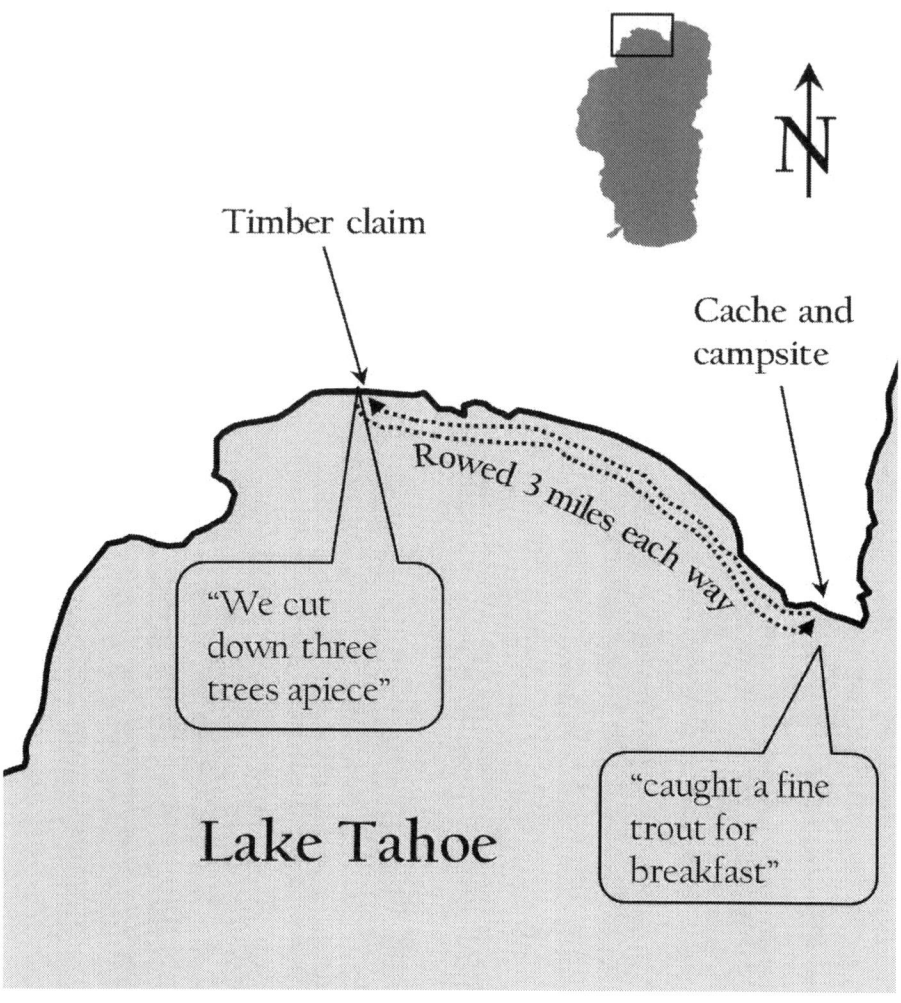

Figure 61. Map showing water route and activities by Clemens and Kinney on the third day

cutting and preparing just two saplings. Finally, and after much discussion, they settled on a brush "house," constructed as a simple lean-to, set back into the forest on a level site. The raw materials would have been the plant species Manzanita, whitethorn, and willow with an underlying support frame composed of sturdy alder

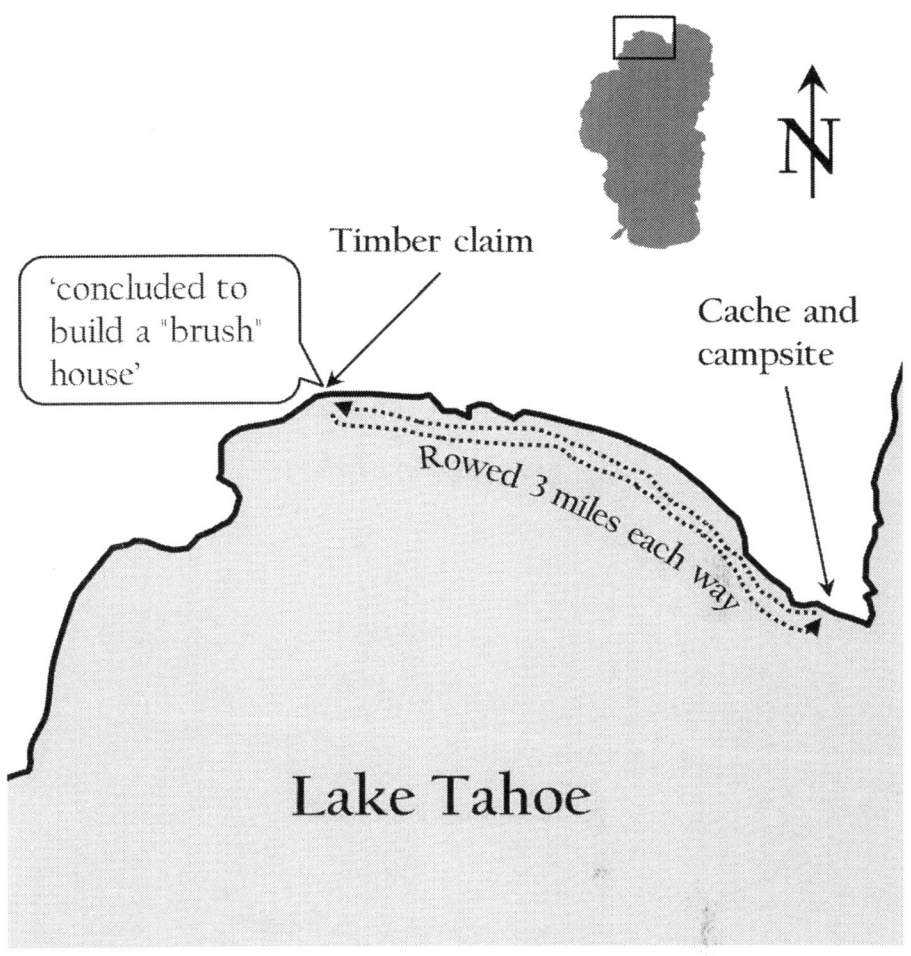

Figure 62. Map showing water route and activities by Clemens and Kinney on the fourth day

and small diameter pines. The illustration, taken from *Roughing It*, shown in Figure 63 depicts the construction of the brush house as interpreted by the illustrator, possibly from Twain's description.

Following a day of start-stop work and debate, the two returned by boat to the cache site for the night.

The fifth day of the trip (Figure 64) and fourth full day at the lake began with the two timber baron hopefuls relaxing and resting at the

Figure 63. Illustration of the lean-to brush house from *Roughing It*

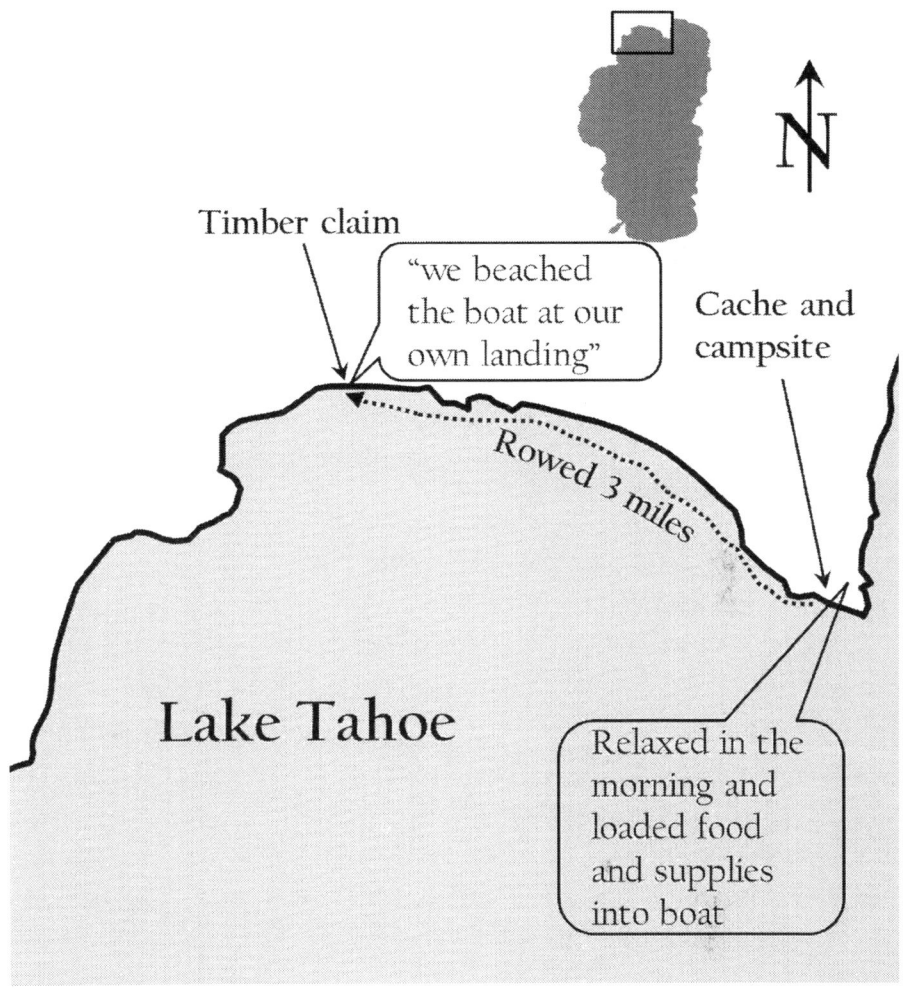

Figure 64. Map showing water route and activities by Clemens and Kinney on the fifth day

cache site. After spending the morning and early afternoon at the cache site, the two men gathered up as much of the food and equipment as they could carry in their boat and set course for the timber claim. Their intent was to set up camp and spend idyllic time enjoying their new timber ranch and Lake Tahoe.

A Tossing, Blinding Tempest of Flame

After arriving by boat at the timber claim just before evening, the two went about unloading and carrying their cargo to the brush house for storage. As the house was some distance from the shoreline and well into the forest, it required a short walk between the boat and the house. Clemens started a campfire near the house, turned his back on the ever-increasing flames and walked back to the boat to get another load. Just as he reached the boat, he heard Kinney yelling and whirled around to see him sprinting through the gauntlet of flames that had escaped the confines of the campfire ring. Figure 65 shows the illustration of the incident from *Roughing It*. The two men stood near the water's edge of the wide beach and observed the quick progress of the flames.

Although we will never know the full circumstances surrounding the escape of the campfire, we can surmise a few relevant factors. September is historically a very dry month, accounting for only 2 percent of the total yearly precipitation and humidity is nearly its lowest for the year at 25 percent. It is the last month following the typically dry summer period beginning in early June. During this time, wildfire danger is abnormally high. Twain recalled the weather as "superb," implying the warm daytime temperatures and low humidity that contribute to increased wildfire danger. The needles, leaves, plant and tree materials on the forest floor, collectively known as duff, would have been very dry and easy to ignite.

Typically, afternoon winds on the North Shore near the timber claim blow vigorously from the south. If Clemens had not cleared to bare soil a sufficiently wide area around the campfire ring, the gusty winds would have easily carried flaming embers into the highly flammable forest duff and understory. The result would have been the wall of flames that Kinney had to cross to safety on the beach. In *Roughing It,* Twain wrote of the dry pine needles igniting like "gunpowder" and with an almost pyromania inspired fascination, he wrote the, "wonderful to see ... fierce speed the tall sheet of flame traveled!"

By today's standards, we cannot excuse Clemens' negligence and ignorance of campfire safety. However, we can understand that in prior days he had camped on the beach at Stateline Point. Here, his campfires were on nonflammable sand and gravel devoid of forest duff and a safe distance from dry brush. Perhaps his experience there coupled with his tenderfoot outdoor skills led to this disastrous outcome.

The escaped campfire engorged itself on dry brush and forest duff so that within one-half hour, it had become a widespread out of control wildfire. In Clemens' letter home, he gave a more subdued and factual account of the fire's progress. Comparatively, in his description in *Roughing It*, he spared no superlatives, vivid imagery or hyperbole in giving a Hollywood-like version of the wildfire's growth.

From the letter,

> ...*The level ranks of flame were relieved at intervals by the standard-bearers, as we called the tall dead trees, wrapped in fire, and waving their blazing banners a hundred feet in the air. Then we could turn from this scene to the Lake, and see every branch, and leaf, and cataract of flame upon its bank perfectly reflected as in a gleaming, fiery mirror. The mighty roaring of the conflagration... rendered the scene very impressive. Occasionally, one of us would remove his pipe from his mouth and say, "Superb! magnificent! Beautiful!*

From *Roughing It*,

> ... [A]ll before us was a tossing, blinding tempest of flame! It went surging up adjacent ridges –surmounted them and disappeared in the canons beyond – burst into view upon

FIRE AT LAKE TAHOE.

Figure 65. Illustration from *Roughing It* showing the start of the wildfire

higher and farther ridges, presently – shed a grander illumination abroad, and dove again – flamed out again, directly, higher and still higher up the mountain-side – threw out skirmishing parties of fire here and there, and sent them trailing their crimson spirals away among remote ramparts and ribs and gorges, till as far as the eye could reach the lofty mountain-fronts were webbed as it were with a tangled network of red lava streams. Away across the water the crags and domes were lit with a ruddy glare, and the firmament above was a reflected hell!

Every feature of the spectacle was repeated in the glowing mirror of the lake! Both pictures were sublime, both were beautiful; but that in the lake had a bewildering richness about it that enchanted the eye and held it with the stronger fascination.

Hidden in the book description is another clue to his location. Where he wrote about the glare of the fire on the crags and domes across the water, he is recalling the illumination of the fire on the western side of Stateline Point. Direct lighting from the flames, the reflection of the flames on the still lake surface toward Stateline Point, or both caused this phenomenon.

The two retreated to the beach to watch the spectacle from a safer distance. They watched the fire spread and progress generally northward to the ridgeline separating the Tahoe Basin from Martis Valley. When they felt safe at about 11 p.m., they bedded down with their blankets on the sandy beach between protecting boulders. In the morning, they were surprised to find themselves covered with ash, discovered the fire had switched directions overnight and found burnt driftwood that had floated back toward their camp. When the colder night air began to sink, it slid downward along the mountain slopes toward the lake, forcing the direction of burn southward to within a few steps of their sandy beach beds. The violent updrafts generated by the advancing line of fire lifted small pieces of burned wood into the air, and they drifted southward with the night air currents. They landed in the lake where waves gently pushed them back ashore and within six feet of the beached boat.

Although the fire had changed directions overnight, Clemens wrote to his mother that they were still safe. He added that no one else was within six miles of his location. This was a possible reference to a Washoe tribal campsite located on Incline Creek (possibly revealed by smoke from cooking fires), the Chinese woodcutters encountered near the summit of the Carson Range during the trip from Carson City, or a few Euro-Americans moving along the Washoe Trail or camped on the North Shore.

Another consideration is the description of the fire itself. The *Roughing It* description seems highly embellished, perhaps for creative literary value, and goes on to state that the wildfire consumed all the trees. However, this is implausible, since the wildfire occurred in a mature forest that was well adapted to periodic fire. This seems to be borne out by the more subdued description in the letter. Here Clemens wrote of *"level ranks of flame,"* seemingly a description of the burning understory. The letter went on to mention standing dead trees that burst into flames, possibly indicating that a considerable period has passed since the last wildfire had burned through this area of the forest. This was most likely a low intensity surface fire; it only burned forest duff, undergrowth and standing dead trees, and left only burn scars on the very large mature trees. Clemens' letter seems to reinforce this conclusion, when he tells his mother, *"In a day or two we shall probably go to the Lake and build another cabin and fence, and get everything into satisfactory trim..."* If the fire had consumed all the trees, as the sensationalized *Roughing It* account would have us believe, then there would have been no reason to return to a forest of worthless fire ravaged trees.

According to the *Roughing It* account, the next morning on the sixth day (Figure 66) the two would-be timber barons boarded their boat for the return trip to Carson City. They encountered rough water with Clemens bailing while oarsman Kinney labored against the oncoming waves. After helplessly passing east of Stateline Point, the situation became dire, and they decided to make a hard landing on a small segment of sandy beach east of the point.

As they made their landing, the boat swamped and high waves washed crew and cargo ashore. The account continues with the two men taking refuge on the shore and shivering in the shelter of a large boulder. Knowing the whole adventure covered only six days away from Carson City, this latter element seems improbable for the first trip. Perhaps, the swamping occurred but not the night spent shivering on the shore, or the incident happened during a subsequent trip, and Twain fused it into the *Roughing It* storyline for dramatic effect. In any event, the two returned to Carson City by boat and foot and prepared for a return trip to complete work on their claim.

Consider that Claim Better than Bank Stock

On October 25, 1861, Clemens wrote his sister, Pamela Moffett, covering a number of his recent undertakings and responding to a September 8, 1861 letter in which his sister inquired about the status of the timber claim filed on behalf of her husband, William A. Moffett.

Clemens wrote that he had laid a claim, *"about two miles in length by one in width" on the shore of Lake Tahoe. He listed the owners of the claim as, '"Sam. L Clemens, Wm. A. Moffett, Thos. Nye" and three others.'* Thomas Nye was the nephew of Nevada Territorial Governor James Nye. Possibly, one of the three other unnamed persons was John Kinney. This claim was in the same location as the claim initially discovered by Clemens and Kinney on their first trip that ended in a wildfire that burned, but did not destroy, the timber. The size of this claim (Figure 67) was 1,280 acres, an amount that

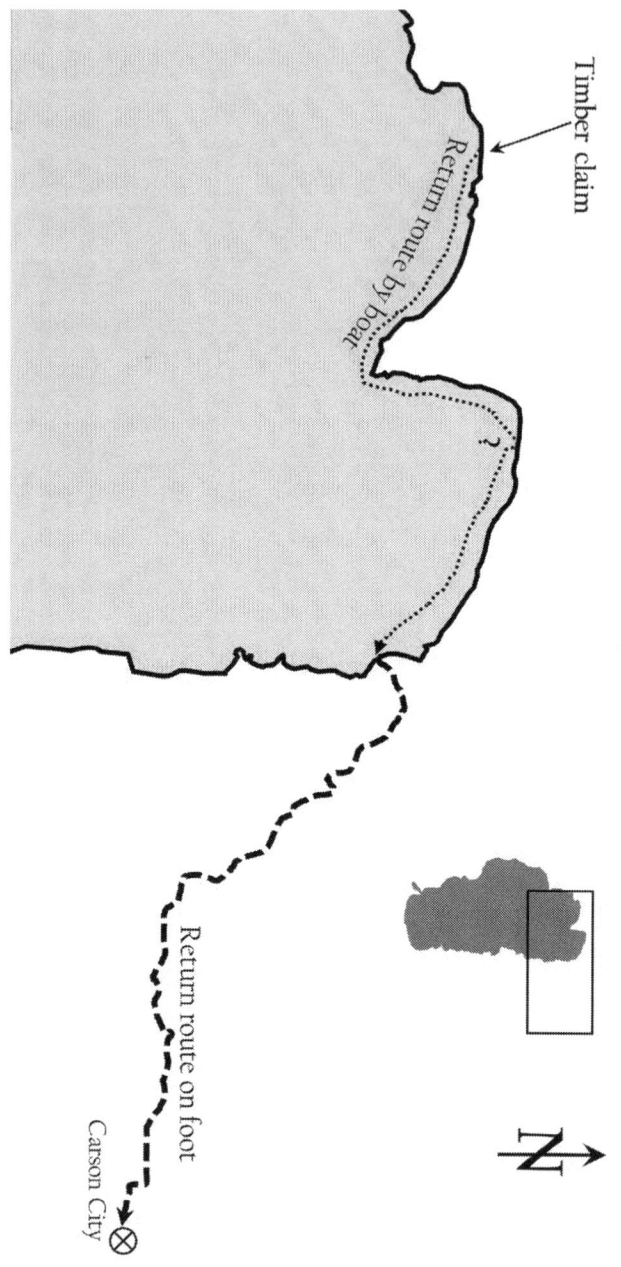

Figure 66. Map showing water and land route followed by Clemens and Kinney on the sixth day.
128 A Wood Ranch or So

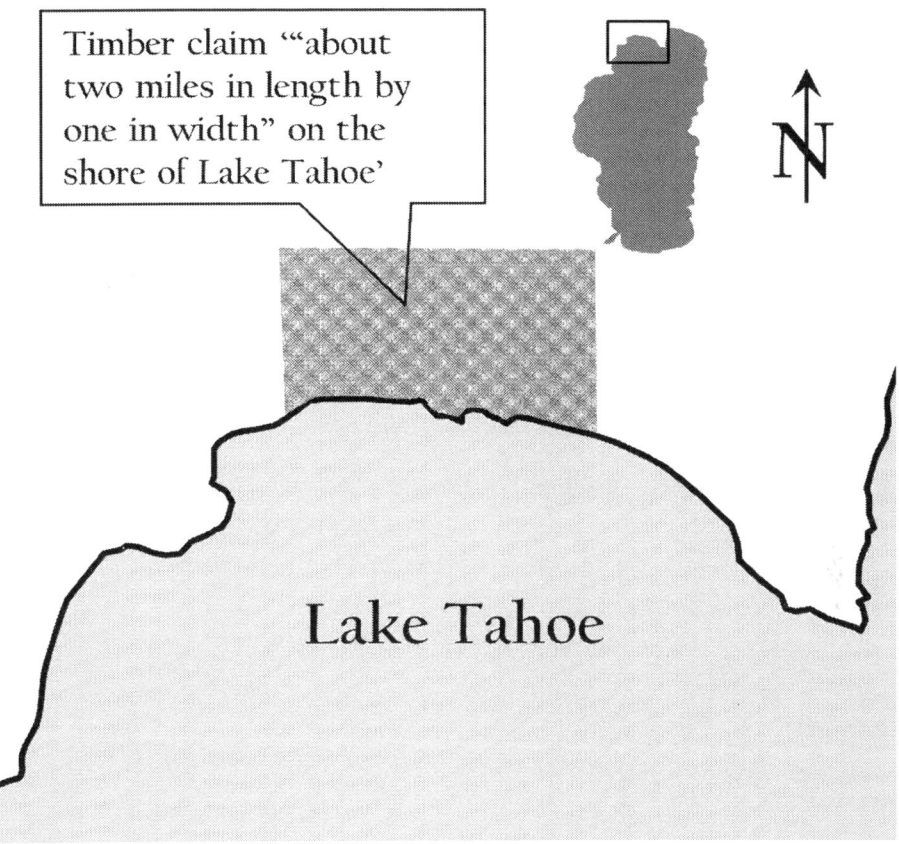

Figure 67. Map showing the location and possible extent of the claim filed by Clemens and five others.

would require at least four claimants at the maximum claim per person of 320 acres. Clemens continued in his letter, saying, '*It* [the timber claim] *is situated on "Sam Clemens' Bay"—so named by Capt. Nye—and it goes by that name among the inhabitants of that region.*' This is a reference to modern-day Agate Bay, as it had no recognized name until 1863.

The latter part of this quote suggested that Euro-Americans were in the general vicinity of the claim (probably spread out along the North Shore) and correlated to Clemens' earlier statement that no one was within six miles of the wildfire. The observation also discredits the statement in *Roughing It* that they did not see another human during the timber claim adventure, since he would have seen the mentioned inhabitants that obligingly used his name for their bay. Alternatively, the mention of naming of the bay was in jest and never really happened.

Clemens foresaw the need to establish a sawmill near his timber claim if he was ever to realize its value. He told his sister that,

> [I]f we succeed in getting one Mr. Jones, to move his saw-mill up there, Mr. [William] Moffett can just consider that claim better than bank stock. Jones says he will move his mill up next spring.

Contrary to the letter's promise, Mr. C. Jones did not move his mill up as Clemens hoped and, instead he and a partner erected a steam-powered mill on the lower reach of Clear Creek, south of Carson City. Another implication of Clemens' comment about a sawmill is that it casts further doubt on the veracity of his statement in *Roughing It* that his first night's campsite was three miles from a sawmill and workmen. Why would Clemens think he needed a sawmill near his timber claim if an existing mill was within a reasonable distance?

The Life We Led on Our Timber Ranch

What we have in the two Lake Tahoe chapters in *Roughing It* is a composite storyline. Twain based the partially true story on two trips that spanned perhaps six days or so each, separated by one or two days back in Carson City. The chronology of the first trip, based largely on his letter home, seems to account for most of the time spent seeking a timber claim or ineffectively working to build a fence and cabin. Only the afternoon of the fourth day offered an opportunity for an open block of time for recreation and relaxation.

We do not know the chronology of the second trip or the actual participants that might have accompanied Clemens. If there were more persons on this expedition, then there might have been time for the recreational pursuits described in *Roughing It*. The details of these pursuits could not have been fabricated by Twain for literary effect; they are based solidly on the 1861 conditions at Lake Tahoe. Moreover, through correlation to known features of the Tahoe Basin, they reinforce the location of his timber claim on the North Shore.

How do we know for sure that the two men were on the North Shore of Lake Tahoe? Twain wrote a defining description of the boulders he saw on the bottom of the lake, "We were on the North Shore. There, the rocks on the bottom are sometimes gray, sometimes white." Twain's reference to white and gray rocks on the bottom is consistent with the unique area between Stateline Point and the eastern extent of modern-day Tahoe Vista. It is only here on the northern half of the lake that gray colored surface volcanic rocks composed of andesite meet the uplifted white granite. Eons of seismic activity and weathering have shed large boulders from the above-water terrain. In Tahoe Vista, boulders along the shoreline are gray and change to white granite as one moves eastward toward Stateline Point. Figure 68 presents a map showing the generalized geology between Stateline Point and modern-day Tahoe Vista.

Another identifying factor was Twain's description of the size of the submerged boulders. While drifting in the boat, he saw boulders the size of a "village church." These boulders offshore of the cache site were of massive size compared to other boulders elsewhere. Consistent with Twain's recollection, the boulders offshore of Stateline Point are extremely large when compared to granite boulders elsewhere on the lake. Figure 69 shows one of these boulders as typical of others near Stateline Point.

We begin with morning and afternoon of the fourth day of the first trip when it is likely that Clemens and Kinney spent time drifting around Stateline Point in their boat and gazed over the sides to peer into the depths of Lake Tahoe. With the mid-day sun still high in the

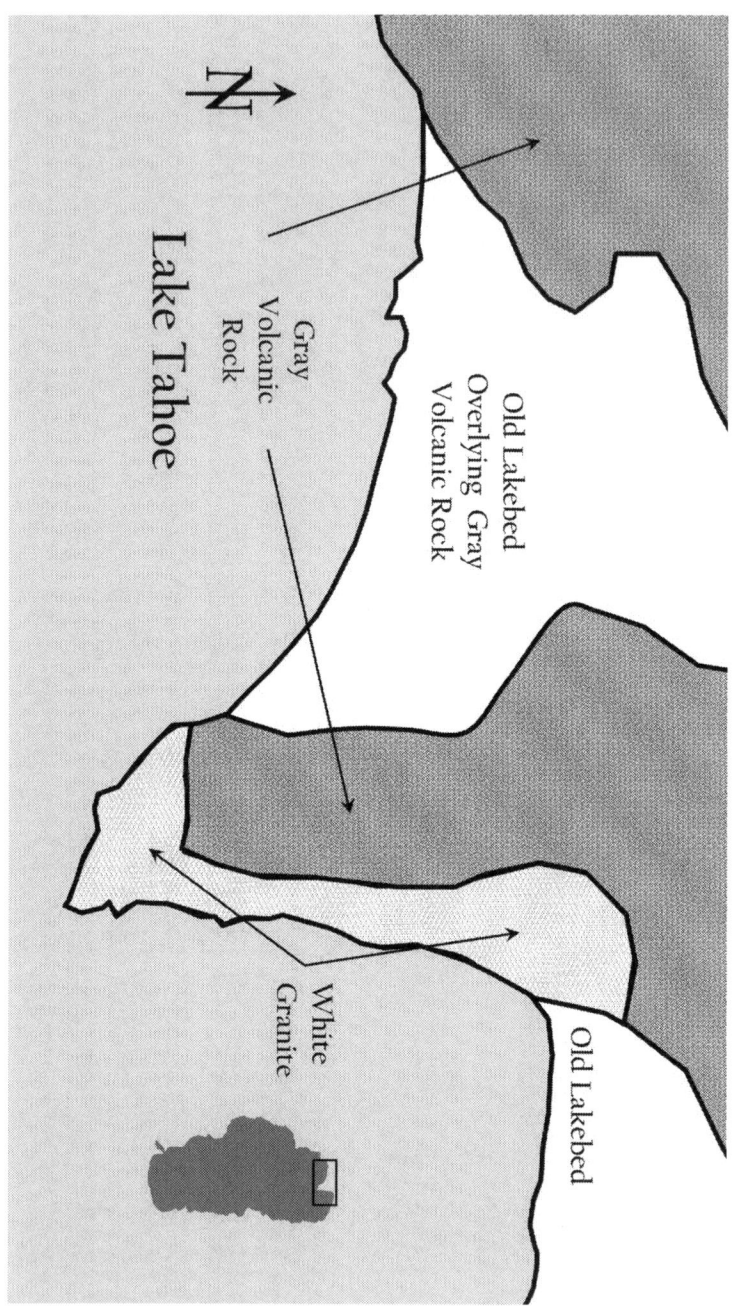

Figure 68. Map showing generalized geology of Stateline Point and the area to the west.

Figure 69. Example of a large 25+ feet diameter boulder offshore of Stateline Point

late-summer sky, light penetrated deeply into the exceptionally clear water and brightly illuminated the bottom features.

Although we can no longer see the boulders the same way Clemens did because of decreased water clarity and growth of attached algae, we know from the large granite rocks found on the shoreline that similar-sized granite rocks occur underwater. We can see the exceptional size of these rocks but attached algae prevents us from seeing their white granite surface. Twain characterized the drifting over the boulder fields as "balloon voyages." His sense of flying over the lake bottom, revealed by the exceptionally clear water, was so strong that it seemed as though it was earthly terrain viewed from an airship. He commented on the large boulders that came into a magnified close view, seemed to threaten to ground the boat, but dropped away as they drifted over. One must read the passage verbatim in Chapter 8 to experience the fullness of his vivid description.

Twain wrote in Roughing It, 'Sometimes we rowed out to the "blue water," a mile or two from shore. It was as dead blue as indigo there, because of the immense depth.' It is a cause backscatter of the residual blue and indigo colored light toward the observer's eye. This is an important point: At the 75-foot depth and deeper, the waters of Lake Tahoe show their characteristic blue and indigo blue colors.

The map in Figure 71 shows the occurrence of blue water as defined

Figure 70. An illustration from *Roughing It* showed Clemens and Kinney drifting and observing large boulders (Wikimedia

by the 75-foot bathymetric contour and the horizontal distance from shore. The blue water line in Agate Bay is the only area in the northeast quadrant of Lake Tahoe that occurs at an offshore distance of 1-2 miles, precisely as described by Twain.

Although Twain never wrote about seeing Sierra Nevada bighorn sheep at Lake Tahoe, he mentioned them in lectures promoting the publication of *Roughing It*. He talked about viewing them far off

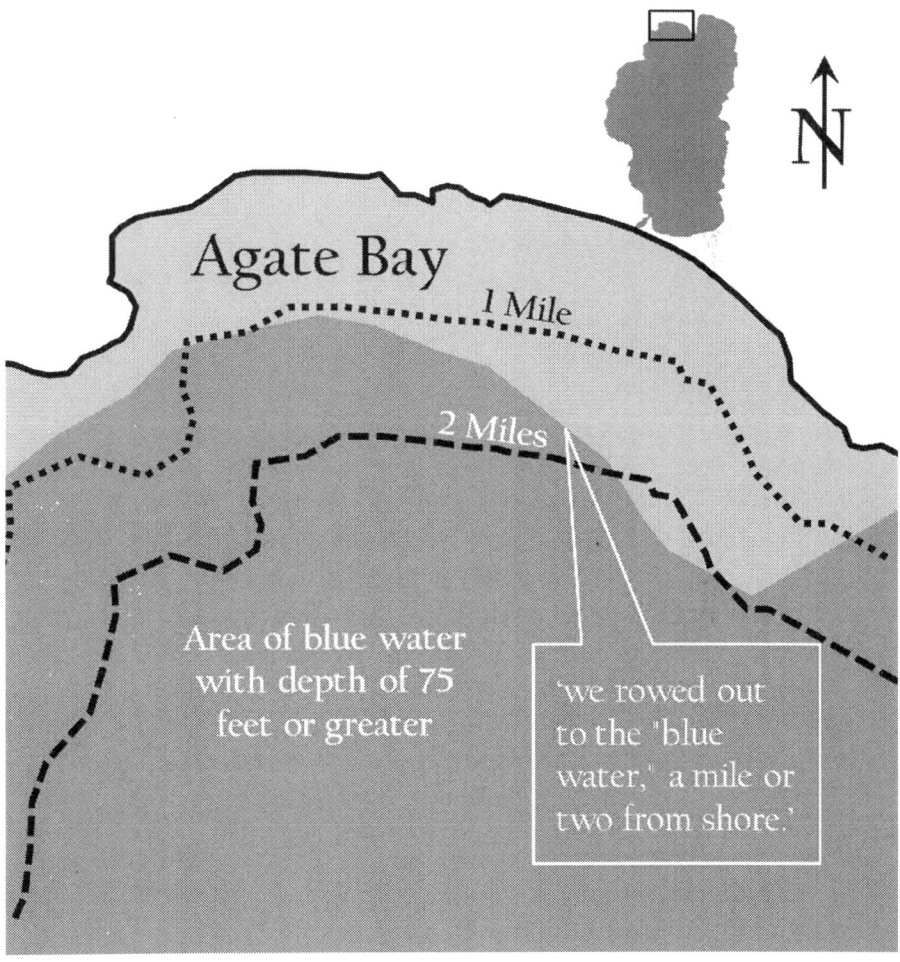

Figure 71. Map of Agate Bay area showing area of blue water occurrence and distance from shore

through a "spyglass." This serves to locate him on the North Shore since the bighorn habitat occurred on the high open meadows north of Stateline Point that would have been visible from the boat as Clemens and Kinney traveled between their campsites.

Twain lamented their unsuccessful attempts at catching Lahontan cutthroat trout:

> We frequently selected the trout we wanted, and rested the bait patiently and persistently on the end of his nose at a depth of eighty feet, but he would only shake it off with an annoyed manner, and shift his position.

The mainstay of the Lake Tahoe Lahontan cutthroat diet was insects and small fish. Understanding that they were using bait-fishing techniques, the two probably did not have live bait or an artificial lure that was appealing to the trout. Twain speculated that the trout could see his line in the clear water. In any event, they "did not average one fish a week…" including the one trout they caught on the third day.

Twain reported, "We bathed occasionally, but the water was rather chilly, for all it looked so sunny." Even with global warming well underway in the 21st century, water in snow-fed Lake Tahoe in September is usually 62° F. In 1861, the water temperature was probably 2°-3° F colder.

In an August 18, 1863 column for the *Territorial Enterprise,* Twain mentioned his recollection of riding, "that razor-bladed beast of Tom Nye's" on a horseback trip to Lake Tahoe. He did not state the date, purpose or destination for the horseback trip. Some scholars believe this was a reference to the second timber claim trip to Lake Tahoe. They infer this from the October 25, 1861 letter to Clemens' sister stating that Nye was one of six co-owners of the timber claim. This seems an unlikely destination since access to the North Shore timber claim and supply cache was by boat, leaving the question of what they did with the horses unanswered.

Given that the two were mounted and the event occurred before mid-1863, the trip had to follow routes accessible by horses. This strongly points to the area south of Glenbrook along the Carson Emigrant Ridge Road as the most likely route for the riders. The Kings Canyon Road and the Glenbrook to Zephyr Cove branch of the Lake Tahoe Wagon Road did not open until 1863. Some scholars even theorize that "Sam Clemens Bay" eventually became Zephyr Cove, if this was, in fact, a timber-scouting trip.

An alternative and more plausible explanation has the trip on Tom Nye's horse unrelated to the timber claim. Absent any new information, we will never know if this trip was timber claim-related or for some other purpose.

Timber Claim Never Completed Because It Was Not in the Nevada Territory

Scholars have long puzzled over Clemens' lack of follow-through to preempt (convert government land to private ownership) the land for the timber claim compared to his aggressive acquisition of mineral rights. This is particularly confounding because he wrote his sister on October 25, 1861 that he had *"laid a timber claim"* at Lake Tahoe on behalf of his sister's husband, himself and four others. Why did he not complete the filing? Perhaps new mining ventures swept away his focus, or the claim partners were unwilling to pay the cost of surveying and mapping the claim. A more likely explanation comes from the inaccurate mapping of Lake Tahoe prevalent in 1861. Clemens had to rely on available crude maps that predated the publication of the General Land Office surveys and maps. From these crude maps, he and others believed they were in the Nevada Territory, when they were actually in California. A portion of a map from that era showing the Tahoe region before the public land survey of 1861 appears in Figure 72.

Government agents would have held in abeyance the approval of Clemens' claim until General Land Office surveys underway at the time could provide plats showing the details of government land ownership and more importantly, the state-territorial boundary between California and Nevada. When these approved plats became available, they showed the location of Clemens' claim was about 2-3 miles inside the State of California and therefore, ineligible for the land preemption program in the Nevada Territory. Twain apparently never spoke on record or wrote about the timber claim after October

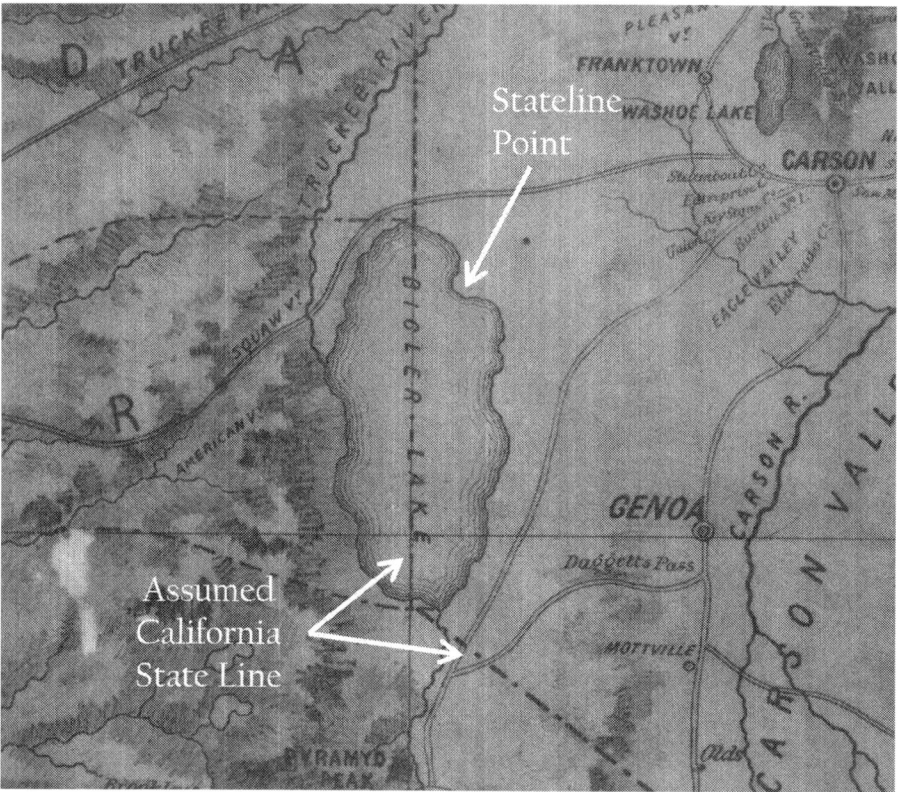

Figure 72. Circa 1860 map of the Western Nevada Territory and Eastern California, showing the area west of Stateline Point at Lake Tahoe (Bigler Lake) incorrectly located within the Nevada Territory.

1861. No other information or public records on the timber claim have been located, so we may never know for sure the reason for the failed enterprise.

A final note about John Kinney, Clemens' companion on his first trip to Tahoe: Kinney returned to his native Ohio and served as a captain in the 7th Ohio Calvary, as Twain reported in the January 6, 1863 *Territorial Enterprise*. Kinney later abruptly resigned from his commission under unknown circumstances. He died in 1878.

Twain Biographical Writer Stated Carnelian Bay Area as the Location

George Wharton James was a late 19th century/early 20th century writer. He wrote on travel, Native American culture, natural history and health. In addition, he wrote Mark Twain biographical pieces for books and magazines. He wrote the seminal *Lake of the Sky* about Lake Tahoe, in addition to numerous books and articles about the natural history of the West.

In 1914, he was a guest lecturer to the Nevada Historical Society on Nevada history, lectured again in 1921 on "Nevada Authors" for the Nevada Department of Education and wrote a Nevada promotional piece for the "All Nevada Edition" of the *Nevada State Journal* in 1922. James wrote three Twain-themed magazine articles, plus portions of two book chapters involving Twain in the West.

In another book by James, *California Romantic and Beautiful*, published in 1914, he pinpoints the location of Mark Twain's campsites as "not far from Carnelian Bay," located on the North Shore of Lake Tahoe. This is the only reference to a specific location for a timber claim location by an author from the same era as Twain lived. In 1914, the community of Carnelian Bay was the largest recognized settlement in that area, so James referenced this geographical location as it was closest to the timber claim and cabin.

James pursued a meeting with Mark Twain to discuss his years in the West and his literature during that period, only to be rebuffed by

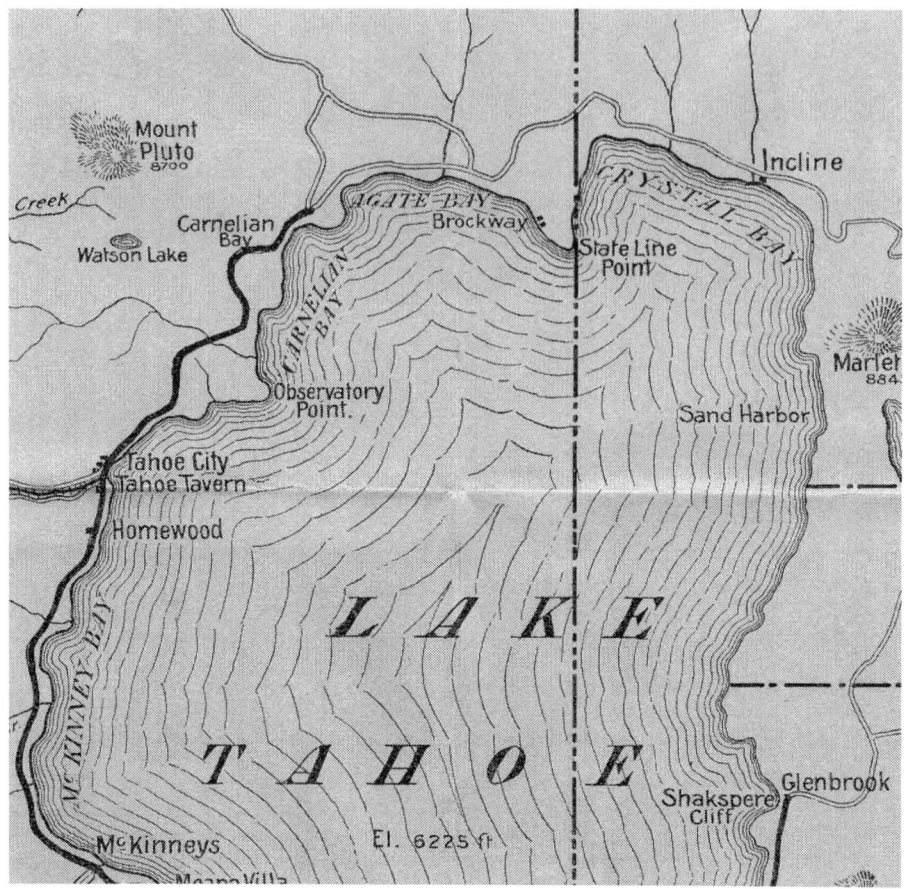

Figure 73. Excerpt of map from George Wharton James' *Lake of the Sky* (1915) showing location of Carnelian Bay in relation to the North Shore of Lake Tahoe (Public Domain)

Twain's secretary based on Twain's very busy schedule. James traveled to New York and was able to wrangle a meeting with Twain, partly to convince him to pose for fundraising photos to benefit Ina Coolbirth. Coolbirth was a dear friend of Twain's from his San Francisco days and she had lost her home in the 1906 earthquake.

James is one of only two persons known to speak personally with Mark Twain (1907) and later write about Twain's Lake Tahoe experiences and location. The other person was Albert Bigelow Paine, Mark Twain's biographer, who gave no specific details on location. James lived in Nevada in the 1880s and was friendly with a number of Twain's Virginia City, Nev. friends. James knew Dan DeQuille, Twain's colleague at the *Territorial Enterprise*, and Marshall Jack Perry. DeQuille and Twain roomed together and later, DeQuille stayed at Twain's home while writing his Comstock history, *Big Bonanza*. As a news source and friend, Perry knew Mark Twain well during his years as a reporter for the *Territorial Enterprise*. Both men could have provided extensive background material to James.

Chapter 4

Restored at Lake Bigler

Mark Twain ventured twice to Lake Tahoe as a destination, first for the cure of a cold, and then again, for restoration of his bedraggled spirit and another cold. Popular 19th century beliefs held that one could restore health and vigor by partaking of fresh pure air, drinking or bathing in clean water, and generally living in a pristine mountain environment.

All the Fun Going at Lake House
In August 1863, Mark Twain was suffering from a respiratory illness that he characterized as a cold. In a brief letter written to the *San Francisco Daily Morning Call* on August 8, he complained of "a cough, and a cold in my head, and a sore throat, and a voice like a trombone." A trip to Lake Bigler (Tahoe), he opined, "will restore me to the full enjoyment of a life of virtue and usefulness." His destination was Lake House on the South Shore of Lake Tahoe in California (see Figure 30).

Already well known among the elite of San Francisco and Virginia City and the first for Lake Tahoe resorts, Lake House offered therapeutic benefits and readily available recreational pursuits. Guests could relax in bathhouses; take a trail ride on a horse, play billiards, or bowl a game or two. Because of its popularity, in 1863 it was undergoing expansion with the addition of a new wing to the original hewn log structure. Co-owners Dean and Martin sought to make Lake House an upscale resort with 'good accommodations and "all luxuries of the season can be had and making it into "a splendid watering-place in the Atlantic style,"' as travelogue writer J. Ross Browne observed in his 1863 visit.

Browne implored the ill and downhearted to visit Lake House for its healthful and spiritual restorative properties.

> To dyspeptics, consumptives, and broken-down stockbrokers I have a word of advice to offer: If you want your digestive apparatus put in complete order, so that brickbats will stick to your ribs without inconvenience, spend a month with my friend Martin [co-owner of Lake House]; if your bronchial tubes distress you, swallow a few thousand gallons of Lake Tahoe air, and you can blow bellows blasts from your lungs forever after; if your nervous system is deranged by bad speculation in stocks, bowl nine pins and row one of Martin's boats for six weeks… It is all a matter of health in the long-run; with good digestion and a sound nervous system, there is no trouble in life; for these ends there is no place like Lake Tahoe.

Lake House was not located on the busy Lake Tahoe Wagon Road but on a spur that veered toward the lake and rejoined the main road. Still, it drew travelers and teamsters who wanted a respite from the rigors of the heavy traffic and rough conditions on the main wagon road. A conversation between two teamsters, recorded in the journal of William Brewer, revealed the sense of the place and its orientation toward rest and relaxation.

> *I was amused at a remark of a teamster who stopped here for a drink—the conversation was between two teamsters who looked at things in a practical light, one a stranger here, the other acquainted:*
>
> *No. 1. "A good many people here!"*
>
> *No. 2. "Yes."*
>
> *No. 1. "What they all doing?"*
>
> *No. 2. "Nothing."*
>
> *No. 1. "Nothing at all?"*
>
> *No. 2. "Why, yes—in the city we would call it bumming (California word for loafing), but here they call it pleasure."*
>
> *Both take a drink and depart for their more practical and useful avocations.*

On August 9, Mark Twain traveled on the Pioneer Stage Company's coach from Virginia City to Lake House. He traveled with a fellow reporter named Adair Wilson from a competing newspaper, the *Virginia Daily Union*. Their stage driver was Hank Monk, a man legendary for his driving skills.

Beginning in 1852, Hank Monk drove stages in California. Later, he drove stages for various companies between Virginia City and Lake Tahoe, for a career that spanned over 30 years. He was briefly associated with *New York Tribune* Editor-in-Chief Horace Greeley when Monk took Greeley on a wild stage ride over the Sierra Nevada to get the time-strapped Greeley to a speaking engagement in Placerville, Calif. The tale of the trip circulated widely through the mining camps and eventually several published versions reached the entire nation, giving Monk a nationwide identity. Twain considered Monk the "king of stage drivers," and parodied the

Greeley trip as a tall tale in *Roughing It*, although the event actually occurred. In December 1863, Twain reported in his column that Monk received from his Virginia City admirers an engraved pocket watch that commemorated the Horace Greeley story.

Once at Lake House, Clemens found the hotel "crowded with the wealth and fashion of Virginia" in addition to guests from San Francisco and Sacramento. Rather than resting his illness-wracked body, Clemens immersed himself in "*all the fun going,*" as he told his mother and sister in a letter. He found the guests at Lake House a "*stirring set*" and accompanied them on excursions such as hunting,

Figure 74. A well-dressed man and woman pose in front of Lake House while a carriage near the hotel awaits them.

fishing, and sailing in addition to dancing at the hotel. In the evenings, he nursed his cold with a sheet bath (a wet cold sheet applied to the body), mustard plaster, and a concoction of onion and gin. Clemens discovered the activity was not conducive to recuperation and the remedies ineffective; his illness simply worsened. Despite failure to obtain a cure, Twain was nonetheless able to parlay the experience into two humorous stories for newspapers in August and September.

Who were these people "of Virginia" that Twain encountered at Lake House? In his other writings, Twain used the term "Virginia" to mean Virginia City. These jubilant folks could have been the wealthy social elite of Virginia City rubbing shoulders with other elites from San Francisco and Sacramento. Another scholar believes these people were expatriates of the State of Virginia, seeking refuge and respite from the hardships and horrors of the Civil War. See the well-regarded *Tahoe Beneath the Surface* by Scott Lankford for more about this view.

A group of the merrymakers at Lake House acquired a town site on the shoreline and gave a lot to Clemens. He told his sister in a letter that he would build her a house on it when she came out for a visit, but nothing ever came of it.

Unsuccessful in curing his cold, Mark Twain's stay at Lake House ended at seven days. In the early morning hours of August 17, he boarded a stagecoach with traveling companion Wilson for the return trip to Carson City. The same day and still carrying his worsening cold, he left Carson City by stagecoach for Steamboat Springs.

Steamboat Springs was an area located approximately 14 miles south of modern-day Reno, Nev. where steam produced by geothermal heat emanated from fissures. In 1863, a Dr. Ellis operated the site using the purported healing properties of the steam and hot spring water to treat patients for a variety of illnesses and infections. The facility included bathhouses built over the fissures and a hotel. Even Steamboat Springs was insufficient to cure Twain's respiratory infection, and he returned to Virginia City still fighting his illness. On September 5, he left for San Francisco, ill and still searching for a cure.

Figure 75. In this photo from about 1865, the Lake House excursion sailboat docks at the pier just west of the hotel

Rest in the Bosom of Logan & Stewart

December 11, 1863 brought the close of the Nevada state constitutional convention. The reportorial entourage, known unofficially as the Third House, convened in the same hall to celebrate (and parody) the just concluded session. They elected Mark Twain President of the Convention and Governor of the Third

House. Again, Twain was suffering from a respiratory illness. As he had done in the past, he planned a trip to Lake Tahoe for rest and recuperation. The next morning, Twain boarded the stagecoach for the Logan Hotel on the East Shore of Lake Tahoe, a little more than a mile south of Glenbrook (see Figure 25). As a sign of his rising celebrity, a competing newspaper, the *Virginia*

Figure 76. This circa 1865 photo showed the view to the south from the site of Logan Hotel. Mark Twain saw this same view during his stay at Logan Hotel in 1863. (Library of Congress)

Evening Bulletin, mentioned on December 17 the newly elected "President" of the Third House had retired to Lake Tahoe.

Twain wrote a December 12, 1863 article for the *Territorial Enterprise* from Carson City in advance of his Logan Hotel stay and was effusive in extolling the features and virtues of the Logan Hotel. This suggests he might have been a complimentary guest courtesy of partners Robert Logan and Wellington Stewart and primed with marketing puffery ahead of the trip. Either the visit was undeserving of a follow up article, or if Twain wrote one, it was lost.

Logan, a rancher, built the hotel building on 640 acres of lakefront and mountain property during the summer and fall of 1863. He formed a partnership with Stewart, a Douglas County, Nev. justice of the peace, to manage his new inn.

The new Logan Hotel sat on a small rise overlooking a shallow cove punctuated with rocks jutting out into the lake. Initially called Glenbrook Rocks, United States Geological Survey officials changed it to Logan Shoals in 1957.

In addition to carrying another cold, Twain seemed downtrodden and sullen when he began the *Territorial Enterprise* article,

> Thither I go to recuperate. I take with me a broken spirit, blighted hopes and a busted constitution. Also some gin. I shall return again, after many days, restored to vigorous health; restored to original purity; free from sin, and prepared to accept any lucrative office the people can be induced to force upon me.

The coach carrying Twain traveled over the 15 miles from Carson City to the hotel on the new Kings Canyon Road, a point of convenience that Twain mentioned in his advance article. He added that upon arrival at the Logan Hotel, "the worn pilgrim may rest in peace in the bosom of Logan & Stewart."

Without having visited before, Twain described the Logan Hotel as,

> ...new, handsomely furnished, and commodious; it stands within fifty feet of the water's edge, and commands a view of all the grand scenery there about; its table is furnished with

the best the market affords, and behold they eat trout there every day.

The hotel did lively business and in 1865 added a pier and excursion boats. However, financial problems forced sale of the property for back taxes in 1866 to an agent acting for owners of the Carson and Tahoe Lumber and Fluming Co., who eventually logged the property.

Chapter 5

Up Among the Clouds

Although technically not a part of the Tahoe Basin, Alpine County, Calif. and Truckee-Donner Summit fall within the greater Lake Tahoe region in the Central Sierra. Both mountainous locations are immediately next to the Tahoe Basin, and both are places visited by Mark Twain during his 1861-68 years in the West.

Flowers to Snow Drifts

In April of 1868, Twain was traveling throughout Northern California and Western Nevada on a lecture tour before departing from California and Nevada for the last time. On May 31, 1868, *The Chicago Republican* published a Twain account of a trip over the still snowy Sierra Nevada entitled, "The Summit of the Sierras—From Flowers to Snow Drifts [:] Up Among the Clouds." Interest in the transcontinental railroad was high in Chicago, which stood to benefit greatly by the coming rail connection with the West Coast. The setting for this story involved the Sacramento Valley and Sierra

Nevada of California and three modes of transportation: railroad, horse drawn sleigh and stagecoach.

President Abraham Lincoln signed the bill allowing for the construction of a transcontinental railroad on July 1, 1862. The bill authorized two companies to construct and operate a railway between Chicago, Ill. and Sacramento, Calif. The Central Pacific Railroad started in Sacramento and worked its way east while the Union Pacific began in Omaha, Neb. with a westward heading. The two met less than seven years later to join the rails at Promontory, Utah on May 10, 1869.

California Governor and Central Pacific director Leland Stanford presided over ground breaking for the initial phase on January 3, 1863. Track reached Cisco, Calif. on the western slope of the Sierra by November 1866. From here, construction slowed considerably as crews attacked the formidable granite fortress of the Sierra Nevada. To expedite construction, during the winter of 1866-67 crews moved over the summit to start a second eastward heading beginning at Coburn Station. Coburn Station was renamed Truckee in July 1867 by Central Pacific.

As part of the railroad construction, Central Pacific completed the Dutch Flat-Donner Lake Road in June 1864 with the dual purpose of supplying its crews and providing toll road service for the mining camps of Western Nevada. The road began in Alta, Calif. and paralleled the railway over Donner Summit. From the summit, it diverged to follow the north shore of Donner Lake, through Coburn Station and then north to join the Henness Pass Road, an established supply route to the Nevada mining region.

Twain lectured in Grass Valley, Calif. the evening of April 21 and returned to Sacramento. He boarded the train in Sacramento on April 23, expecting to lecture in Virginia City on Saturday evening, April 25. The April 22 edition of the *Virginia City Daily Trespass* reported Mark Twain would lecture "on 'Pilgrim Life,' being a sketch of his notorious voyage to Europe, Palestine, etc., on board the steamship Quaker City. The mere announcement will be quite sufficient to fill the house to overflowing." Twain's agent, Sam Wetherill, rescheduled the Saturday lecture at the Athletic Hall to Monday, April 27 at the Opera House to accommodate a larger than originally expected crowd. Following this lecture to an overflow crowd, Twain presented another lecture in Carson City on April 29, lingered to visit with friends and then returned to California.

Writing in the *Chicago Republican* article in advance of his departure from Sacramento, Twain spoke of his dread over the inconvenience of having to change the modes of his transportation. The trip would involve railroad, horse drawn sleigh over snow and finally, stagecoach to his destination. He seemed to pine for the days of rattling across the countryside by stagecoach in a 30-hour nonstop journey.

Twain boarded the 6:30 a.m. Central Pacific train in Sacramento for the 89-mile ride on the rails to the temporary terminus at Cisco, Calif. at an elevation of 5,923 feet. As he departed Sacramento in the morning, the area had been experiencing extended summer-like weather and Twain wrote that he, "…left grassy slopes and orchards of cherry, peach and apple in full bloom—left strawberries and cream and vegetable gardens, and a mild atmosphere that was heavy with the perfume of flowers…"

By mid-day he was at the temporary terminus, where

> …we stood seven thousand feet above the sea, with snow banks more than a hundred feet deep almost within rifle-shot of us. We were at Cisco, the summit of the Sierras, where for miles the railway trains rush along under tall wooden sheds, built to protect them from snows and the milder sort of avalanches. We had been running alongside of perpendicular snow-banks, whose upper edges were much above the cars. At Cisco the snow was twenty or thirty feet deep.

Here, Twain confused the summit location and elevation with the temporary terminus. While it was true he was at Cisco, he was still over 13 miles and 1,100 feet below the 7,056 feet summit at Donner Pass.

Snowfall records for Donner Summit for the winter of 1867-68 do not exist, but total precipitation for Sacramento from July 1867 through June 1868 was about 150% of average, suggesting that snowfall had been a comparable amount above normal.

Figure 77. Snowplow near Cisco in 1868 when Mark Twain passed through (Wikimedia Commons)

At Cisco, the rail passengers transferred to sleighs drawn by four horses for the 24-mile trip on the Dutch Flat-Donner Lake Toll Road to Truckee. Sleigh passengers crossed over the summit at Donner Pass, and then descended the eastern escarpment of the Sierra

Nevada to follow the northern shore of Donner Lake to Truckee, just east of the lake. As the sleigh passed Donner Lake, Twain was able to observe it directly and thus was able to speak with first-hand knowledge when he mentioned it in *Roughing It* lectures four years later.

Figure 78. Winter view of Cisco in 1868 when Mark Twain crossed over the summit (Wikimedia Commons)

At Truckee, passengers made yet another transfer, this time to a stagecoach that took them to the Henness Pass Road and eastward into Nevada. Twain has enough time in Truckee to send a telegram

Figure 79. Cisco in winter in 1868 during a brief visit by Mark Twain (Wikimedia Commons)

to the *Territorial Enterprise*, "I am doing well, having crossed one divide without getting robbed anyway. Mark Twain."

Twain was amused with the sleigh ride during what he considered the summer season and made a point in his article to focus on the humorous contradiction of sleigh riding in the summer-like weather.

> Taking the advice of people I deemed wiser than myself, I had wrapped up myself in overcoats, and put on overshoes. It was a perfect tropical day. ...All I wish to say is, that I do not despise to go sleighriding in the summer time. But here in the

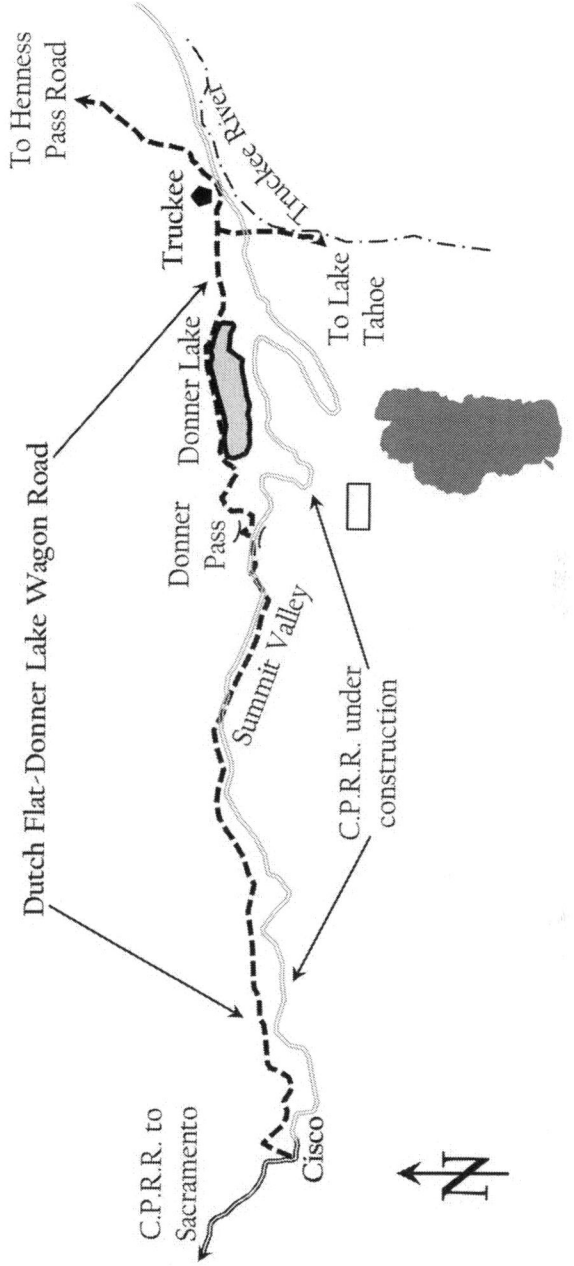

Figure 80. Map showing route of Mark Twain from Cisco to Truckee in 1864

midst of these snowy wastes the sun flamed out as hot as August, and I had to take off everything I could. And the next time I have to do such a thing I mean to have a fan, and some ice cream, and a suit of summer linen along.

Figure 81. Portrait of Mark Twain circa 1867 (Wikimedia Commons)

Twain concluded by reporting that railroad construction was progressing nicely and by July, travelers could expect to make the journey to Chicago by rail and Overland Mail Stage in eight days.

I Depart for Silver Mountain

The story of Twain's visit to cover the mining excitement in Silver Mountain City in Alpine County begins several days before in Virginia City. According to a humorous but factual story written by Dan DeQuille in a late April edition of the *Territorial Enterprise*, Twain suffered a nose injury while fooling around with boxing gloves at the "Club Room" in Virginia City. The Club Room was a gymnasium in the back of a French restaurant on C St. in Virginia City. Twain tangled with an experienced boxer who delivered a powerful punch, resulting in a bloody nose and considerable swelling. Recalling the incident years later, DeQuille said Twain volunteered to go to Silver Mountain City to remove himself from potential ridicule in Virginia City over his swollen nose.

On April 25, 1864, Twain was in Carson City and filed an informative and eclectic report that covered everything from his brother Orion's new offices to the telegraph monopoly to social events. He concluded the dispatch skeptical of his expected early morning departure,

> I depart for Silver Mountain in the Esmeralda stage at 7 o'clock to-morrow morning. It is the early bird that catches the worm, but I would not get up at that time in the morning for a thousand worms, if I were not obliged to.

Twain was referring to the Pioneer Stagecoach Lines owned by Wells, Fargo & Co. that ran between Carson City and Aurora, Esmeralda County, Nev. The stage service to Silver Mountain was irregular and ended there, forcing passengers and freight to transfer to pack trains to continue the journey. Twain would have passed over Jacob Marklee's toll road and though his toll station 10 miles from Silver Mountain City.

Figure 82. The main street of Silver Mountain City, Alpine County, Calif. circa 1865 (Wikimedia Commons)

Following Twain's departure from Virginia City for Silver Mountain, Dan DeQuille wrote a parody in the *Territorial Enterprise* about the arrival of Twain's puffed-up nose in Silver Mountain City. DeQuille had him peering out of the stagecoach window as it entered town and townspeople noticing the enlarged snout assumed its owner was here to give a show. DeQuille said the curious townsfolk gathered at the hotel to cheer the nose as its owner stepped off the coach with one woman touching it and declaring her good fortune, "the happiest moment of her life."

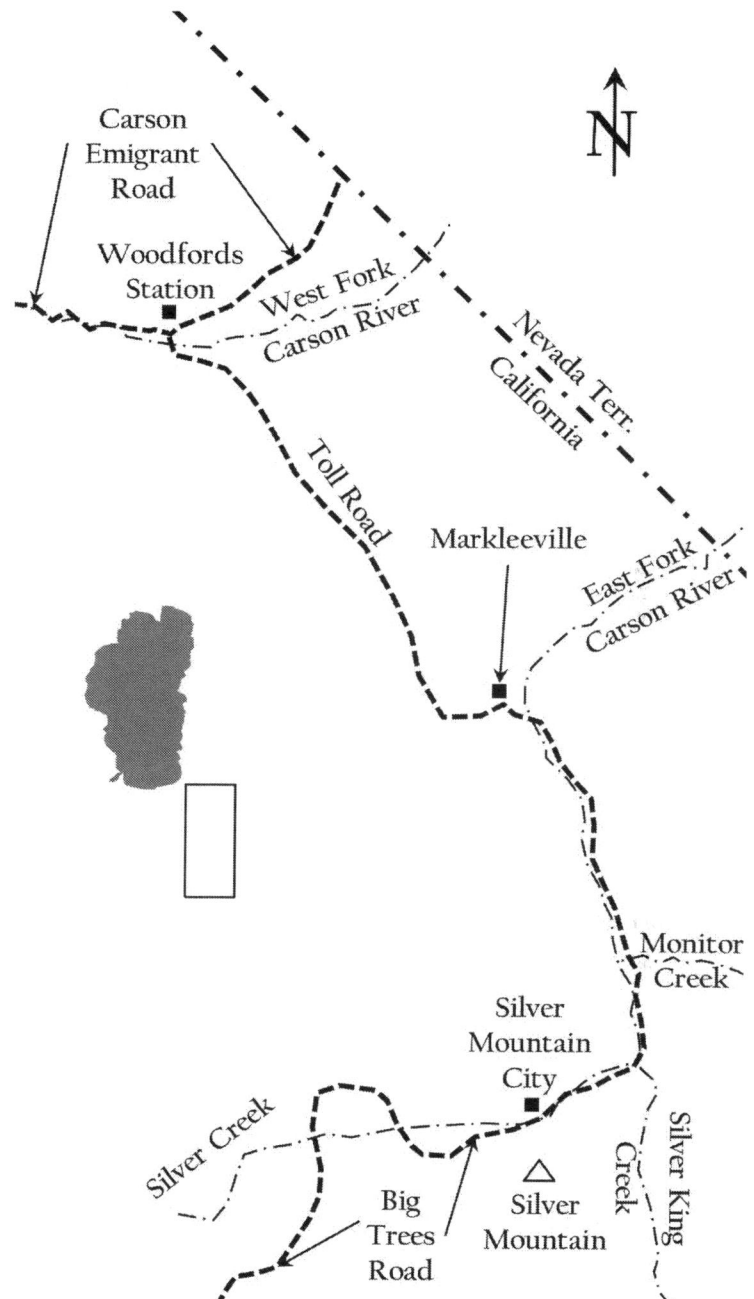

Figure 83. Map showing 1868 features in Alpine County and Mark Twain's route to Silver Mountain City

Twain's report of his visit for the *Territorial Enterprise* was lost, but we have an article from a *Daily Alta California* reporter named "Traveler" who visited Silver Mountain City on May 24, a few weeks after Twain. The reporter found miners working more than 15 claims with shares selling from $20 to $100 per foot. A new mill was under construction and a healthy business district, including a Wells, Fargo & Co. office, had sprung up in the valley. Traveler pointed to the town's inherent advantages: abundant timber and water, location within California beyond the reach of the corrupt Nevada judiciary, and reachable by road from either the Carson Valley or Esmeralda Mining District in Nevada.

When voters created Alpine County in 1863, they selected Silver Mountain City as the county seat. At the time of Twain's visit in 1864, the town had perhaps as many as 3,000 inhabitants. By 1866, the silver mining had played out and demonetization of silver in 1873 sealed the town's fate. The town was on a steep decline, and in 1875, Markleeville became the county seat. Silver Mountain City was all but a ghost town by 1878. New owners dismantled one of its hotels and moved it to Markleeville in 1883, but the jail remained for years until a new facility replaced it in Markleeville.

Chapter 6

I Measure All Lakes by Tahoe

The known written record of descriptions of Lake Tahoe by Sam Clemens and Mark Twain spans the years 1861 through 1891. While his "fairest picture," "singularly clear water" and "grasshopper soup" statements are the most often quoted, he had much else to say about the lake. His comments begin with the therapeutic effects of the lake and its surroundings in 1861. He then raises the volume and intensity of his writings with his vehement opposition to the changed name of the lake. Finally, he accepts the name change and returns his focus to the uniqueness and beauty of Lake Tahoe as he weaves it into his nonfiction book *Roughing It* and lectures following.

The material presented in this chapter reveals two of Twain's many gifts as a writer. He had a keen ability to observe the most subtle aspects of the natural environment and the literary skill to translate these observations into meaningful prose that connected with the emotional side of the reader. One need only read his *Roughing It* accounts (Chapter 8) of the sunrise lighting of the mountains and canyons of the Sierra Nevada on the West Shore of Lake Tahoe and his vivid descriptions of water clarity and bottom features in the lake to understand fully his exceptional talent.

Here we present a collection of excerpts of Lake Tahoe oriented writing from Clemens and Twain together with context and interpretation. The inventory of quotations is probably not complete since previously undiscovered text or accounts still surface and add to the database of the author's literary legacy. We omitted repetitive news reports of his *Roughing It* lectures that mentioned Lake Tahoe.

The Masterpiece of the Creator – Letters 1861-63
The earliest mention of the lake's therapeutic benefits and stunning beauty appeared in letters Clemens wrote to his mother and sister in September and October of 1861 following his first visits to Lake Tahoe, then called Lake Bigler. "*I intend that Pamela shall live on Lake Bigler until she can knock a bull down with her fist--say, about three months.*" In this context, Clemens was suggesting relatives come out for a visit. Pamela was his ailing sister. The implication was that the mountain air and water would have a restorative effect on Pamela's health.

Shortly after the letter to his mother, Clemens wrote his sister Pamela on October 25, 1861 from Carson City.

> *I had better stop about "the Lake," though, --for whenever I think of it I want to go there and die, the place is so beautiful. I'll build a country seat there one of these days that will make the Devil's mouth water if he ever visits the earth.*

The sublime beauty of the lake had now settled into Clemens' thoughts, and he was beginning to appreciate the aesthetic values of this special place.

In a February 16, 1863 letter to his mother and sister, Clemens returned to the presumed therapeutic benefits of life at the lake and the continued poor health of his sister when he wrote,

> *Pamela, you do not say whether you are getting well or not? I think you will have to spend next Summer at the fountain of Youth – the fabled spring which the weary Spaniards sought with such a hopeful yearning, and never found. But I have found it, and it is Lake Bigler. No foul disease may hope to live in the presence of such beauty as that.*

Continuing with the presumption of curative and inspirational properties of the lake and suffering from a respiratory illness himself, Twain wrote in August 13, 1863 San Francisco *Morning Call*, "However, Lake Bigler will restore me to the full enjoyment of a life of virtue and usefulness tomorrow."

On August 19, 1863 and following his failed therapeutic stay at Lake House, Clemens wrote his mother and sister from Steamboat Springs, Nev. Still entranced with the stunning magnificence of Lake Tahoe, he remarked, *"The Lake seems more supernaturally beautiful now than ever. It is the masterpiece of the Creator."*

Bigler vs. Tahoe – Commentary 1863-64

The year 1863 also marked the beginning of Mark Twain's public rants about the federal name change from Lake Bigler to Lake Tahoe. In this dispatch to the August 19, 1863 *Territorial Enterprise,* he insinuates the name "Tahoe" is a less than a worthy appellation for such a magnificent work of nature. The piece was written from Steamboat Springs, Nev. where Twain was attempting to cure a raging cold after a failed attempt at a cure at Lake Tahoe.

> I went to the lake (Lake Bigler I must beg leave to call it still, notwithstanding, if I recollect rightly, it is known among sentimental people as either Tahoe Lake or Yahoo Lake - however, one of the last will do as well as the other, since there is neither sense nor music in either of them),

Just as the lake's history has gone through distinct phases, so has it name changed with the preference of explorers, cartographers, political winds and local inhabitants. The Washoe called it *da ow a ga*, meaning "edge of the lake" or simply, *da ow*. Henry Preuss affixed the label "Mountain Lake" to the first map of the Fremont 1844-45 expedition but Fremont preferred "Lake Bonpland" after the French botanist who accompanied an earlier western exploration party. Others added assorted odd names, but none ever stuck. The California Surveyor General named it "Lake Bigler" after California's third governor who had led a mission to rescue emigrants trapped there. That name seemed to persist on some maps for years. Nevertheless, even that name fell into disrepute when Bigler came under suspicion as a southern sympathizer during the Civil War. While there was a widespread desire to rebuke Bigler and rename the lake, the political path to the final naming was ambiguous.

One account of the name change has federal cartographers Henry DeGroot and William Knight researching the common name "Lake Tahoe" and applying it to their map in 1862. Most people believed the word "Tahoe" descended from a Euro-American mispronunciation of the first two syllables of the prehistoric Washoe name, but had a large number of conflicting translations. Bigler stood as the official name of the lake until California finally relented in 1945 and officially recognized the name "Lake Tahoe."

Scholars suspect that during this time, Twain harbored closeted sympathy toward the Confederacy during the Civil War and his outbursts of criticism toward the name change reflected this. (See Scott Lankford's *Tahoe Beneath the Surface* for more on this view.) Another theory, and not necessarily exclusionary of the closeted Confederate notion, is that Twain's ingrained racism toward Native Americans was laid bare during his objections to the name because of its Native American origins.

The essay, "Bigler vs. Tahoe" appeared in the September 13, 1863 edition of the San Francisco *Golden Era* as a reprint from the *Territorial Enterprise*. In this piece, Twain was lecturing "Grub," a letter writer to the *Territorial Enterprise*, who had written Twain directly with a "Letter from Lake Bigler." The exchange probably appeared in *Territorial Enterprise* around the first week of September 1863, but both source *Territorial Enterprise* editions were lost.

Twain used a racial slur for Native American but it was not clear whom exactly he meant to be the target of the slur. Either he was directing it at the local Washoe tribe or he was directing it at California Native Americans, who some thought might be related to the Washoe.

> I hope some bird will catch this Grub the next time he calls Lake Bigler by so disgustingly sick and silly a name as "Lake Tahoe." I have removed the offensive word from his letter and substituted the old one, which at least has a Christian English twang about it whether it is pretty or not. Of course Indian names are more fitting than any others for our beautiful lakes and rivers, which knew their race ages ago, perhaps, in the morning of creation, but let us have none so repulsive to the ear as "Tahoe" for the beautiful relic of fairy-land forgotten and left asleep in the snowy Sierras when the little elves fled from their ancient haunts and quitted the earth. They say it means "Fallen Leaf" - well suppose it meant fallen devil or fallen angel, would that render its hideous, discordant syllables more endurable? Not if I know myself. I yearn for the scalp of the soft-shell crab - be he [derogatory name for a California or Nevada Native American] or white man - who conceived of that spoony, slobbering, summer-complaint of a name. ... "Tahoe" - it sounds as weak as soup for a sick infant. "Tahoe" be - forgotten!

On December 12, 1863, and writing a promotional piece in advance of his visit to the Logan Hotel, he took another shot in the *Territorial*

Enterprise at the new name. He threw in a racial epithet (omitted in the quote), possibly directed at the local Native American tribe, the Washoe, whose language was thought to be the likely source of the new name. "The Logan Hotel is situated on the banks of Lake Bigler - or Lake Tahoe, which signifieth "grasshopper" in the [derogatory name for a California or Nevada Native American] tongue." His statement about the English translation of the name is not true.

Scant two months after the gratuitous Logan Hotel piece, Twain vented his spleen again, complete with the racial slur, on the Bigler controversy and at the same time denigrated its native source. He used the pretext of reporting in the February 12, 1864 *Territorial Enterprise* on a new law that regulated the taking of fish.

> It is a good law, and calls our lake by its right name Lake Bigler - and rejects the spooney appellation of "Tahoe," which signifieth "grasshopper" in the [derogatory name for a California or Nevada Native American] tongue, and "breech clout" [a garment that provides covering for the loins] in the Washoe lingo. Bigler is the legitimate name of the Lake, and it will be retained until some name less flat, insipid and spooney than "Tahoe" is invented for it. I am sorry, myself, that it was not called in the first place by some cognomen that could be persuaded to rhyme with something, because, you see, every sentimental cuss who goes up there and becomes pregnant with a poem invariably miscarries because of the unfortunate difficulty I have just mentioned. I speak of the matter lightly, but it is not a frivolous one, for all that.

Again, his translations of the meaning were wrong, perhaps deliberately so, to imply a belittling definition to the name "Tahoe" that would be an insult to such a magnificent lake. This was his last shot at the naming controversy until the publication of *Innocents Abroad* in 1869. He then turned his attention to writing about the lake in ways that were more constructive and commercially viable.

Fish in Lake Tahoe Are Not Troublesome – 1864 Article

After maintaining literary silence on the subject of Lake Tahoe for 12 months, Twain wrote publicly about the lake and used the name "Lake Tahoe" without regressing into his naming polemics. Maybe he saw the new name as more or less permanent, suspected the public had tired of his rants, or he had simply run his course on the subject for now.

Drawing at least partially on his lack of fishing success during the timber claim adventure, he noted in this September 4, 1864 commentary in the San Francisco *Daily Morning Call* that fishing at Lake Tahoe would not be demanding on the featured person. The subject of the commentary was Charles Henry Webb, who had just sold his weekly publication, *Californian*, to which Clemens had been a paid contributor.

> After faithfully laboring night and day for about four months, and publishing fifteen numbers of the best paper in its particular department ever issued on this coast, Mr. Webb will now go and rest a while on the shores of Lake Tahoe. He has chosen to rest himself by fishing, and he is wise; for the fish in Lake Tahoe are not troublesome; they will let a man rest there till he rots, and never inflict upon him the fatigue of putting on a fresh bait.

I Measure All Lakes by Tahoe – *Innocents Abroad* 1869

In 1868 and for the first time, Twain made the comparison of another body of water to Lake Tahoe. The comparison was between the Sea of Galilee and Lake Tahoe in a dispatch written from the Holy Land to the *Daily Alta California* newspaper. Twain naturally gravitated toward Tahoe as the gold standard of large world lakes. A year later, he would announce in his first book, *Innocents Abroad*,

> I measure all lakes by Tahoe, partly because I am far more familiar with it than with any other, and partly because I have such a high admiration for it and such a world of pleasant

> recollections of it, that it is very nearly impossible for me to speak of lakes and not mention it.

In his January 19, 1868 dispatch from the Holy Land, excerpted here, he drew stark and unflattering comparisons between the two water bodies.

> The celebrated Sea of Galilee is not so large a sea as Lake Tahoe by a good deal— it is just about two-thirds as large. And when you speak of beauty, this sea is no more to be compared to Tahoe than a meridian of longitude is to a rainbow. The dim waters of this puddle cannot suggest the limpid brilliancy of Tahoe… Silence and solitude brood over Tahoe; and silence and solitude brood also over this lake of Gennesaret. But the solitude of the one is as cheerful and fascinating as the solitude of the other is dismal and repulsive.

The balance of the dispatch appeared in *Innocents Abroad* the following year, but without this introductory paragraph.

The publication of *Innocents Abroad* brought the first vivid descriptions of Lake Tahoe in book form to the public at large and resurrected Twain's five-year old ranting about the Tahoe name. The book, based on a series of letters sent from Europe, the Holy Land and North Africa to the *Daily Alta California*, sold well in its first year and was a bestseller among all of Twain's books.

This and the following passage appeared in *Innocents Abroad* as a digression to his memories of Lake Tahoe in the context of describing the Sea of Galilee.

> In the early morning one watches the silent battle of dawn and darkness upon the waters of Tahoe with a placid interest; but when the shadows sulk away and one by one the hidden beauties of the shore unfold themselves in the full splendor of noon; when the still surface is belted like a rainbow with

broad bars of blue and green and white, half the distance from circumference to centre...

Here Twain was writing about the transition of colors in the waters of pristine Lake Tahoe as one moved from the shoreline toward the center of the lake. The white color to which he referred was actually the shallows where the light-colored bottom dominated the nearly full spectrum reflected light giving it a white appearance. The white

Figure 84. The Sea of Galilee in 1900 (Library of Congress)

was more striking than it is today because of decreased clarity and the growth of attached algae since Twain's early 1860s visits. As Twain reached deeper water, the red, orange, yellow and magenta colors were absorbed by water molecules and particles shortened the light path before it could develop its blue color. This left green as the predominate color he saw bounced back from the water. Farther out and at a depth of 75 feet, the green was absorbed, leaving only blue and indigo colored light in the original spectrum and giving the lake its characteristic and world famous blue and cobalt blue colors.

> ...when, in the lazy summer afternoon, he lies in a boat, far out to where the dead blue of the deep water begins, and smokes the pipe of peace and idly winks at the distant crags and patches of snow from under his cap-brim; when the boat drifts shoreward to the white water, and he lolls over the gunwale and gazes by the hour down through the crystal depths and notes the colors of the pebbles and reviews the finny armies gliding in procession a hundred feet below...

In this passage, Twain was recalling his time spent drifting about in a boat over the boulder field off Stateline Point during his first trips to Lake Tahoe to stake a timber claim.

In his description of Italy's Lake Como in *Innocents Abroad*, Twain again reverted to the lake he knows best for comparison – Lake Tahoe. This time he used water clarity as his measuring rod, and humorously exaggerated his ability to see details at a depth of 180 feet in Lake Tahoe such as the imperceptible scales on a trout.

> That is all very well, except the "clear" part of the lake [Como]. It certainly is clearer than a great many lakes, but how dull its waters are compared with the wonderful transparence of Lake Tahoe! I speak of the north shore of Tahoe, where one can count the scales on a trout at a depth of a hundred and eighty feet.

> As far as I am privately concerned, I abate not a jot of the original assertion that in those strangely magnifying waters one may count the scales on a trout (a trout of the large kind,) at a depth of a hundred and eighty feet--may see every pebble on the bottom--might even count a paper of dray-pins. People talk of the transparent waters of the Mexican Bay of Acapulco, but in my own experience I know they cannot

compare with those I am speaking of. I have fished for trout, in Tahoe, and at a measured depth of eighty-four feet I have seen them put their noses to the bait and I could see their gills open and shut. I could hardly have seen the trout themselves at that distance in the open air.

As I go back in spirit and recall that noble sea, reposing among the snow-peaks six thousand feet above the ocean, the conviction comes strong upon me again that Como would only seem a bedizened little courtier in that august presence.

Figure 85. Lake Como, Italy from an 1834 painting by Jean-Baptiste-Camille Corot (Wikimedia Commons)

Continuing with his comparison of Como to Tahoe,

> Como is a little deeper than Tahoe, if people here tell the truth. They say it is eighteen hundred feet deep at this point, but it does not look a dead enough blue for that. Tahoe is one thousand five hundred and twenty-five feet deep in the centre, by the state geologist's measurement. ...Tahoe is from

ten to eighteen miles wide, and its mountains shut it in like a wall. Their summits are never free from snow the year round. One thing about it is very strange: it never has even a skim of ice upon its surface, although lakes in the same range of mountains, lying in a lower and warmer temperature, freeze over in winter.

Twain reasonably doubted the quoted depth of Como. Lake Como is actually 1,320 feet in maximum depth. The depth and dimensions he cited for Tahoe were equally inaccurate but probably based on the best measurements available at the time. He noted that Lake Tahoe does not freeze over in winter, a natural phenomenon that perplexed him. The lake's resistance to forming ice cover was the product of a relatively mild climate and its surface-to-volume ratio that allowed it to retain sufficient heat over winter to prevent freezing.

Grasshopper Soup – *Innocents Abroad* **1869**
Lying dormant for at least five years was Twain's still simmering irritation over the renaming of Lake Bigler to Lake Tahoe. In this passage from *Innocents Abroad*, he invoked a furious curse on the politicos responsible for this desecration, raised Lake Tahoe to supernatural status, and as he had done before, denigrated the Native American origins of the modern name.

> Sorrow and misfortune overtake the legislature that still from year to year permits Tahoe to retain its unmusical cognomen! Tahoe! It suggests no crystal waters, no picturesque shores, no sublimity. Tahoe for a sea in the clouds: a sea that has character and asserts it in solemn calms at times, at times in savage storms; a sea whose royal seclusion is guarded by a cordon of sentinel peaks that lift their frosty fronts nine thousand feet above the level world; a sea whose every aspect is impressive, whose belongings are all beautiful, whose lonely majesty types the Deity!

Tahoe means grasshoppers. It means grasshopper soup.[2] It is Indian, and suggestive of Indians. They say it is Pi-ute [Paiute]--possibly it is [derogatory name for a California or Nevada Native American]. I am satisfied it was named by the [derogatory name for a California or Nevada Native American tribe]--those degraded savages who roast their dead relatives, then mix the human grease and ashes of bones with tar, and "gaum" it thick all over their heads and foreheads and ears, and go caterwauling about the hills and call it mourning. These are the gentry that named the Lake.

People say that Tahoe means "Silver Lake"--"Limpid Water"--"Falling Leaf." Bosh. It means grasshopper soup, the favorite dish of the [derogatory name for a California or Nevada Native American] tribe,--and of the Pi-utes [Paiutes] as well.

Twain's attack on the Tahoe name showed he was still seething with resentment and harbored a belittling attitude toward Native Americans, who played no role in the official naming action. However, it was his grand finale, and we heard nothing more of it afterward, in any of his writings or lectures.

Fairest Picture – *Roughing It* 1871-72

The next time Lake Tahoe emerged in Twain's writings was in conjunction with the 1872 publication of *Roughing It* (two chapters) and his ensuing lecture series that promoted the book. When it came to Lake Tahoe, *Roughing It* marked a return to the original themes of the lake's therapeutic effect on body and spirit, astounding water clarity and the intrinsic beauty of its surroundings.

Roughing It was a fountain of effusive and vivid descriptions of the beauty of Lake Tahoe, even as lumbermen, hunters, anglers and

---

[2] Grasshoppers were a nutritional food source for Washoe and other Native American tribes and may have been prepared in a broth.

THE INVALID.　　　THE RESTORED.

Figure 86. Images from *Roughing It* showing "before" and "after" therapeutic benefits of life at Lake Tahoe

water seekers plundered the Tahoe Basin to satisfy the mining industry's insatiable appetite for natural resources. Twain may have been aware of these developments by reading newspaper and magazine accounts. However, the prevailing philosophy of the era was that these activities were necessary for progress, and they were beneficial by preventing waste of an unexploited resource. In the latter 20th century, *Roughing It* provided frequently used quotations for commercial marketing, as if Mark Twain's endorsement was the only thing one needed to make the decision to buy a building site or book a vacation at Tahoe.

The most frequent quote from *Roughing It* was Twain's recollection of seeing Lake Tahoe for the first time as he emerged from the forest along Tunnel Creek above the east side of Crystal Bay. With Twain having the reputation of a globetrotting writer, his conclusion that Lake Tahoe was the most beautiful region in the world carried considerable weight.

> ...at last the Lake burst upon us--a noble sheet of blue water lifted six thousand three hundred feet above the level of the sea, and walled in by a rim of snow-clad mountain peaks that towered aloft full three thousand feet higher still! It was a vast oval, and one would have to use up eighty or a hundred good miles in traveling around it. As it lay there with the shadows of the mountains brilliantly photographed upon its still surface I thought it must surely be the fairest picture the whole earth affords.

In this quote, he was closer to the actual elevation (6,225 feet) but overshot the circumference of the lake, which was actually 75.1 miles. He was generally correct about the elevation of the surrounding peaks, although several reach more than 4,000 feet above the lake's surface.

Speaking in *Roughing It* to the restoration of spiritual strength and cure of physical infirmities, Twain injected humor to make his point in this passage.

> Three months of camp life on Lake Tahoe would restore an Egyptian mummy to his pristine vigor, and give him an appetite like an alligator. I do not mean the oldest and driest mummies, of course, but the fresher ones. The air up there in the clouds is very pure and fine, bracing and delicious. And why shouldn't it be?--it is the same the angels breathe.

In his *Roughing It* descriptions of Lake Tahoe and its surroundings, Twain grabbed the reader's emotions by taking the reader to Lake Tahoe in a mental image to see its beauty and experience its moods.

> The forest about us was dense and cool, the sky above us was cloudless and brilliant with sunshine, the broad lake before us

was glassy and clear, or rippled and breezy, or black and storm-tossed, according to Nature's mood; and its circling border of mountain domes, clothed with forests, scarred with land-slides, cloven by canons and valleys, and helmeted with glittering snow, fitly framed and finished the noble picture. The view was always fascinating, bewitching, entrancing. The eye was never tired of gazing, night or day, in calm or storm; it suffered but one grief, and that was that it could not look always, but must close sometimes in sleep.

Twain's fascination with the extraordinary clarity of the water and its optical properties showed in these two passages from *Roughing It*. When Twain was gazing down through the depths in 1861, water clarity was probably 125 feet or more as measured by sighting an eight-inch diameter disk lowered into the water. Today, average clarity hovers around half that depth.

So singularly clear was the water, that where it was only twenty or thirty feet deep the bottom was so perfectly distinct that the boat seemed floating in the air! Yes, where it was even eighty feet deep. Every little pebble was distinct, every speckled trout, every hand's-breadth of sand.

Down through the transparency of these great depths, the water was not merely transparent, but dazzlingly, brilliantly so. All objects seen through it had a bright, strong vividness, not only of outline, but of every minute detail, which they would not have had when seen simply through the same depth of atmosphere.

In the latter part of 1871, Twain embarked on a lecture series to promote *Roughing It*. In this account published in the December 16, 1871 Grand Rapids *Daily Morning Democrat* he touched on three aspects of Lake Tahoe that were not mentioned in the book.

He described Lake Tahoe, in Nevada, as the noblest, loveliest inland sea in the whole world -- a master work of nature -- a hundred miles in circumference, six thousand feet above the sea -- an oval mirror framed by snow-capped mountains ten thousand feet high, and whose waters were so clear that the smallest pebbles were distinctly visible at the bottom, eighty feet from the surface. This lake, he said, never freezes, though Lake Donner, in the immediate vicinity, does; and that was a question for science -- not why Lake Donner does freeze, but why Lake Tahoe don't. He advised all invalids to go there; and he earnestly urged all sportsmen to shoulder their rifles and proceed to Tahoe at once, for it is "the best hunting ground in the world; you might hunt a year -- and never find anything. There's no game there, except mountain sheep and seven-up." The sheep are American chamois, have big horns, and you can see them -- with a spy-glass; but it's hard to shoot them -- with a spy-glass.

He mentioned Donner Lake, the nonfreezing conundrum, and sighting bighorn sheep, none of which found their way into *Roughing It*. Donner Lake does develop an ice cover during winter because its microclimate is much colder than Tahoe and the lake lacks the favorable surface-to-volume ratio that helps Tahoe remain free of ice during winter. The old growth and mature forest that experienced low-intensity fires lacked the shrubs that could support significant herds of larger game such as deer. Deer were only transient visitors anyway, since the deep winter snow drove them to lower elevation each winter. Only the bighorn sheep (incorrectly referred to in the lecture as "chamois") could survive the harsh conditions above timberline on the North Shore.

Trout from Tahoe – ***A Tramp Abroad*** **1880**
Long after his Tahoe experiences, Twain in *A Tramp Abroad*, his 1880 travelogue sequel to *Innocents Abroad*, listed, "Lake trout,

Figure 87. A frozen Donner Lake as seen from the Donner Summit area circa 1868 (Wikimedia Commons)

from Tahoe" on a long list of favorite fare he looked forward to eating upon returning home.

> It has now been many months, at the present writing, since I have had a nourishing meal, but I shall soon have one--a modest, private affair, all to myself. I have selected a few dishes, and made out a little bill of fare, which will go home in the steamer that precedes me, and be hot when I arrive--as follows:

...
Lake trout, from Tahoe.
...

His characterization as "lake trout" was a reference to the Lahontan cutthroat trout and not the species commonly known as lake trout or mackinaw. It was not until 1910 that fish and game officials introduced lake trout species into Lake Tahoe. His preference most likely came from dining on the cutthroat trout served at Lake Tahoe hotels and widely shipped to the mining camps of Nevada.

Figure 88. Lahontan cutthroat trout (R. Halden)

A Sea in the Clouds – 1891

One final Lake Tahoe quote emerged in 1891 in *King's Handbook of the United States*, "A sea in the clouds, whose royal seclusion is guarded by a cordon of sentinel peaks that lift their frosty fronts 9,000 feet above the level of the world." As far as the written record was concerned, this was the final enduring statement of Mark Twain on Lake Tahoe.

Chapter 7

In the Footsteps of Mark Twain

The Tahoe Basin and adjacent areas have massive amounts of public lands managed as national forests and state and local parks. The Tahoe Basin is 87% publicly owned and nearby Alpine County, briefly visited by Twain in 1864, is 96% in public ownership. This provides the unique opportunity for Twain scholars and enthusiasts to visit most of the sites associated with Sam Clemens and Mark Twain that are mentioned in this book. A bonus is the public land protections and strict environmental protection measures on the public lands have preserved the surrounding environment so that it resembles in many ways the conditions in the 1860s. The opportunity to stand where Twain stood, see what Twain saw and experience the same feelings that Twain felt adds new dimensions to the appreciation of the author's works.

Refer to the area map (Figure 89) for the general locations and identification of the Mark Twain sites. Use the written directions and

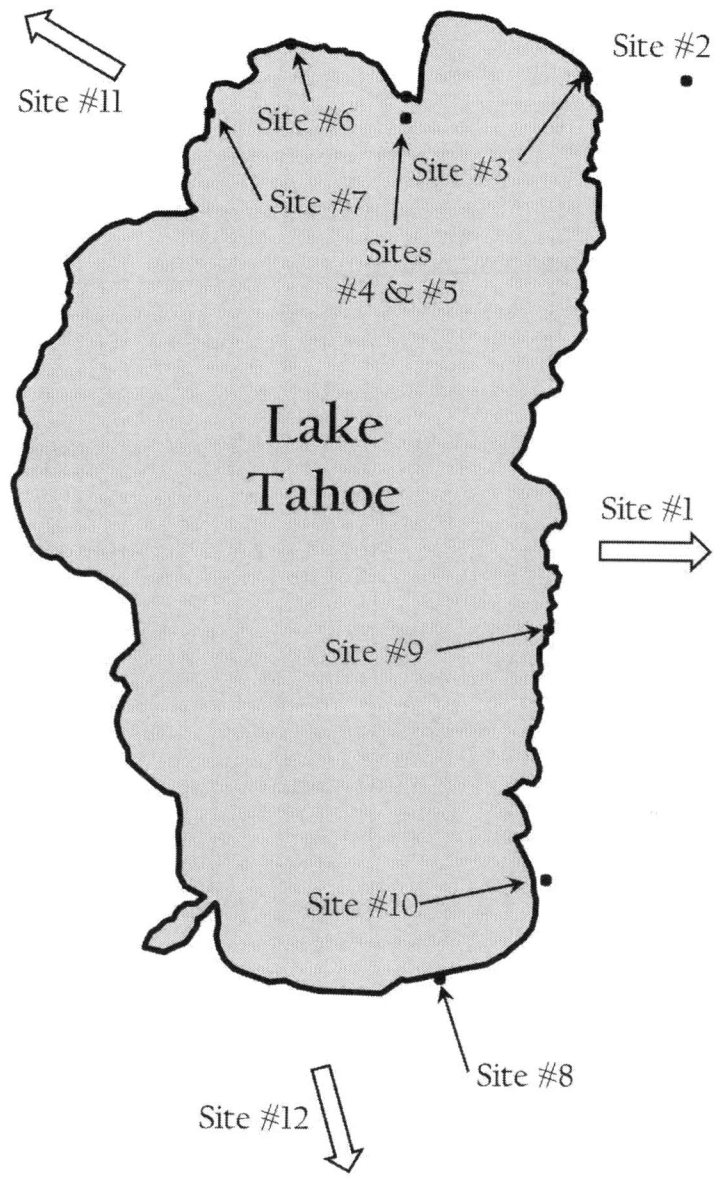

Figure 89. Area map showing points of interest associated with Mark Twain.

detail maps to find the site. Consult online maps and guide books to get specific directions to many of these locations.

Site #1 Ash Canyon-Washoe Trail from Carson City to Lake Tahoe

For the most adventurous and physically fit, the route from Carson City to Lake Tahoe is a major challenge and not recommended for many people. Maintenance of the Ash Canyon road is largely nonexistent and many parts are downright dangerous for vehicles. There are no services. Interested persons can drive a portion of the Ash Canyon road using a 4WD vehicle, ride all of it on a mountain bike or simply hike the distance, as Clemens did in 1861.

Figure 90. Entrance to Ash Canyon from Wellington West Road

Motor vehicles will encounter a locked gate at the boundary to Lake Tahoe Nevada State Park, just past the Franktown Creek-Ash Creek watershed divide. Check on road conditions with the Carson City Public Works Division before attempting this route. Only persons who are knowledgeable on outdoor survival skills, carry emergency equipment and supplies and are familiar with the terrain should

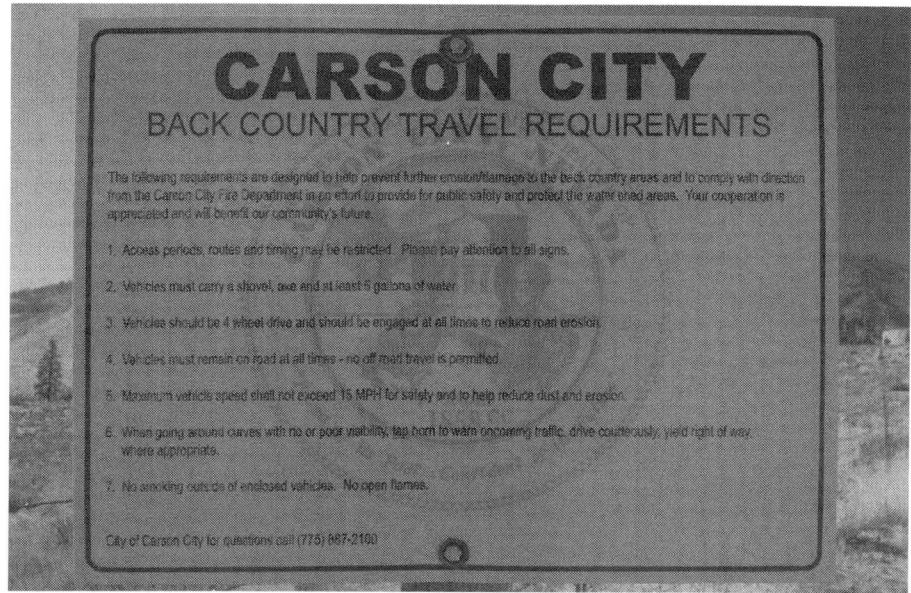

Figure 91. A sign at entrance to Ash Canyon gives many precautions for persons using the Ash Canyon Road

consider this trip. The entrance to Ash Canyon is west of Carson City through an easement from Wellington West near the intersection of Ash Canyon Road and Wellington West. The GPS coordinates at the entrance are 39.1739°,-119.7975°.

Site #2 Fairest Picture Vista Point and Washoe Trail

On a public easement to Lake Tahoe Nevada State Park, one can hike 1.4 miles to the point where Sam Clemens emerged from the forest to see Lake Tahoe for the first time. It was this magical view from the Washoe Trail (approximated by the modern-day Tunnel Creek Road) that inspired him to write that Lake Tahoe is the "fairest picture the whole earth affords."

Where legal to do so, park on the Highway 28 roadway shoulder near the intersection of Lakeshore Drive in Incline Village, Nev. Start at the intersection of Ponderosa Ranch Road and follow the Tunnel Creek Road that starts on the right. The vista point is at GPS coordinates 39.22747°,-119.92019°.

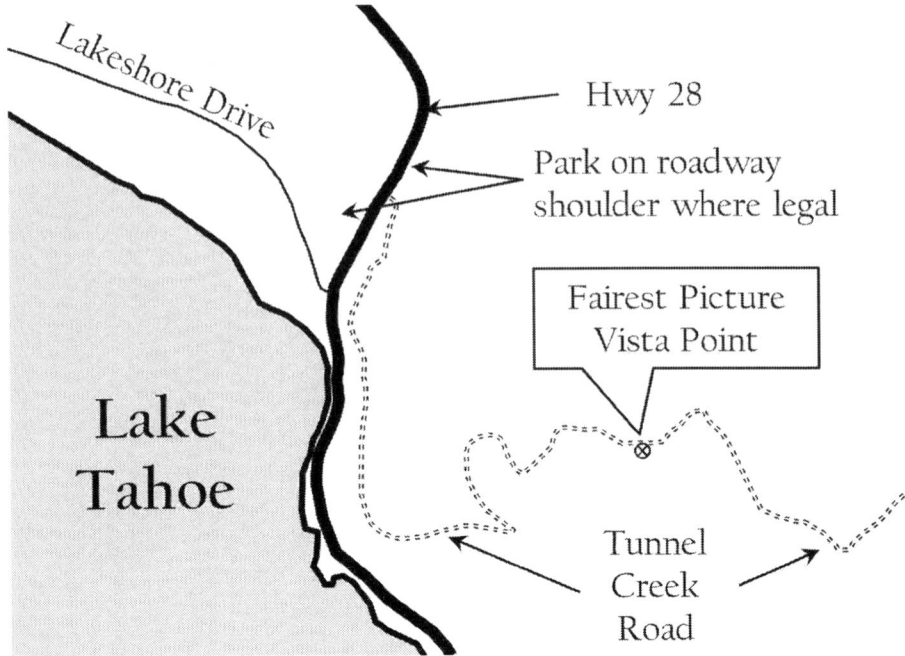

Figure 92. Detail map for hiking to the Fairest Picture Vista Point

Site #3 Hidden Beach (Found a Skiff)

The beach where Sam Clemens and John Kinney found the skiff they used to cross Crystal Bay is a public beach now called Hidden Beach and part of Lake Tahoe Nevada State Park. Looking westward from the beach, one can see "across a deep bend of the lake [Crystal Bay] toward the landmarks [Stateline Point] that signified the locality of the camp." One can visit the beach after a short walk from the roadside parking area, about 0.5-mile south of the intersection of Highway 28 and Lakeshore Drive. Look for parking on the lakeside of the road only and past the last house. From the parking areas, follow a path 0.4 to 0.6-mile on the lakeside just inside the highway guardrail and look for interpretive signs about Lake Tahoe. The GPS coordinates for Hidden Beach near Incline Village are 39.22132°,-119.92893°.

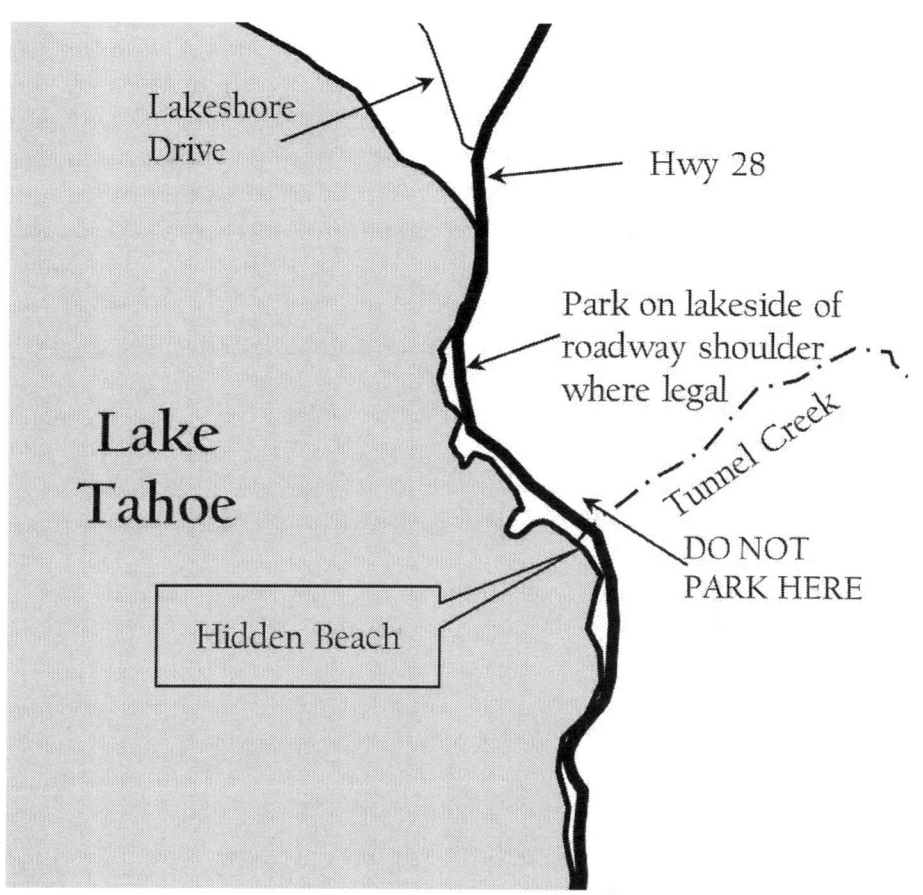

Figure 93. Detail map for locating Hidden Beach

Site #4 Speedboat Beach (Supply Cache Campsite)

At the tip of Stateline Point is a small public beach owned by the Placer County. It was here that Clemens and Kinney found the Brigade's cache of food and supplies and played faro on a flat rock. The public beach is entirely in California. Once on the beach, you may move westward along the public trust zone below the high-water rim of Lake Tahoe. No such public trust zone exists in Nevada, and you will encounter "no trespassing" signs east of Speedboat Beach. Obey them.

You may visit Speedboat Beach by turning south off Highway 28 onto Harbor Avenue. Follow Harbor Avenue until it ends near Lake

Tahoe. Park where legal on Harbor Avenue or Speedboat Avenue. The GPS coordinates for Speedboat Beach on Stateline Point are 39.22296°,-120.00722°. Parking is very limited, so arrive early or park on the state highway and walk in if you wish to visit this site.

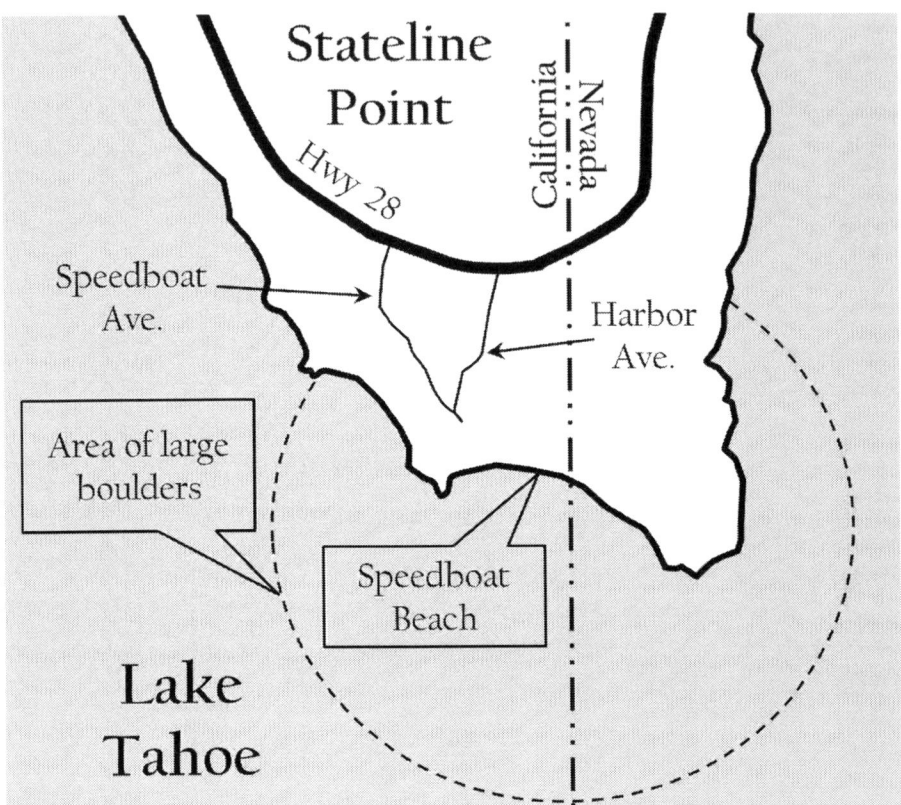

Figure 94. Detail map showing location of Speedboat Beach and the offshore area where large submerged boulders occur.

Site #5 Recreate Sam Clemens' Balloon Voyage over the Submerged Boulders (Offshore of Stateline Point)

If you brought an inflatable boat or a small kayak, you can drift offshore of Speedboat Beach on Stateline Point. Here you can see the massively large boulders that Mark Twain wrote about in *Roughing It* as his "balloon voyages." Alternatively, you can rent a kayak at one of the several Kings Beach locations and paddle out to

Stateline Point yourself. Refer to Figure 94 for the general location of the large submerged boulders. The GPS coordinates for the submerged boulder field are 39.2208°,-120.0071°.

Site #6 Sandy Beach (Timber Claim Campsite and Wildfire Location)

Although we do not know the exact location of Clemens and Kinney's campsite and brush house, you can get a feel for the area at Sandy Beach, on public land managed by the California Tahoe Conservancy. The public beach lies on the lakeside of the highway between Anderson Road and National Avenue in Tahoe Vista, Calif. You may park on the shoulder of Highway 28 where legal to do so. The GPS coordinates for Sandy Beach are 39.23966°,-120.05111°.

Figure 95. Photo of Sandy Beach showing large boulders offshore

It was in this area that Clemens and Kinney staked their timber claim. Later, their untended campfire ignited a wildfire. The boulders you see out in the water are similar to the two protecting boulders that the two men slept between during the fire. Recall that the shoreline extended much farther out than today. You may move east and west along the shoreline in this area below the high-water rim of Lake Tahoe. Across Highway 28 and on private property, you will see some examples of the large trees in excess of five feet about which Twain wrote.

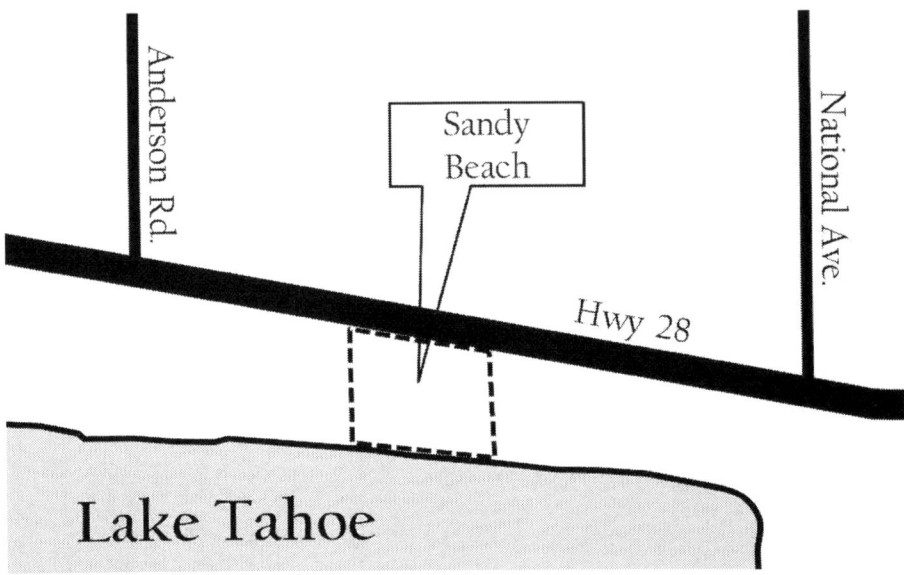

Figure 96. Detail map showing the location of Sandy Beach in the Tahoe Vista area and on or near the timber claim and wildfire locations

Site #7 Carnelian West Beach (Cabin and Dugout Canoe Site)

The Carnelian Bay cabin where Clemens and Kinney played cribbage and then paddled back in the cabin owner's canoe is long gone. However, the location is on a Placer County roadway right-of-way that parallels the Lake Tahoe shoreline with parking and access at the California Tahoe Conservancy Carnelian West Beach. Please stay on the defined pathway and do not cross onto private property, including the pier. The area below the high-water rim of Lake Tahoe is a public trust zone, and you may cross over this to the lake.

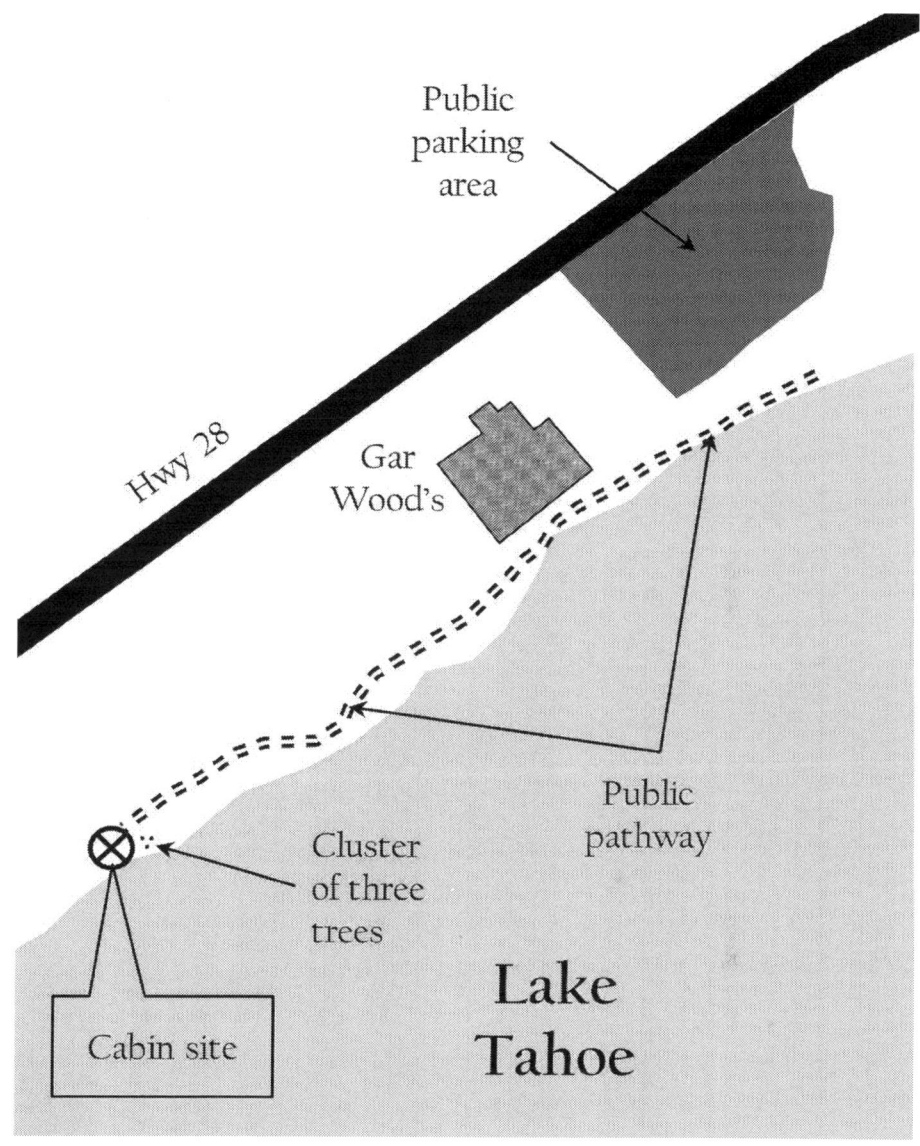

Figure 97. Detail map showing approximate location of the Carnelian Bay cabin site near Carnelian West Beach

Walking about 450-500 feet southwest of Gar Wood's pier, you will come to a cluster of three old-growth trees – two cedars and Jeffrey pine. See Figure 98 for a picture of these trees. These trees mark the approximate location of the cabin. Keep in mind the shoreline extended much farther out than today and has receded because of erosion caused by the Tahoe Dam. If you look to the east, you can imagine

Clemens and Kinney watching for the moonrise over the Carson Range before beginning their canoe trip back to camp at Stateline Point. The GPS coordinates for this site are 39.22433°,-120.08466°.

Figure 98. Cluster of old growth trees (center) that mark the approximate location of the cabin site.

Site #8 Lake House Location

The now vacant site where Lake House once stood is easily accessible by a surface street in the Al Tahoe area of South Lake Tahoe. In 1863, Mark Twain stayed here while attempting to cure a severe cold.

A short walk along a pleasant trail bordering Upper Truckee Marsh takes you to an area enclosed by a low fence. The meadow and access trail is on public land managed by the California Tahoe

Figure 99. Modern-day photo showing the site of Lake House marked by the rustic fence.

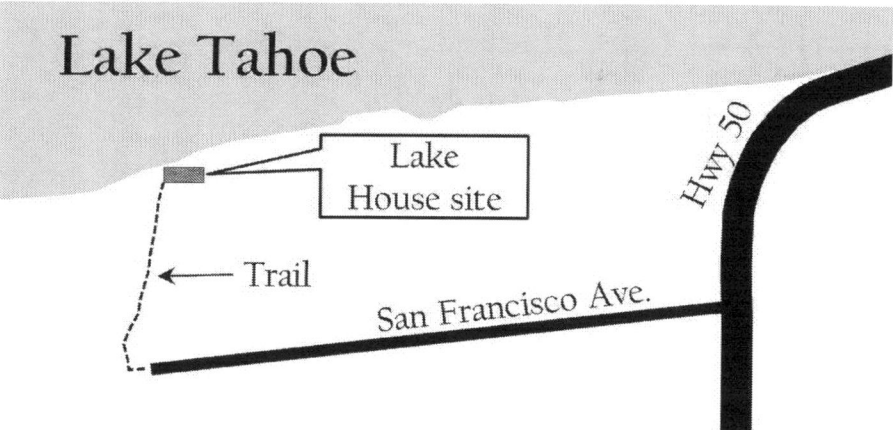

Figure 100. Detail map showing public access and trail to the Lake House site on Upper Truckee Meadow in South Lake Tahoe

Conservancy. This is the probable site of Lake House. To the west of this site, was the location of the Lake House pier that docked the excursion sailboat boarded by Mark Twain.

To access the site of Lake House for U.S. Highway 50, follow San Francisco Ave. to its end and park where legal. Enter the meadow through the gate at the end of the street and follow the trail toward Lake Tahoe and the site of Lake House. The GPS coordinates for the trailhead at the end of San Francisco Ave. are 38.93945,-119.99137 and the coordinates for site of Lake House on the edge of Upper Truckee Meadow are 38.94314°,-119.99111°.

Site #9 Lake Tahoe Wagon Road Remnant near Logan Shoals
The United States Forest Service operates a Lake Tahoe vista point and lake access at Logan Shoals on the East Shore. Here, you can hike down to a surviving remnant of the Lake Tahoe Wagon Road, traveled at least 12 times in a stagecoach by Mark Twain. The road is still passable and one can walk it about 0.3-mile until it ends at

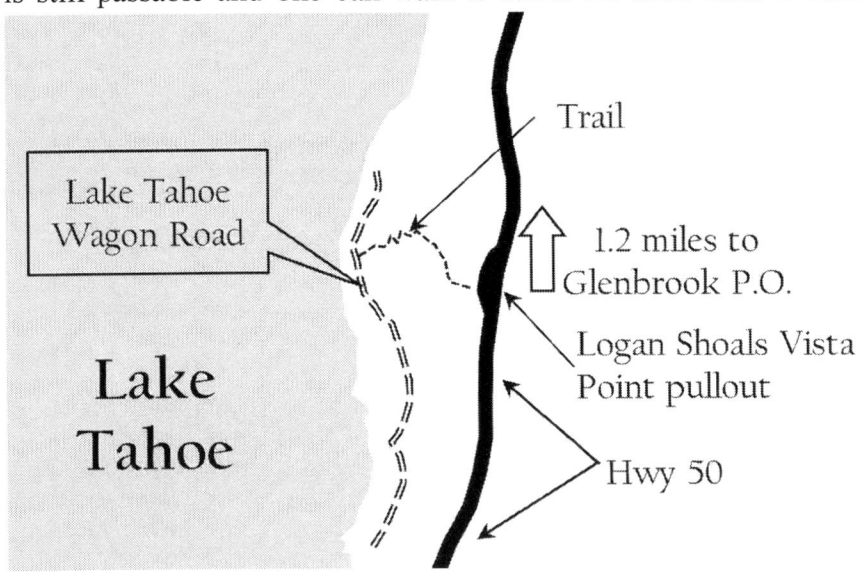

Figure 101. Detail map showing the location of the Logan Shoals Vista Point and access to the Lake Tahoe Wagon Road remnant

private property. Imagine rumbling along in a stagecoach while absorbing the magnificent Lake Tahoe scenery as Mark Twain did.

From Highway 50 on the East Shore, watch for the Logan Shoals Vista Point sign on the lakeside of the highway about 1.2 miles south of the Glenbrook Post Office at 1785 U.S. Highway 50. One may park along the highway at the vista point pullout where legal. Follow one of the several steep trails leading down to the lake; these trails will intersect with the remnant of the Lake Tahoe Wagon Road. The GPS coordinates for the Logan Shoals Vista Point on the East Shore are 39.05802°,-119.94324°.

Figure 102. Lake Tahoe Wagon Road remnant near Logan Shoals Vista Point

Site #10 Lake Tahoe Wagon Road Remnant near *Lam Watah*
The *Lam Watah* interpretive site, operated by the United States Forest Service, honors a historic Washoe cultural site where families camped for centuries. Here again, another surviving segment of the

Lake Tahoe Wagon Road and a small section of the Lake House Road, both traveled by Mark Twain, is visible and accessible.

You can reach the *Lam Watah* cultural site, by turn onto Kahle Drive from U.S. Highway 50 near Stateline, Nev. Park in the small parking area to the right. Looking out toward the meadow, you will see a dirt road that threads between two sets of boulders. This is the remnant of the Lake Tahoe Wagon Road. Another dirt road leads toward the lake. This is possibly the remnant of a meadow road/trail that lead to Fish & Ferguson's landing for the freight schooner *Iron Duke*.

In the meadow toward the highway is a large grouping of boulders. You will find evidence of ancient Washoe encampment here in the form of well-worn grinding rocks use to process seeds and nuts. The GPS coordinates for the *Lam Watah* cultural site entrance are 38.97058°,-119.93524°.

Figure 103. Remnant of the Lake Tahoe Wagon Road

Relive Mark Twain's western experience as portrayed in *Roughing It* by the Ghost of Mark Twain, McAvoy Layne

Noted Mark Twain impressionist McAvoy Layne regularly performs Mark Twain monologues in a Chautauqua-style setting at various venues throughout the Lake Tahoe and Western Nevada region. Layne has been preeminent in preserving the wit and wisdom of "The Wild Humorist of the Pacific Slope," Mark Twain. Visit the website www.ghostoftwain.com for location information and a schedule of performances.

Figure 104. A Washoe family circa 1870s (Wikimedia Commons)

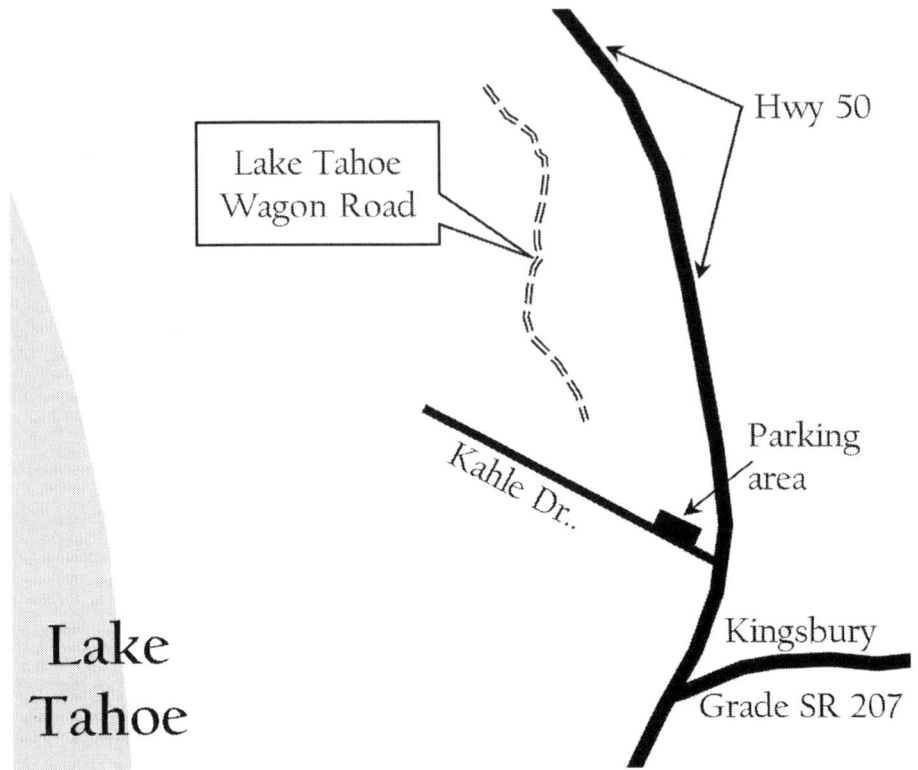

Figure 105. Detail map showing the location of Lam Watah cultural site and the Lake Tahoe Wagon Road remnant

Site #11 Dutch Flat-Donner Lake Wagon Road Route Over Donner Summit

You can drive your car or ride your bike along a section of old Highway 40 where it closely followed the Dutch Flat-Donner Lake Wagon Road. Mark Twain came over the snow-covered wagon road in April of 1868 in a horse-drawn sleigh.

Your route will follow Hampshire Rocks, Donner Pass and Prosser Dam Roads. Check highway conditions in winter, as these roads can close for brief periods due to snow. Consult online road maps for more detailed mapping information.

To follow the Dutch Flat-Donner Lake Wagon Road historical alignment, begin by taking the Big Bend Exit #166 off ramp from

Interstate 80 (east bound) about 32 miles west of Truckee, Calif. and at GPS coordinates 39.30430°, -120.52045°. (If west bound on Interstate 80, take the Cisco Grove Exit #165 and follow Hampshire Rocks road east toward Big Bend.) From Big Bend, drive east bound on Hampshire Rocks Road. This road follows the old route of the wagon road. Continue under the freeway to Donner Pass Road; it follows the wagon road alignment to about Soda Springs. From Soda Springs, the wagon road alignment was south of Donner Pass Road in the broad meadow called Summit Valley, or formerly, Lake Van Norden.

Once over Donner Pass, the wagon road followed a circuitous route between the paved road and railroad. Parts of the Dutch Flat-Donner Lake Wagon Road east of Donner Summit are still visible and accessible but extremely hard to locate on the ground. Check with Truckee area trail websites for updates to mapping and directions to follow this section of the road on foot from Donner Summit to Donner Lake.

Continue along Donner Pass Road until you reach the west end of Donner Lake where the wagon road route rejoins the paved road. Donner Pass Road follows the wagon road to Historic Downtown Truckee. It was here that Mark Twain left his horse-drawn sleigh, sent a telegram to Virginia City and boarded a stage for the last leg of his final trip to Nevada.

Continue along Donner Pass Road through Truckee to its intersection with Highway 89. Turn left onto Highway 89 and follow it about 0.75-mile until the junction of Prosser Dam Road, which continues to follow the alignment of the wagon road. Follow Prosser Dam Road about 2.5 miles until you reach Prosser Reservoir at GPS coordinates 39.37671°,-120.14142°. This concludes your 25-mile journey retracing Mark Twain's route along the Dutch Flat-Donner Lake Wagon Road.

Site #12 Silver Mountain City Town Site

The town site for Silver Mountain City, visited by Mark Twain in 1864, is easy to find on Highway 4. Look for a few interpretive signs and remnants of the old rock-walled jail.

Figure 106. Interpretive panel and site marker at Silver Mountain City

Consult online road maps for more detailed mapping information. Begin at the junction of Highways 88 and 89 in Woodfords, Alpine County, Calif. Take Highway 89 south to Markleeville. Your route will follow the general corridor of the wagon road and stagecoach route to Silver Mountain City. About 4.8 miles past Markleeville, Highway 4 begins. On Highway 4 and about 10.5 miles from Markleeville is the location of the abandoned town of Silver Mountain. As you enter the town site, watch for a Forest Service sign and interpretive information marking its former location. The GPS coordinates for the site of Silver Mountain City in Alpine County are 38.55998°,-119.8100°.

Chapter 8

Debunking the Mark Twain-Lake Tahoe Myths

Mark Twain once wryly remarked, "Often, the less there is to justify a traditional custom, the harder it is to get rid of it." One can add to this another of Twain's incisive observations, "Loyalty to petrified opinions never yet broke a chain or freed a human soul in this world – and never will." Both quotes are dense with meaning and sensibility. In the general sense, they reinforce the view that a long-held belief, irrespective of justification or rationality, is an impediment to progress, new ideas and expansion of knowledge. He probably had in mind the larger notions of society, religion and governance as he contemplated the inflexibility of human nature. The same concept applies at the micro level to the various Mark Twain-Lake Tahoe myths that have embedded themselves in the ethos of the region.

Where might one expect to encounter Mark Twain-Lake Tahoe myths? The worst offenders are commercial websites where naive webmasters simply feed on each other's ignorance and create a perpetual motion machine of Mark Twain and Lake Tahoe misinformation. Add to this marketing literature for real estate, hotels and recreation pursuits. Authors who fail to do thorough research repeat the myths in their guidebooks and Tahoe history volumes. Even knowledgeable tour guides embellish and misspeak about Mark Twain.

The myths trace back to one or more rationales for their existence. In the most elementary case, a myth may be the result of flawed historical research or mistaken identity. In other cases, misinterpretation of Twain's sometimes-vague writings may be the culprit. In the extreme case, the desire to associate one's self or a region with Mark Twain for financial or prestigious advantage lies at the heart. Irrespective of the reason for the myth and because of the limitless popularity of Mark Twain, these myths persist despite their spurious origins.

In this digital age of broadly and indiscriminately distributed information, the Mark Twain-Lake Tahoe myths find repetition with reckless unrestraint over a modern-day digital path paved with laziness, naivety and fallacy. The more repetition a myth receives and the more often it appears in otherwise credible sources, the more deeply ingrained in Tahoe history the belief becomes. Likewise, the more vehement the denial becomes from those who have an ego-centered ownership stake in the myth.

As we dissect these myths and examine the entrails of their sources, we use for guidance the principle of "preponderance of evidence." The principle states that the explanation that garners the preponderance of evidence in support based on weight and credibility denotes the most likely factual explanation. This is a common standard for burden of proof in civil court cases. The principle fits the analysis of Mark Twain-Lake Tahoe myths well because of inherent uncertainties. Historical records can be murky and contradictory. Often, there is absence of clear and convincing evidence that alone is insufficient to stand as proof. Finally, the ongoing addition of Mark Twain-related documents and primary source information to existing collections makes it impossible to certify an accurate and comprehensive record of all relevant facts.

Myth: Mark Twain Stayed at the Lake Shore House in Glenbrook in 1863.

This myth is a simple case of flawed historical research by a primary source. Lake Shore House was Augustus Pray's 19th century hotel in Glenbrook, Nev. The erroneous conclusion that Mark Twain stayed there in 1863 appears in a footnote added by Mark Twain Project (MTP) editors to *Mark Twain's Letters, Volume I, 1853-66*. The letter in question is the August 19, 1863 letter from Mark Twain to his mother and sister. As previously explained in Chapter 4, Twain was writing about his stay at Lake House on the South Shore. In the footnote, the MTP editors looked to E.B Scott's *The Saga of Lake Tahoe* as their primary source for guidance. Based on this lone source, they determined that Twain really meant "Lake Shore House" when he wrote "Lake House."

Scott states in *The Saga of Lake Tahoe*, Augustus Pray was rushing the Lake Shore House in Glenbrook to construction in 1863. Scott references the August 26, 1863 edition of the *Sacramento Daily Union* as the foundation for this statement. Actually, the *Sacramento Daily Union* article states that Pray had sold five acres to Colbarth for construction of a hotel. The hotel in question was the upscale Glen Brook House that opened later in 1863. According to Thompson & West's *History of Nevada*, it was not until the spring of 1876 that Pray converted part of his lakefront sawmill to a hotel and named it Lake Shore House.

Mark Twain passed through Glenbrook about 12 times each way while traveling through Tahoe by stagecoach to and from California. He was surely familiar with the community, and he may even have made day trips to Glenbrook for pleasure. However, no writings by

Twain or others exist to document any such day-use or overnight visits.

Myth: Mark Twain Stayed at Lake House at Hobart on the East Shore in 1863.

This myth stems from a secondary author's misinterpretation of historical research by a primary author. This myth appeared in the Margaret Sanborn's *Mark Twain: The Bachelor Years* and was a variation of the Lake Shore House myth. Despite getting the hotel correct, the location is in error. Lake House was on the South Shore (see Figure 30 for the correct location) and the logging camp of Hobart did not appear until the 1880s when the Sierra Nevada Wood and Lumber Co. entered the southernmost extent of the East Shore to conduct timber harvest operations there. The original Lake House burned in 1866 and was replaced by Rowland's roadhouse in 1868.

Sanborn appears to conflate across 20 years a narrative in *The Saga of Lake Tahoe* that speculated a picture of an abandoned boat was the same boat mentioned in the 1861 journal of artist Joseph Lamson. Lamson had written that he had walked three miles east from Lake House and encountered men working on a boat. The workers were in a location that 20-plus years later would be the site of the Hobart logging camp. The camp was the namesake for the surname of one of the Sierra Nevada Wood and Lumber Co. owners, Walter Hobart. Sanborn overlooked the three miles distance between Lamson's starting point and the location where he encountered the boat workers to conclude erroneously that Lake House was farther east than it was actually.

Myth: Mark Twain Visited Cascade Lake in the 1880s.

Cascade Lake is a small body of water south of Emerald Bay (Figure 30). This appears to be a myth rooted in storytelling or mistaken identity. The persistent myth about a Mark Twain visit appears in several places: *The Saga of Lake Tahoe* and various local history books and guidebooks. None of these cites a primary source.

The problem with the story is that there is no record that Mark Twain ever returned to Tahoe or any other place in the Sierra Nevada region after his final visit in April-July 1868 for a lecture tour in northern California and western Nevada. Afterward, the closest he came was his 1895 world lecture tour beginning in the upper Midwest, then on to Washington State and British Columbia before continuing the tour overseas.

A similar but true account has John Muir visiting Cascade Lake in 1878 and perhaps, the central characters became transposed during repeat storytelling.

Another possibility is a visit by a Mark Twain impostor who conned the well-respected residents of Cascade Lake. The venerable TwainQuotes.com website documents a fair amount of 19th century Mark Twain lookalikes and wannabes. Site author Barbara Schmidt sums it up succinctly, "Throughout his lifetime, Mark Twain was a target for impostors and doubles [that] played upon his well-known appearance and reputation. Untangling all of their trails and establishing their identities [have] yet to be accomplished."

Myth: Mark Twain Described Lake Tahoe as the "Jewel of the Sierra"

Commercial copywriters often credit Mark Twain with describing Lake Tahoe as the "Jewel of the Sierra." There is no evidence in the written record that Twain ever said this. The earliest written mention of the phrase appears in David Starr Jordan's 1922 memoir, *Days of a Man*, in which he declares Lake Tahoe "the jewel of the Sierra." Jordan was a prominent naturalist, president of Stanford University, and a director of the Sierra Club. He first visited Lake Tahoe in 1880 and was the likely source of this famous quote.

Myth: Mark Twain Resided at Friday's Station While He Wrote Parts of *Roughing It*

At least one corporate website makes this erroneous statement in an attempt to boost the status and value of their properties. Mark Twain did pass through Friday's Station on his dozen or so trans-Sierra trips, and two chapters of the book are set at Lake Tahoe. However, there is no evidence he resided or even stayed briefly at Friday's Station. Twain wrote *Roughing It* in 1870-71 while he was living in Buffalo and Elmira, N.Y.

Myth: Mark Twain Attempted to Stake a Timber Claim and Accidentally Started a Wildfire on the East Shore Near Glenbrook in 1861.

Without question, this is by far the biggest and most over-hyped myth involving Mark Twain and Lake Tahoe. Widely circulated and repeated for such a long period, this myth became the epitome of Mark Twain's "loyalty to petrified opinion." While the basic storyline has some aspects connected to reality, the Glenbrook and East Shore settings are the mythological elements.

A synopsis of the most recent version of this mythical story unfolds something like this: Starting at an arbitrary point west of Carson City, Sam Clemens and friend John Kinney walked up a 1850s era wagon road/trail. They followed Kings Canyon and Clear Creek over Spooner Summit and down a road along Glenbrook Creek to Lake Tahoe. They found a rowboat on the shore, rowed three miles north to Skunk Harbor where they found a food and supply cache in the rocks, and slept on a sandy beach. Over an undetermined number of days, they established their timber claim three miles further north of the cache site, slept on a sandy beach, walked six miles back to Glenbrook, borrowed a dugout canoe found at vacant cabin at Glenbrook, paddled back to the timber claim site, suffered a wildfire and returned to Carson City. Figure 107 presents the general sense of the East Shore timber claim scenario. The myth was so strongly rooted that even the *Nevada Historical Society Quarterly* published two papers that attempted to confer legitimacy on the story.

The myth originated with the financial advantage rationale as its underpinnings. In the early 20th century, tour boats loaded with enthralled passengers circled the lake. The boat captains liked to

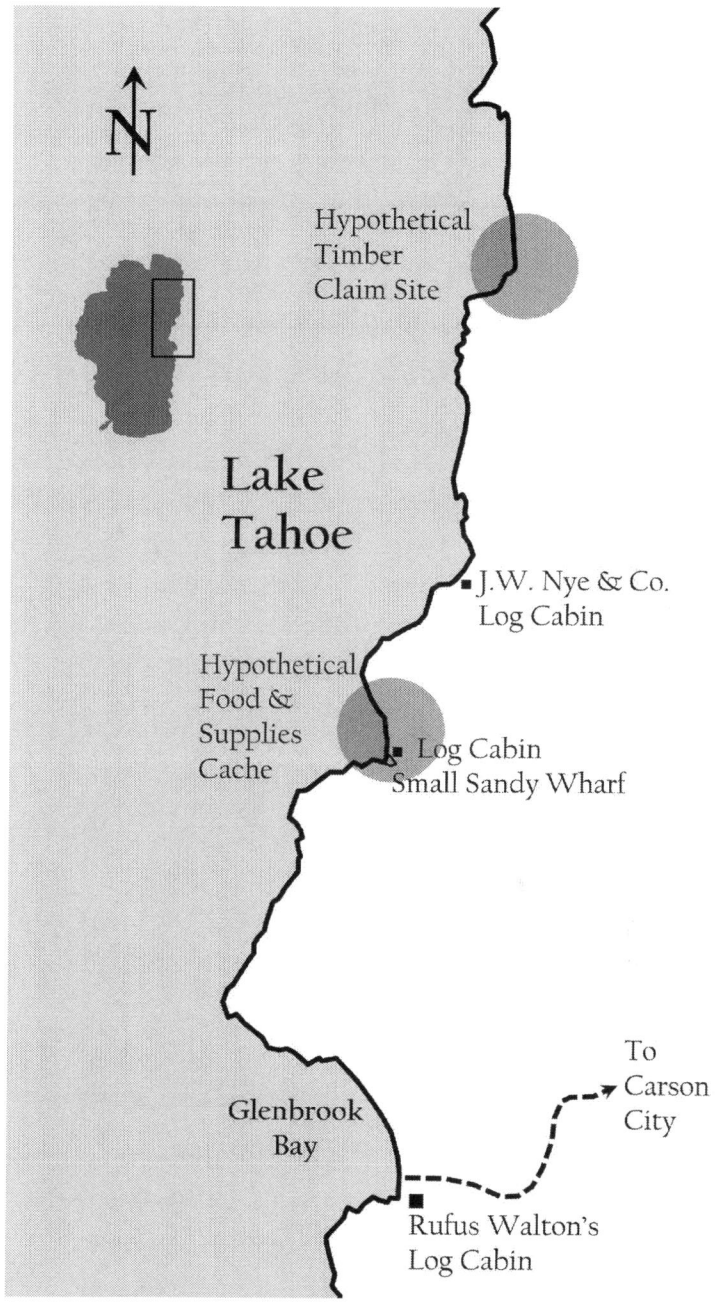

Figure 107. Location map and points of interest for East Shore timber claim myth

entertain their guests with Native American legends and Tahoe-specific myths to enrich their Tahoe vacation experience. For example, one captain told his passengers that the vertical scars on the slopes above the East Shore near Sand Harbor were "bear slides" worn into the hillside each winter by generations of playful Tahoe bears. In truth, breaks in a 19th century water flume triggered massive landslides that created the still-visible scars.

In much the same way, early 20th century tour boat captains pointed to one of a few dilapidated shacks visible on the East Shore north of Glenbrook, and pronounced one of them the remnant of the cabin built by Mark Twain. Never mind that Mark Twain clearly states in *Roughing It* that he quit building his log cabin shortly after starting it and his "cabin" was nothing more than a pile of brush that was consumed in a wildfire anyway. With this creative storyline firmly implanted in the imaginations of generations of Tahoe tourists, it became an element of Tahoe history.

Others took a simplistic approach. They reasoned that Glenbrook was the first site at Tahoe for a Nevada lumber mill in 1861, so Twain must have been lurking nearby with his short-lived timber ranch. Others opted for folk wisdom over logic and reasoned the simplest explanation was the best, irrespective of the contradicting facts. They argued that one road leading to Glenbrook was the most direct from four available routes from Carson City to Tahoe, though it was not, so he must have gone that way.

The myth deeply entrenched itself in Tahoe history when it first appeared in print in 1949 in *Sierra Nevada Lakes*. Paradoxically, authors George and Bliss Hinkle cited the tourism origins of the myth but went on to repeat the myth as though it was a fact on the same pages. E.B Scott noticed the *Sierra Nevada Lakes* information and cemented it into the minds of readers. He repeated it in *The Saga of Lake Tahoe, Volume I* as an undocumented statement, absent any other supporting rationale. Then, others simply paraphrased Scott's account in their books, newspaper articles, blog posts, websites, newsletters, brochures and nearly every other conceivable form of communication media and promotional literature. The result was a supernatural conversion from myth to "truth" by the process of repetition.

Undoing over 100 years of Mark Twain-Lake Tahoe mythological dogma is no small task, and with that in mind, we begin.

Brigade Cache and J. W. Nye Timber Claim and Cabin Were Not Located Near Each Other

Twain wrote in *Roughing It*, "Three or four members of the Brigade had been there [Lake Tahoe] and located some timber lands on its shores and stored up a quantity of provisions in their camp." We start here because proponents of the East Shore location myth point to this lone quote as the lynchpin of their argument. They say it locates the first night's campsite and thus, determines the general location of the timber claim adventure. This one assumption restricts all that follows.

The implied assumption is this: When Twain talked about the Brigade claim, he was actually referring to the J.W. Nye & Co. timber claim and cabin. However, the evidence-based nexus that the sites are near each other is nonexistent. Twain is talking about a different claim in a different location.

Twain describes finding, 'In a "cache" among the rocks... the provisions and the cooking utensils...' Later, in the text, he mentions sleeping on the beach. Both aspects are inconsistent with an East Shore cache site. Although East Shore proponents do not acknowledge this, there were already a cabin and landing at the same location they say was the undeveloped Brigade cache site.

Why would one store scarce and valuable food and supplies in the exposed rocks instead of the protected and secure cabin? Twain recalled, "It is always very cold on that lake shore in the night," and endured, "the procession of ants that passed in through rents in our clothing and explored our persons." Why would one sleep on the beach in the cold air pestered by insects when a comfortable and available cabin was within sight?

Another inconsistency that weakens any geographical relationship between the Brigade camp and the existing cabin and landing is Twain's omission of any reference to this highly relevant cabin in the context of his campsite descriptions in either *Roughing It* or his letters. The reason is clear: Clemens was never at a cabin site, nor is this cabin site the location of the cache in the rocks.

Clemens' Route Was Not the Kings Canyon-Clear Creek Alignment

The written description of Clemens' route from Carson City to Lake Tahoe occurs in only one place: Chapter 22 of *Roughing It*. In lectures, he mentioned only the distance and twice quoted 10 miles, a figure less than the 11 miles distance cited in *Roughing It*. As Twain recalled, the key elements of the hike were, 11 miles in length, began on level ground, scaled two summits and crossed a valley between the summits.

The actual route was the Ash Canyon road/trail to the Washoe Trail. However, East Shore timber claim believers speculate on the Kings Canyon-Clear Creek road/trail, known as the Johnson's Cutoff, as their preferred route explanation.

The Johnson's Cutoff east of Spooner Summit does not appear on the 1861 General Land Office maps, though the Kings Canyon and Walton Toll Roads do. This suggests that because of use of other preferred routes, the old Johnson's Cutoff had fallen into disuse, and traceable remnants had disappeared by 1861 or the surveyors overlooked it as inconsequential, though the route did exist at one time.

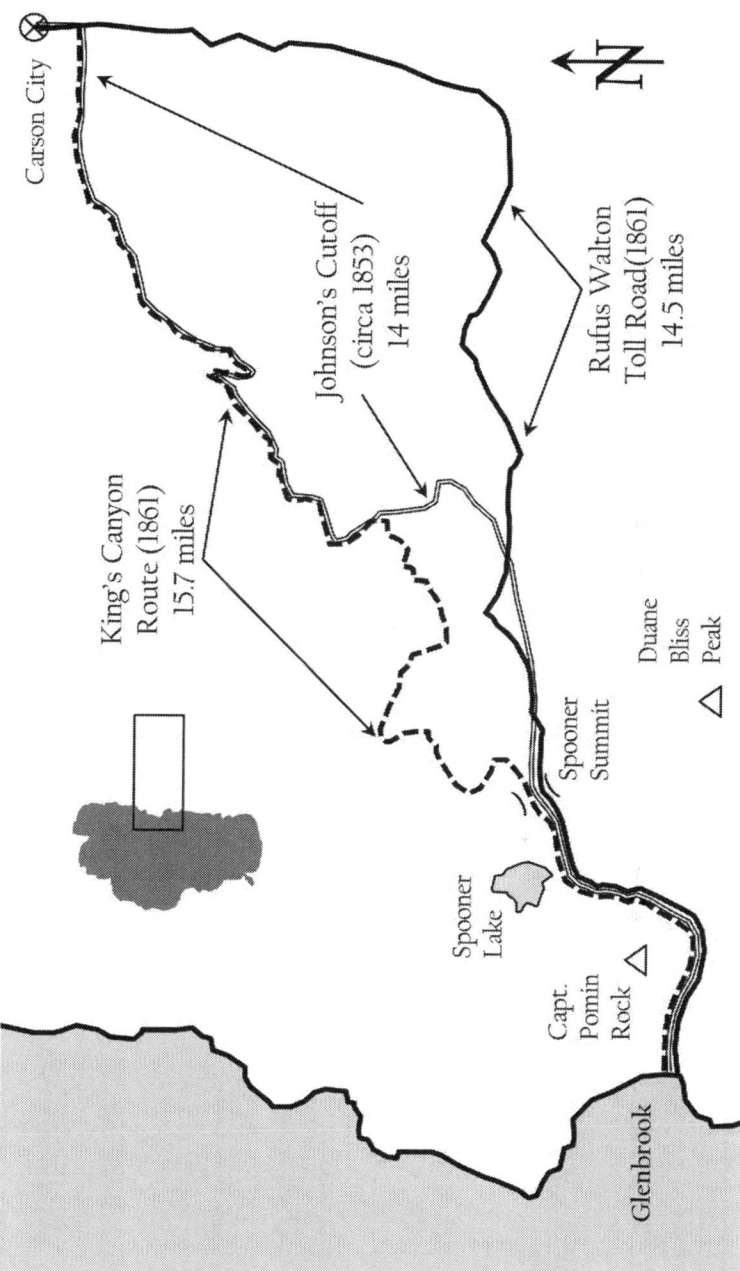

Figure 108. Map view of alternative routes from Carson City to Glenbrook in 1861.

Mark Twain Myths Debunked 211

Only a rough alignment based on emigrant diaries and an 1853 handbill serve to document the Johnson's Cutoff route. Using the work of original researcher, Dana Supernowicz, we plotted his mapped route for the Johnson's Cutoff as shown in Figure 108. We found that while the route did meet the two summits with valley criteria, it came in at 14 miles travel distance from Carson City to Lake Tahoe at Glenbrook.

The Nevada Department of Transportation has weighed in with their determination of the possible 1861 alignments that Clemens could have walked. In 2010, they published a historical map analysis, "Mark Twain in Tahoe 1861: Which Way Did He Go?" that presented the 1861 alignments of the Ash Canyon-Washoe Trail, Kings Canyon Road and the Rufus Walton Toll Road as the candidate routes. They rejected the alternative Johnson's Cutoff route as a viable possibility since it did not appear on the 1861 map. In the NDOT historical booklet on the Highway 50 corridor, "Foot Path to Four Lane," the author concludes that the Johnson's Cutoff followed Clear Creek all the way to the valley floor.

Despite its problems, the Johnson's Cutoff route seems to be the lesser of two viable routes for Clemens, but there are characteristics that make it even less probable, e.g., overland distance, better choices for travel to Glenbrook, and the absence of a sufficiently discernable trail.

From Carson City to Glenbrook, three routes present themselves: Kings Canyon Road, Johnson's Cutoff and Rufus Walton Toll Road. For a person traveling to Glenbrook, the Rufus Walton Toll Road made the most sense since it was nearly the same distance and sustained heavy travel by wagons and pack trains between Walton's Landing (Glenbrook) and Carson City. The heavy travel would enable one to catch a ride with one of the returning empty carriers by paying a small fare and toll.

If one was committed to foot, then one would have to weigh the disadvantages of the greater distance of the Kings Canyon Road at 15.7 miles to the slightly shorter, but more difficult to traverse and navigate, Johnson's Cutoff.

Deep Bend of Lake Was Not Glenbrook Bay

In *Roughing It*, Twain writes that after finding the skiff on the shore, they set "across a deep bend of the lake toward the landmarks that signified the locality of camp." In Figure 53, one clearly sees the "deep bend of the lake" (Crystal Bay) Twain recounted and the visible landmark of Stateline Point that demarcated the location of the first night's encampment.

Figure 109. Overview of Glenbrook Bay shows a probable rowboat course out of Glenbrook Bay. Deadman Point obscures the landmarks that signify the location of the alternative first campsite.

Some believe that Glenbrook Bay is a deep bend of the lake. Compared to Crystal Bay, it was not a deep bend and Twain used the term "bay" elsewhere in the text to describe portions of the shoreline similar to small coves.

In Chapter 3, we learned that Twain knew that the term "bay" did not fit and he likely drew on his memories of deep sweeping bends in the banks of the Mississippi River as inspiration for this descriptive phrase.

Twain said they rowed "across" the deep bend, instead of rowing "out of" the deep bend that is the case for exiting Glenbrook Bay into the open waters of Lake Tahoe. The absence of the visible "landmarks that signified the locality of camp," at the start, as Twain states, further disqualifies Glenbrook Bay. In Figure 109, an overview photo of Glenbrook Bay, it is clear one does not go "across" Glenbrook Bay, nor is one able to see any landmarks that denote the hypothetical East Shore campsite, as the extension of Deadman Point hides them from view.

From use of the terms "deep bend" instead of "bay" and "across," contrary to a term implying "out of," and considering the lack of visibility of campsite landmarks, we determine that Glenbrook Bay was not the location of Mark Twain's "deep bend of the lake."

Population Estimate Does Not Describe the East Shore

As we mentioned in Chapter 2, Twain erroneously estimated the population of Tahoe at a very low number. His faulty conclusion was a reasonable outcome as he was on the sparsely populated North Shore and would not have observed many other Euro-Americans. He wrote in *Roughing It*, "We did not see a human being but ourselves during the time…" In addition, he wrote in a letter to his mother, "*…there was no one within six miles of us…*" from the timber claim site. All these are indicative of few encounters with other persons.

If he was on the East Shore and had followed the Kings Canyon-Clear Creek route to Glenbrook, he would have encountered a stream of wagons and pack trains carrying goods and travelers on the road between Walton's Landing and Spooner Summit. Once at Glenbrook Meadow, he would have been in the middle of the lively activity associated with receiving shipments and passengers through Walton's Landing. Glenbrook was within six miles of the timber claim site, yet none of this finds its way into *Roughing It* or any of the letters for the simple reason that Clemens was never there in 1861.

From this, we conclude Sam Clemens did not pass through Glenbrook on his timber scouting trips.

Glenbrook Sawmill Was Not in Operation

After arriving at his first night's campsite, Twain recalled in *Roughing It*, "Three miles away was a saw-mill and some workmen." Some say this was the Lake Bigler Lumber Co. mill built at Glenbrook in 1861 and make this their sole defining landmark that fixes the location as the East Shore. In Chapter 2, we showed that the sawmill was a misremembered feature of the story.

Considering the presence of workers at a sawmill as a critical indication of mill operation, we must conclude that the mill Twain referenced in *Roughing It* was not the Lake Bigler Lumber Co. mill at Glenbrook because it could not have been in operation in September 1861.

The Kings Canyon Road and the Johnson's Cutoff used the same alignments for the first six miles. For Clemens' to use the Johnson's Cutoff, it required that he leave the main Kings Canyon Road, descend into Clear Creek canyon, climb out of the canyon and rejoin the Kings Canyon Road near Spooner Summit.

While the Johnson's Cutoff remains a very remote possibility, its distance, availability of better alternatives and lack of a well-defined trace relegate it to unproven status. In comparison, the Ash Canyon-Washoe Trail route was 11.7 miles and much closer to the distance cited by Twain.

Logical reasoning tells us that if the first step of a journey likely did not occur, then, the subsequent steps of the journey that depend on the initial step could not have occurred. In other words, if Clemens did not go to Tahoe over one of three routes leading to Glenbrook, he could not have traveled across the East Shore from Glenbrook. Diehards will not accept that Clemens did not travel to Glenbrook, so we continue our analysis to show the continuing discrepancies and contradictions that defeat the East Shore timber claim story.

Campsites Do Not Fit the Description

To support the assertion that Clemens camped north of Glenbrook on the East Shore, several mistaken assumptions must occur about the order of campsites.

The assumption begins with Clemens traveling north from Glenbrook Bay. However, there was no information in the text of either the letters or *Roughing It* that indicated a direction of travel from an assumed Glenbrook starting point. Other Mark Twain writers have done just the opposite, arbitrarily presuming Clemens turned south to claim timber at Zephyr Cove, six miles down the shore from Glenbrook. Finally, the nonexistent connection between the Brigade cache site and the Nye & Co. cabin site cannot support Clemens turning northward.

To complicate further this reasoning, some implicitly assign an erroneous geographical meaning to Clemens' use of "upper camp" and "lower camp" to make their campsite sequence seem logical. In principle, they mistakenly affix "upper camp" as the northerly site and "lower camp" as the southerly site.

In Appendix II, we demonstrate that Twain was referring to the height of adjacent terrain when he chose the "upper camp" and "lower camp" monikers. He did not intend a geographic, directional or a hierarchical meaning. Both the hypothetical East Shore campsites adjoin equally steep and high shoreline topography as shown in an elevation view of the campsites in Figure 110 and cross-section profiles in Figure 111.

There is not a discernible height distinction between the sites and therefore, no justification to place upper camp to the north and lower camp to the south. Compare this situation to the North Shore destination. Here, the upper campsite is at the foot of the steep Stateline Point while the lower campsite is on the flat beach at the end of a valley that spills out to Lake Tahoe.

Arbitrary choice of a direction from Glenbrook, failure to disprove other possible directions of travel and confusion about the meaning and intent of upper and lower campsites, invalidates the rationale for East Shore campsites.

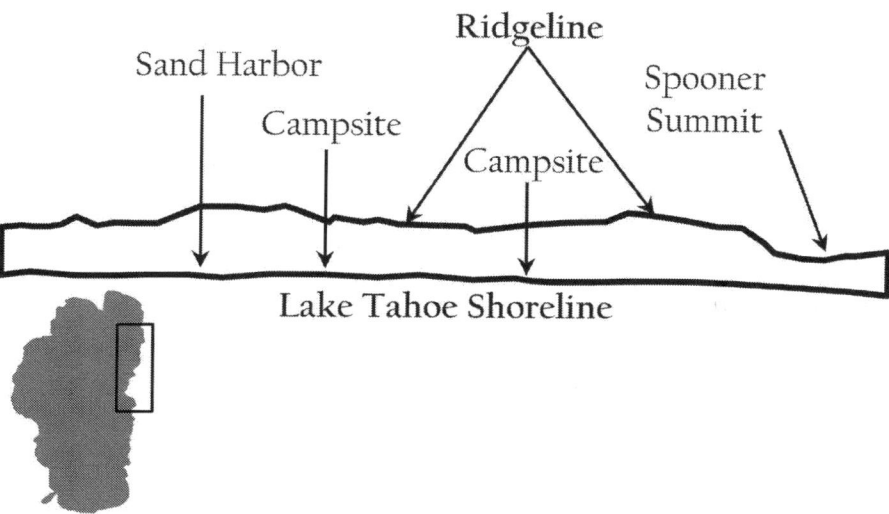

Figure 110. Elevation view of Carson Range ridgeline above hypothetical East Shore campsites shows both sites adjoin similar high terrain.

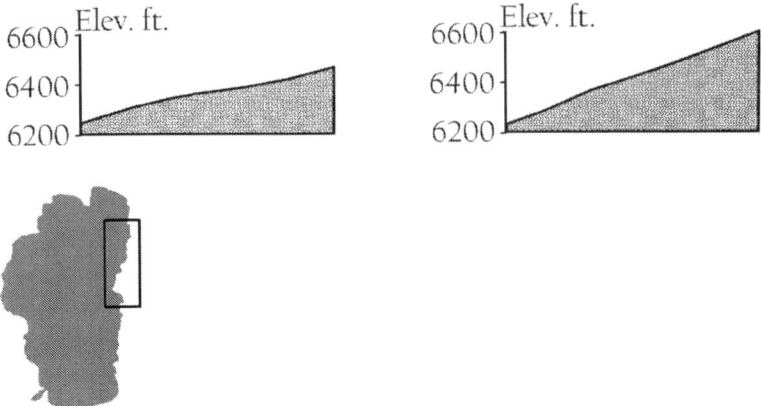

Figure 111. Profiles of hypothetical cache site (left) and timber claim site show similar adjoining height

Campsite Chronology is Erroneous

Because of the mistake in identification of the campsites (reversing upper camp and lower camp), East Shore advocates are not able to fit correctly Twain's sequence of campsites to their locations on the East Shore. Comparative maps best explain this inconsistency. Recall that Appendix II showed that Clemens' description in his letter characterized "upper camp" as the cache site and "lower camp" as the timber claim location.

Figure 112 shows the Day 1 travel, starting from Glenbrook Bay. Clemens and Kinney rowed three miles to the cache site where they found food and supplies and spent the first night at the lake in this location.

Figure 113 shows the Day 2 travel according to Clemens' letter. They started in the morning from the "upper camp" cache site and travel by foot three miles to the "lower camp" timber claim and then

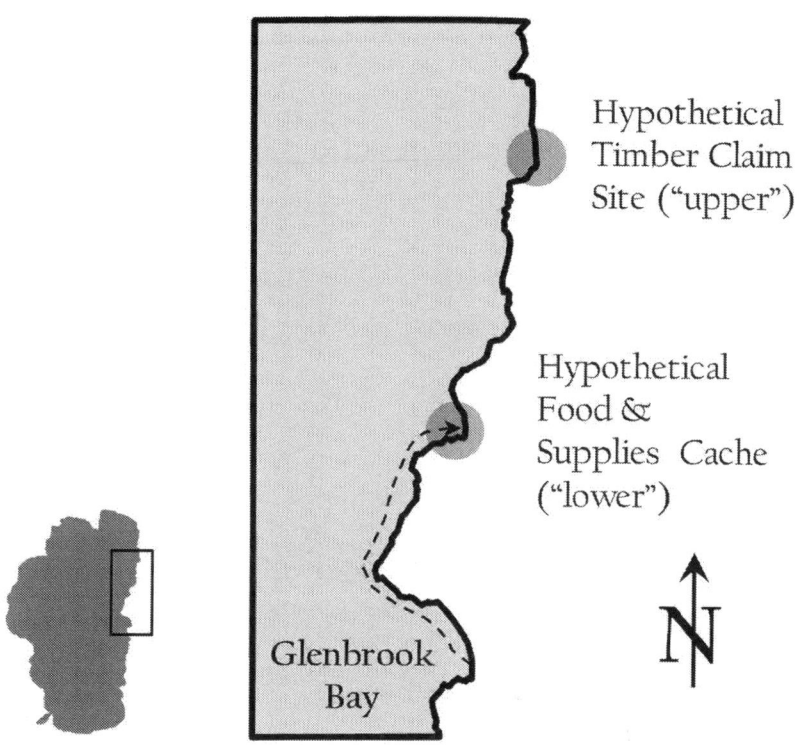

Figure 112. Theoretical first day travel by skiff from Glenbrook to "upper camp" food and supplies cache site

continued another three miles to a cabin. The problem that arises with the East Shore scenario is that proponents start the Day 2 travel from the lower campsite (their definition for "southern"), meaning Clemens and Kinney bedded down at the cache site on Day 1 but miraculously awoke three miles farther north at upper camp (their definition for "northern") to begin Day 2. Proponents must make this erroneous step in order to force-fit the chronology that follows to

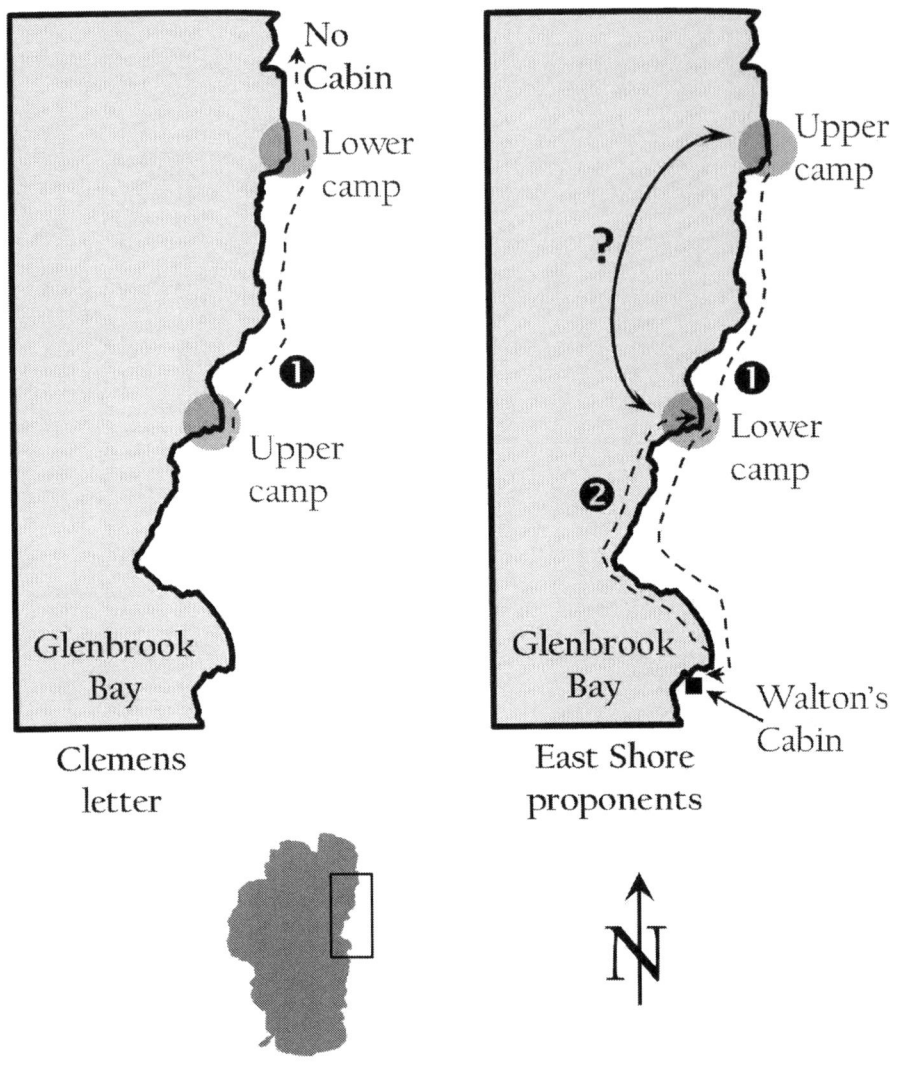

Figure 113. Comparison of campsites showing the sequence according to Clemens' letter on the left and the East Shore scenario on the right; numbers denote necessary steps on second day of travel

match the need to travel across six miles to a cabin, since no cabin existed north of East Shore proponents' upper camp in 1861. Incongruously, they have the two men looking for food, but passing by the food cache on their way to the cabin and then double backing to the cache site – an impossible situation according to Clemens' letter. Further, Clemens' letter says it was six miles from the cabin site back to the food cache, but under the East Shore timber claim scenario, it can only be three miles or less.

No Cabin Existed on the East Shore Where Clemens Said He Found a Cabin

Another critical clue is the cabin entered by Clemens and friend Kinney where they played cribbage and commandeered the owner's dugout canoe. From the campsite sequence chronology in Appendix II, we know that Clemens walked a total of six miles from his starting point at the hypothetical cache site on the second day. Figure 114 shows the points of interest on the East Shore north of Glenbrook Bay in 1861. No such cabin existed on the 1861 plat in a location six miles north of the Day 2 starting point. Thus, the East Shore does not fit Clemens' description for the location of the cabin.

Vacant Cabin Was Actually Occupied and Was Not the Only Cabin on the East Side of the Lake

Ignoring for the moment the problem exposed in the previous section regarding the nonexistence of a vacant cabin, East Shore advocates point to a cabin located near South Point at Glenbrook as the vacant cabin Clemens mentioned in his letter (Figure 113). However, we know that this cabin was the Rufus Walton home and occupied by him as late as August when the artist Joseph Lamson visited the second time. Lamson recorded the visit in his diary. Since business was brisk at Walton's Landing in the fall of 1861, Walton and his family would have been present when Clemens was in the area in September. Twain makes no mention of any other occupants at the cabin, and this precludes Walton's cabin as the unoccupied cabin

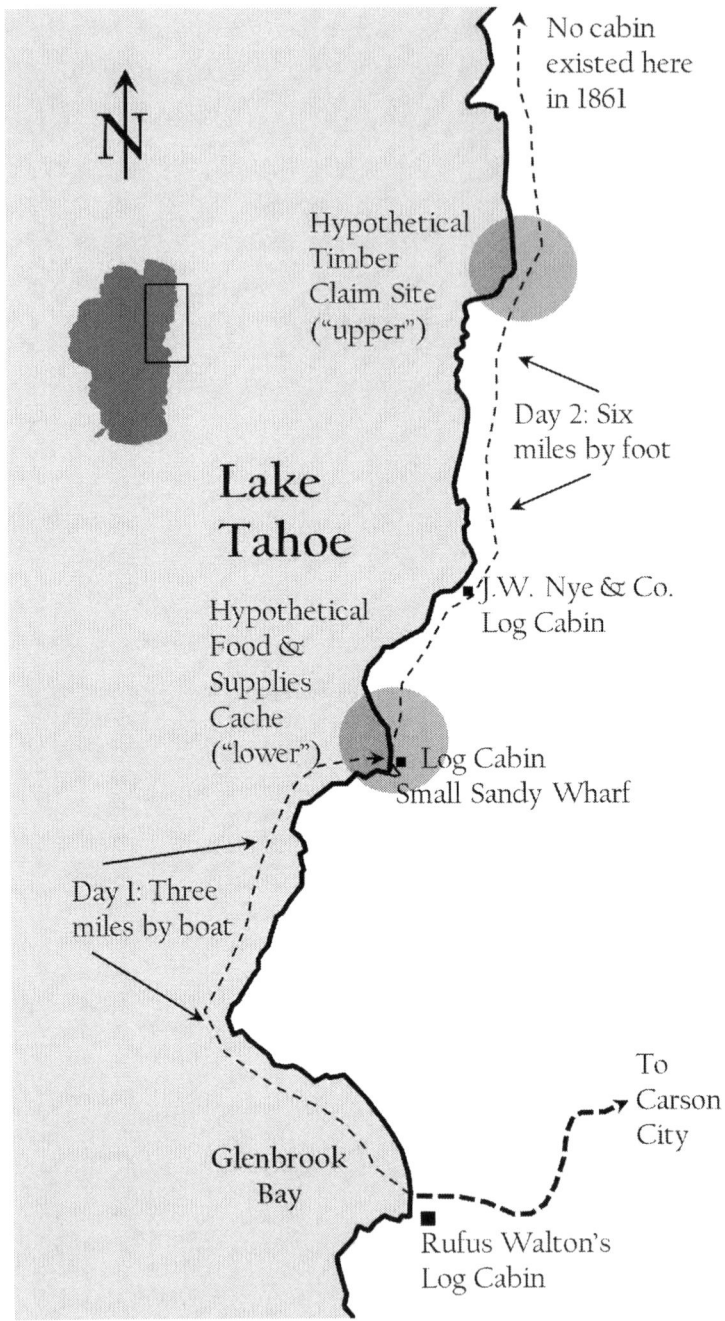

Figure 114. No cabin existed at the location described by Sam Clemens after he had walked six miles on Day 2

entered by Clemens and Kinney. Added to this, Clemens and Kinney took the cabin owner's dugout canoe, an act that would have engendered an owner's protest, or a mention in the letter, if the owner had been present.

Another fact contradicting the Walton cabin as the vacant cabin is Clemens' statement in the letter that it was, "... *the only house on this side of the Lake.*" We know from the 1861 plats, there were three cabins visible on the east side of the lake and these appear on Figure 114.

The lack of an unoccupied cabin, as Clemens described, and the presence of other cabins contradicts Clemens' observations and is evidence enough that the East Shore was not the scene of the timber claim.

Flat Granite Rock is Not Unique, Not at the Location Described by Clemens and Not Exposed in 1861

East Shore timber claim followers like to point to a flat granite boulder at their hypothetical timber claim site as conclusive evidence Clemens camped there. In his letter, Clemens wrote at upper camp, he "*established a faro bank (an institution of this country,) on our huge flat granite dining table...*" The problems with this assertion are threefold. A flat granite rock is not rare enough to be conclusive, the rock itself is not in the correct location and in 1861 the rock was part of the backshore hillside, covered with boulders and soil, and thus, not even visible.

Proponents suggest others should believe that a flat rock found on the East Shore at the hypothetical timber claim site was unique among all other rocks, so its existence was the "capstone" of their proof. In fact, the flat rock does not prove the site because of the widespread occurrence of flat granite rocks on the north and east shores of Tahoe. Fracturing in this granite occurs at depth, beginning as cracks due to extreme stress. The cracks open more widely as the rock reaches the surface and surrounding pressures are less, yielding common flat surface fracture planes.

Figure 115 is a photo of a field of flat surface granite rocks near Stateline Point. These are indicative of the preponderance of such rocks in the northeast quadrant of Lake Tahoe.

Figure 115. Field of flat surface granite rocks along the backshore at Stateline Point

Clemens' letter places the location of the flat granite rock at the site of the food and supplies cache he calls, upper camp. Figure 116 shows the location and identification of campsites and illustrates the wrong location for the granite slab by East Shore proponents.

East Shore Forest Size Was Too Small

In *Roughing It*, Mark Twain described the forest at his timber claim site, "It was yellow pine timber land – a dense forest of trees a hundred feet high and from one to five feet through at the butt." Devotees to the East Shore timber claim myth assert this description of the forest represents much of the Tahoe shoreline, including the

East Shore. Scientific studies of the pre-contact forest conclusively disprove this unsupported statement.

Scientists examined Comstock-era stump fields on the East Shore at the supposed Twain timber claim site. The stump fields represented the condition of the forest before logging, as Sam Clemens might have seen it. None of the sampled stumps showed trees anywhere

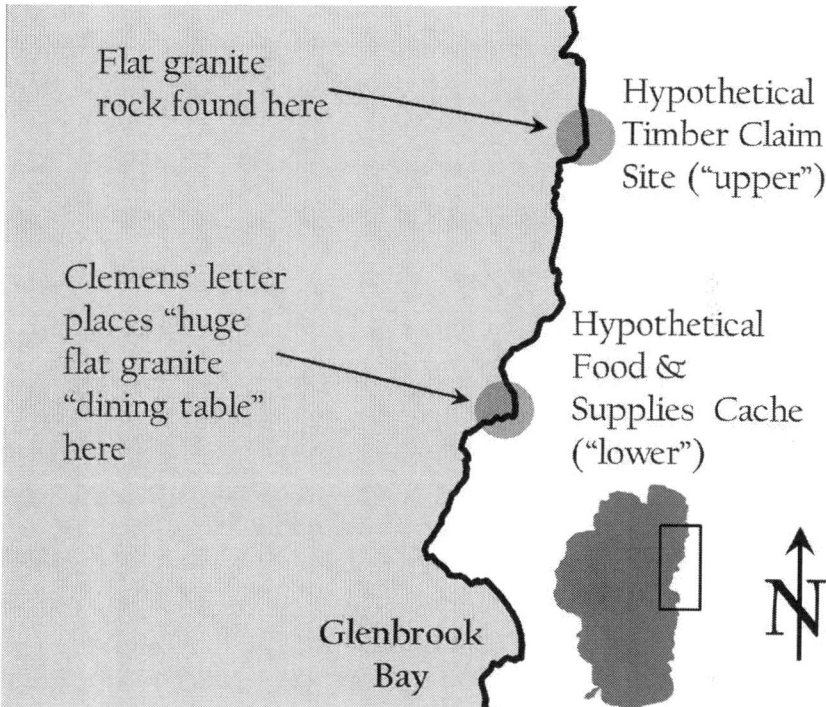

Figure 116. Location of flat granite rock conflicts with Clemens' description

near the size described by Twain. The largest was only 2.8 feet. This is consistent with the Tahoe Regional Planning Agency policy that classifies surviving old growth East Shore trees as substantially smaller in diameter compared to old growth trees growing on the North and West Shores.

The smaller East Shore trees, compared to the North Shore trees, are the result of harsher growing conditions on the East Shore influenced by lower moisture availability and fewer fertile soil conditions, even though the growing season is longer. Much larger trees in excess of five feet in diameter occur around Tahoe Vista on the North Shore.

The statement that the East Shore forest was the same size as described by Twain is not accurate, nor is it based on any historical research or scientific facts. Using the scientific determination that tree size was inconsistent with Twain's description, we conclude that the East Shore was not the location of the timber claim described in *Roughing It*.

Initial View of Lake Tahoe Could Not Have Occurred from Glenbrook

One of the important clues to location in *Roughing It* is Twain's vivid description of his first sighting of Lake Tahoe. The East Shore timber claim believers inexplicably ignore this critical clue to location. They downplay the importance of view description as a clue or insinuate what is not there, is there, if only one uses some imagination.

Twain's description has four key elements: The lake "…burst upon…" them into view, it appeared "…walled in by a rim of snow-clad [sic] mountain peaks…," looked like "…a vast oval…" and exhibited a reflection of "…shadows of the mountains brilliantly photographed upon its still surface…" As other writers have concluded from this passage, Twain was viewing the lake from a distant, high elevation vantage point.

Along the original Glenbrook Canyon road, one traveled along the stream bottom where the forest would block the view from a distance. As one approached the Glenbrook Meadow, the observer would have gradually seen the lake through the well-spaced trees and sparse understory in the old growth forest before emerging into the open meadow. The lake does not "burst" into view in this setting.

Once in Glenbrook Meadow, snowcapped mountains are viewable behind the narrow bay bounded by South Point and Deadman Point. However, it is impossible to have seen the "walled in rim" that Twain recalls because of the low elevation of the viewpoint and the panoramic constraint of the two points that define Glenbrook Bay. Further, these limitations and constraints did not allow the sense of the lake's "vast oval" aspect in Twain's description. Figure 117 is an illustration from the point of emergence from the forest into

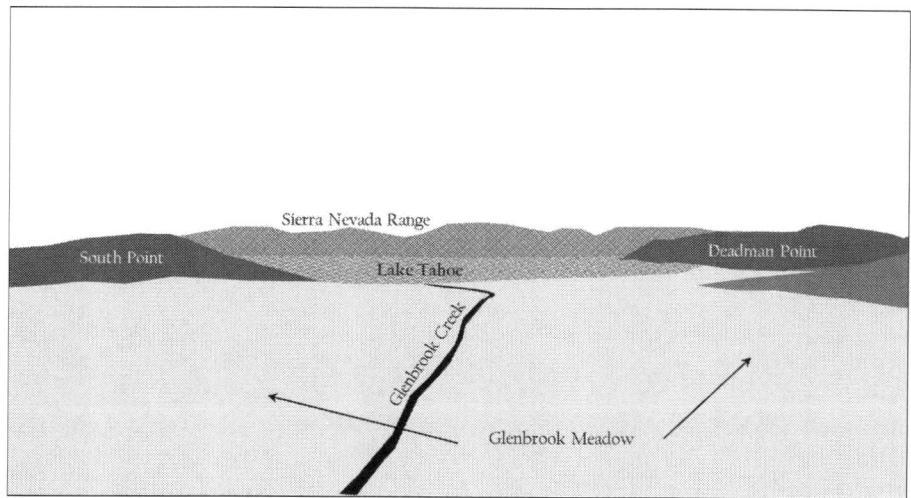

Figure 117. Computer-generated view from the edge of the forest at Glenbrook showing the constrained view of Lake Tahoe; trees have been removed to provide the best possible view

Glenbrook Meadow and shows the low-level and constrained view from this location.

If we treat Lake Tahoe as a flat mirror by neglecting the minor effects of water surface curvature and refraction, we see that the Glenbrook Meadow observation point is too low and too close to afford a full and intense view of the snowcapped mountain range on the opposite shore. Figure 118 illustrates this point. The observation point is too low.

The proximity to the shore forces the reflected image to spread over the 12.1 miles of the lake surface, making it too diffused to be clearly visible with the naked eye.

We use knowledge of old growth forest conditions, historical road alignments, topography and basic physics of light reflection to analyze the lake view from the Glenbrook area. Here, it was impossible in 1861 to obtain a view from Glenbrook anywhere close to what Twain described in *Roughing It*.

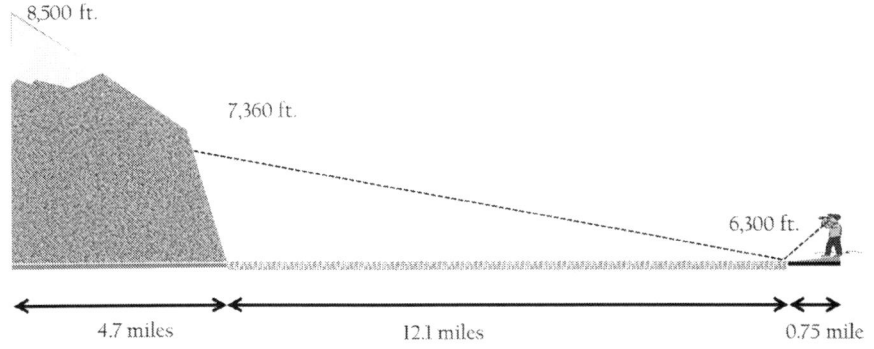

Figure 118. A full reflection of the Sierra Nevada from Glenbrook Meadow is not physically possible

On the North Shore, Not the East Shore

In *Roughing It*, Mark Twain places the setting of his timber claim adventure concisely: "We were on the north shore." Undeterred, East Shore timber claim advocates invoke skewed geography to say Twain meant the East Shore when he wrote "north shore."

In an earlier work, *Innocents Abroad*, Twain referred to seeing fish on the North Shore, "I speak of the north shore of Tahoe, where one can count the scales on a trout at a depth of a hundred and eighty feet." This reference came from his initial timber scouting experience at Lake Tahoe. The timber scouting trips are the only possible sources of the North Shore geographical reference.

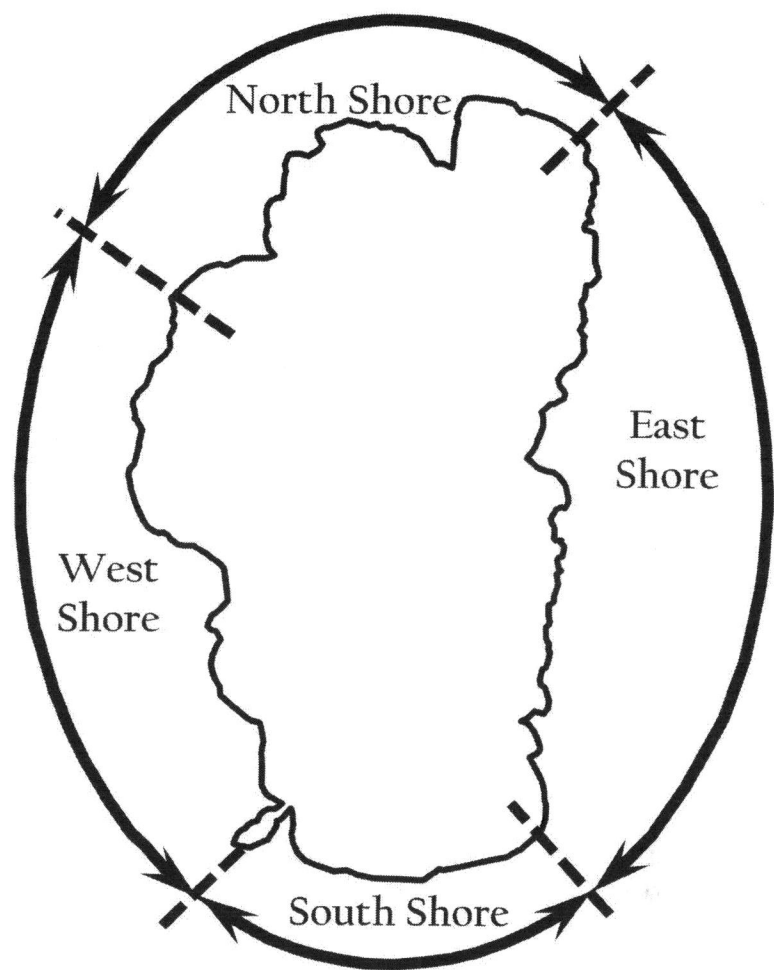

Figure 119. Diagram showing the natural division of geographic names for the Lake Tahoe shoreline

No records show that he traveled to the North Shore after his two visits in 1861. Two independent geographical reference statements using the term "north shore" and Twain's experience in riverboat navigation make this clear: Twain means the North Shore when he says it.

The rounded rectangular shape of Lake Tahoe lends itself to the well-defined geographical zones of the shoreline, as illustrated in Figure 119. We know that Sam Clemens and later, Mark Twain, made many visits to Lake Tahoe and saw the lake from its north, south and east vantage points, including views from high elevations. These visits provided the perspective for him to understand fully the geography of Lake Tahoe. In *Innocents Abroad,* Twain affirmed his knowledge of Lake Tahoe, "I measure all lakes by Tahoe, partly because I am far more familiar with it than with any other …"

East Shore timber claim boosters create their own version of Tahoe geography and declare that the East Shore is really the North Shore. They do this by dividing the lake into a northern half and a southern half based on an arbitrary east-west dividing line running from Glenbrook to Homewood. Doing this ignores the convention of referring to the East and West Shores as distinct geographical areas. It crudely breaks the lake into two halves as though it were circular, and not a rounded rectangle. Applying their geographical principles, one could, with equal validity, divide the lake into east and west halves and thus, declare the North and South Shores nonexistent.

Another explanation offered by East Shore supporters for Mark Twain's description of the setting as the North Shore instead of the East Shore is that Clemens misunderstood a compass reading. Those, whom believe this, assume without the benefit of any supporting evidence, that Clemens had a compass and misunderstood its meaning. They imagine he stood on the East Shore with the compass pointed to the magnetic north, leading him to believe he was on the North Shore, even though there is no mention of a compass or compass readings in any of the relevant Twain writings.

In 1861, the magnetic declination at Tahoe was about 16 degrees east of true north. The magnetic declination is the difference between the direction of the north end of a magnetic compass needle and true north. This amount of declination is enough to mislead a person as to their true location if they did not understand the difference between magnetic north and true north. To accept this as an explanation for the "north shore" statement, one must completely ignore Clemens' training as a riverboat pilot that included navigation skills – and certainly – a basic understanding of the difference between magnetic north and true north. In *Life on the Mississippi,* he discusses the use of a chart and compass as navigation aids in darkness, indicating his fundamental understanding of the critical difference between true north and magnetic north.

Neither irrational geographical revisionism, nor alleged incompetent compass reading by former riverboat pilot Clemens is sufficient to prove that the North Shore is really the East Shore.

White and Gray Rocks Did Not Exist on the East Shore

In *Roughing It,* Twain writes of drifting in a boat while admiring the boulders on the bottom of the lake. He states, "There, the rocks on the bottom are sometimes gray, sometimes white."

In Chapter 3, we examined the geology of the North Shore from Stateline Point and three miles west of location. The rocks in that area are in fact, gray and white consistent with Twain's description.

For the East Shore north of Glenbrook, there is only one natural source of rocks on the bottom of the lake: the white granite of the Carson Range. From this geology, we know the rocks on the bottom are white and do not exhibit any overall gray coloring.

However, it is not now possible to determine the color of rocks on the bottom of the lake because of the growth of attached algae due to human-caused pollution. Despite this well-known fact, East Shore timber claim advocates curiously maintain that the rocks on the bottom of the lake next to the East Shore are white and gray, even though they cannot see the color of the rock.

We can objectively ascertain the color of submerged rocks by examining the natural above-water rocks sitting on the shore as an indication of the types of natural rocks that lie below the water line. In this case, the above-water natural rocks along the North Shore from Tahoe Vista to Stateline Point are white and dark gray. The above-water line rocks along the East Shore north of Glenbrook are uniformly white.

Here, science and geology trump an illusion of what one wishes was true; white and gray rocks only occur naturally on the North Shore, at Stateline Point and west of that location. Mark Twain's description applies only to the North Shore and excludes any possibility that it was the East Shore.

Distance to Blue Water Was Too Far Away

Twain recalls in *Roughing It*, 'Sometimes we rowed out to the "blue water," a mile or two from shore. It was as dead blue as indigo there, because of the immense depth.' Recall from Chapter 3 that it is a known physical principle of water that all but blue and indigo colored light are absorbed at a depth of 75 feet in clear water, free of significant suspended matter. Microscopic particles in the water cause backscatter of the residual blue and violet light toward the observer's eye. This is an important point: At the 75-foot depth and deeper, the waters of Lake Tahoe show their characteristic blue and indigo colors.

This map in Figure 120 shows the occurrence of blue water as defined by the 75-foot bathymetric contour and the horizontal distance from the East Shore. As the map clearly shows, nowhere on the East Shore does the condition of blue water occur anywhere within one mile from shore and is usually within 0.2 mile from shore. In contrast, the blue water line on the North Shore in Agate Bay (Figure 70) meets the 1-2 miles offshore distance mentioned by Twain.

At no point on the East Shore north of Glenbrook is the distance to blue water anywhere near the 1-2 miles cited by Twain. This characteristic alone eliminates anywhere on the East Shore north of Glenbrook as a possible timber claim location.

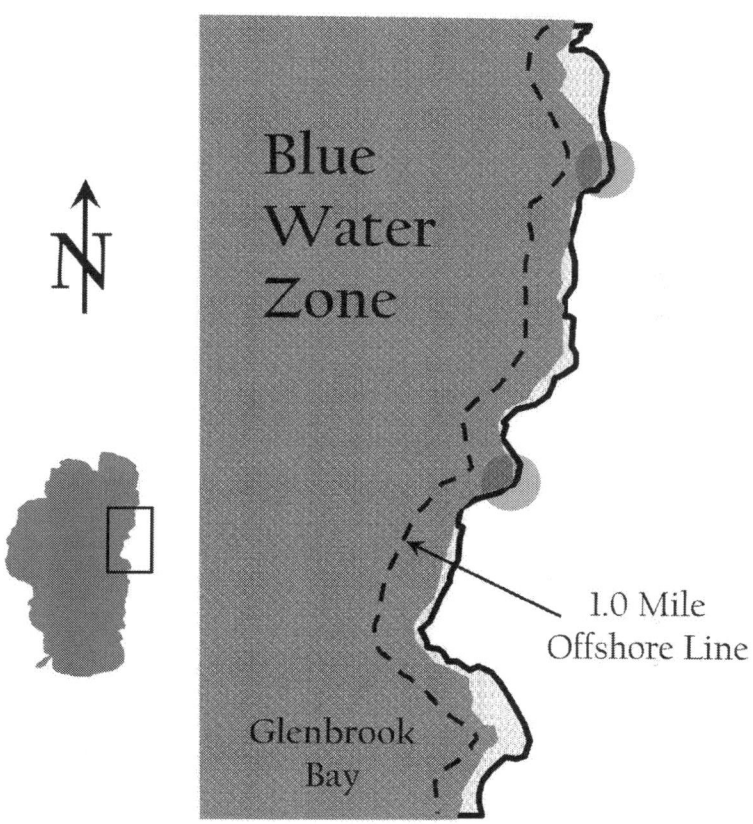

Figure 120. Map showing the distance to "blue water" on the East Shore is about 0.2 mile, much less than the 1-2 miles from shore cited by Twain

Could Not Have Slept on a Nonexistent Beach

The more recent proponents of the East Shore timber claim myth insist Twain camped and slept on the beach at his timber claim camp along a straight section of shoreline north of Thunderbird Lodge. The area in question has about a 30-foot wide beach when the lake is four to five feet below its high water mark. The mistake proponents make is that they assume this beach was present in 1861, when, in fact, it was not. According to the 1861 map for that area, the zone was rocky shoreline with no beach present. A 1985 scientific study

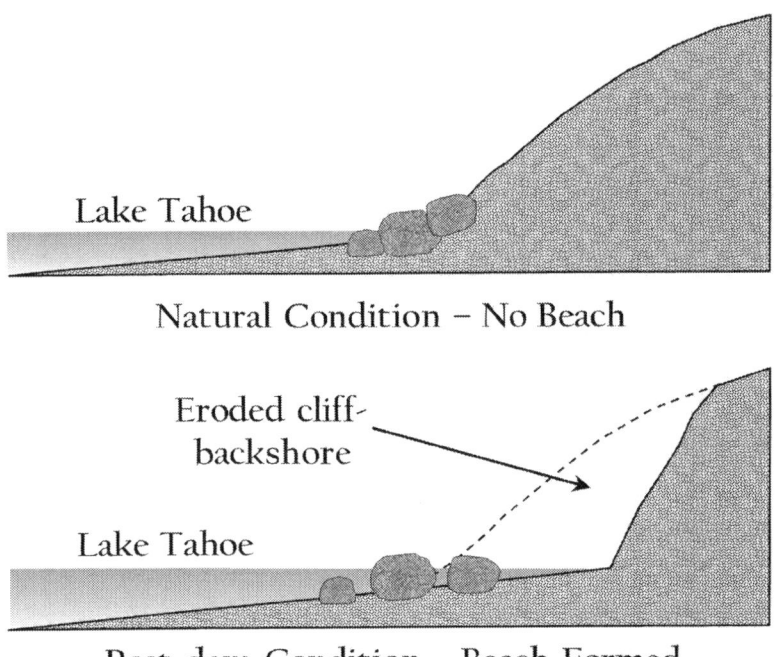

Figure 121. Cross-sectional view of beach in 1861 and formation of 30 ft. wide beach at hypothetical timber claim location after construction of Tahoe Dam

of the Lake Tahoe shoreline before damming classifies the area of the hypothetical timber claim site as a natural boulder shoreline with no sandy beach.

According to the 1985 scientific study, existing beaches at Lake Tahoe formed in one of two ways. The sediment discharges of nearby streams nourished the formation of beaches under natural, pre-Tahoe Dam conditions. Other beaches formed more recently, when the Tahoe Dam raised the lake to an unnatural level that initiated erosion of the otherwise stable waterfront cliffs and backshore.

In this case, erosion from cliff-backshore sources supplied the sediment that created the beach we see today. Figure 121 illustrates this process at the hypothetical East Shore timber claim location.

Creation of the beach by cliff-backshore erosion is the case for this site where, proponents contend Twain slept on a sandy beach. There are no significant streams in the vicinity to supply the sediment necessary to have a naturally formed beach because of the relatively small tributary watershed above. Any sand that might have accumulated was swept northward by near shore water currents where it became trapped at Sand Harbor.

The loose assemblage of submerged boulders now resting about 100 feet offshore from this beach roughly marks the former location of the shoreline under pre-dam conditions. The flat rock that proponents offer as the "capstone" of their argument was behind the boulder line. Therefore, in 1861 the backshore hillside high above the lake contained the flat rock. When the dam raised the water level, wave action eroded the soil holding the boulders in place, they collapsed into the lake, and wave action further exposed boulders embedded in the pre-dam hillside. No beach existed here in 1861 and it would be difficult to land a wooden skiff there without sustaining damage on the rocks.

At the cache site, the situation is slightly different. There, a small tributary drainage feeds sediment to the small cove to create two small slivers of natural beach supplemented by cliff-backshore erosion. Underwater canyon heads at both ends of the cove restrict any new sediment transport into the area, keeping any beach development minimal. The 1861 land office map noting a small landing here confirms this.

Using scientific studies that document the shoreline formation process and classify the shoreline, confirmed by historical mapping, we conclude no beach that would accommodate two men sleeping existed at the hypothetical timber claim site in 1861. Clemens and his friend could not have slept on the shoreline since no beach existed. There was a very small existing beach at the hypothetical cache site.

Wildfire Scars Absent
When it comes to the wildfire described in *Roughing It* and the September 1861 letter, no one disputes that Sam Clemens accidentally started a wildfire at the site of his timber claim. Wildfires can leave a record of their occurrence in the form of a fire scar on tree trunks. Decaying stumps from the Comstock era are an archive of fire history and reveal a significant problem with the veracity of the East Shore timber claim myth. Without knowing about previous fire scar research that was contrary to their theory, proponents made an absolute statement that a fire scar survey would prove their theory.

At the site where proponents say Clemens staked his timber claim, researchers found no 1861 fire scars on Comstock-era stumps, but did find fire scars recorded for 1855 and 1873. The absence of any 1861 fire scar record is a serious obstacle to prove that such a fire occurred.

Researchers have not conducted a fire scar survey for the North Shore, but they have identified candidate stump fields and fire scar studies may occur in the future.

Wildfire Advancement Description Did Not Fit

The East Shore timber claim scenario depends on Twain's description of the wildfire advancement in *Roughing It* to be possible from a boat sitting well offshore. However, we know from the letter of September 1861 that Twain observed the fire from the shore and not from an offshore boat, as he erroneously recalled in *Roughing It*. East Shore timber claim believers state that Clemens could observe the fire advancement from their site, but they erroneously assume he was offshore in a boat with a better view of the mountainside.

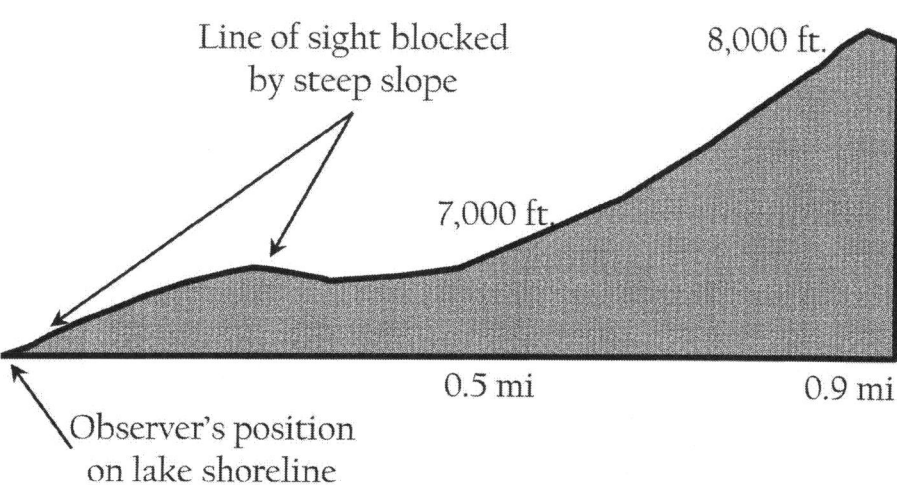

Figure 122. Cross-sectional view of hypothetical timber claim site showing inability to see wildfire advancement as described by Clemens and Twain

Figure 122 shows a cross-section for the East Shore near the supposed timber claim site. It did not allow for a line of sight of the wildfire advancement following Twain's description of the well-spaced standing dead trees bursting into flames. A person standing at a point on the old boulder shoreline cannot see farther than the steep hillside about 50 feet beyond.

Boulders at Supposed East Shore Timber Claim Were Not Present and Are of Insufficient Size

East Shore timber claim supporters point to a field of submerged boulders scattered offshore of their supposed campsite as the boulders that Clemens and Kinney drifted over. In fact, these are mostly the remnants of the boulder shoreline that collapsed into the lake after the construction of the Tahoe Dam. The field did not exist in 1861 as extensively as it does now. In any event, the size of these boulders does not measure up to the size description given by Twain and are far smaller than the massive boulders found offshore of Stateline Point.

Twain Biographical Writer: Carnelian Bay Was the Location

In Chapter 3, we detailed the statement by author George Wharton James in the 1914 book, *California Romantic and Beautiful,* that Twain was camped not far from Carnelian Bay. This conclusion is extremely damaging to the East Shore timber claim myth. This is because it is the only instance where a person who actually met Mark Twain and researched his early writing career in the West, had identified a specific location.

East Shore timber claim devotees fall back on an arsenal of logical fallacies and misrepresentation of history to counter James. One adherent summarily dismisses the 1914 statement in *California Romantic and Beautiful* as not valid because publication occurred after Twain's death. In this one proclamation, he dismisses as invalid not only James, but also by implication, the 40-plus scholarly biographical works written about Twain after his death. The same adherent engages in an *ad hominem* attack against James by characterizing James as a "California booster." This insinuates

James would deliberately lie about Mark Twain to benefit California, in spite the fact he had written extensively about Nevada's history and lectured there at least twice.

Another adherent says James was including the East Shore when he cited the Carnelian Bay location as the closest location. His reasoning? People traveled only by boat in 1914, so locations were broadly geographical. This questionable rationalization is wrong on both counts.

First, a wagon road nearly encircled Lake Tahoe in 1914 except for the section between Incline and Glenbrook. Resort owners had relegated their steamers mostly to tour boat status and longer distance transportation around the lake. Further, people were already mobile using carriages and wagons and automobile tourism was already in full swing by 1914.

As early as 1906, automobiles were being barged across the lake from Tahoe Tavern to Glenbrook. In 1908, Al Sprague built his Al Tahoe Hotel where it was, "advantageously located on the State and National automobile boulevard." In 1911, the Tahoe Tavern held an auto derby, awarding a cash prize to the first automobile to arrive at the hotel for the season.

Second, James published a map of Lake Tahoe in 1915 that showed Sand Harbor and Glenbrook, two locations much closer to the imaginary East Shore campsites. Therefore, James was aware of the specific geography of the North and East Shores. He would have used these latter localities as geographical reference points if he meant the East Shore.

As the only specific location given by a person who actually spoke with Twain, James' writing is particularly problematic for fervent East Shore timber claim supporters. James' description stands as the only credible and sourced statement of the specific location of Mark Twain's timber claim.

Concluding Summary and Comparative Analysis

As a final proof and for demonstration of the preponderance of evidence principle, we compare in tabular form the various indications from letters and book text to determine the location of the early trips to Lake Tahoe and the unrealized timber claim. The findings for the North Shore column come from information presented in Chapter 3.

Evidence	East Shore	North Shore
Route reasonably close (± 10%) to cited distance of 11 miles	No	Yes
Route surmounted two summits	Yes	Yes
Route crossed a valley	Yes	Yes
Route followed all or part of a documented alignment	Yes	Yes
Deep bend of lake with visible landmarks that located first campsite	No	Yes
Population estimate consistent with location	No	Yes
Nye & Co. cabin and Brigade cache in rocks are geographically separated locations	No	Yes
Beach at Brigade cache site	Yes	Yes
Campsites fit upper and lower description	No	Yes
Cabin existed six miles from second-day's starting point	No	Yes
Cabin was unoccupied	No	?
Forest size consistent with description	No	Yes
Lake Tahoe "bursts" into view	No	Yes
Initial view of lake was a "vast oval" with "walled in rim"	No	Yes
Reflection of mountains in initial view of lake	No	Yes
"We were on the north shore."	No	Yes

Evidence	East Shore	North Shore
White and gray rocks on lake bottom	No	Yes
Distance to "blue water" 1-2 miles	No	Yes
Beach at second campsite existed in 1861	No	Yes
1861 wildfire scars found	No	?
Advancement of wildfire visible from campsite	No	Yes
Field of massive boulders offshore in 1861	No	Yes
Site identified by a biographical writer who spoke with Twain	No	Yes

Summary	East Shore	North Shore
Evidence is in Support	4	21
Evidence is in Opposition	19	0
Evidence is Unknown	0	2
Preponderance of Evidence in Support	No	Yes

Note: "?" indicates unknown

Using the preponderance of evidence principle, we find the overwhelming amount of confirming evidence falls in favor of the North Shore as the location of the campsites, timber claim and wildfire.

Epilogue

On September 14, 2010, the Nevada Board on Geographical Names voted to name a random inlet on the East Shore after Sam Clemens. Their flawed reasoning was that Mark Twain was in the general region around Lake Tahoe anyway, and the board was not interested in settling a historical dispute over the location of his campsites.

In the aftermath of the naming action, news stories and photographs appeared that identified the inlet as the actual site of Clemens' timber claim and wildfire and cited the board's action as a reference. Consequently, this myth found renewed life through repetition in mainstream media. However, on May 12, 2011, the United States Board on Geographical Names rejected the proposed naming for two reasons: United States Forest Service opposition to the naming and reasonable doubt regarding the location of Samuel Clemens' campsite.

A final admonition to Mark Twain scholars and enthusiasts: Carefully examine and weigh the evidence. Do not be fooled by false stories and deceptive site names that claim to have a Mark Twain association. They are often a misrepresentation of the life and experiences of Mark Twain at Lake Tahoe that taints his literary legacy and tarnishes the factual basis of history.

Chapter 7

Epilogue – A Final Farewell

Following his lectures in Virginia City and Carson City in late April 1868, Mark Twain lingered to visit with old friends. He left Nevada on May 4. Though he vowed to return, he never did.

From Carson City, he journeyed to Sacramento by stagecoach and then on to San Francisco the next day. His stage trip from Carson City took him through Lake Tahoe; it would be the last time he would gaze upon "the fairest picture the whole earth affords."

I Remember, as if It Were Yesterday

As Twain approached the milestone of his 70th birthday, his fans and friends honored and besieged him with appearance requests. The patriotic citizens of Reno, Nev. planned a weeklong Independence Day celebration in 1905 and selected Mark Twain as their guest of honor. The organizers tasked Robert Fulton with the job of inviting Twain to attend. Fulton came to Nevada in 1877 as the land agent for the Southern Pacific Railroad. He later owned the *Reno Evening Gazette* and was an early advocate of a Truckee River diversion project to support irrigated agriculture. Fulton's May 12, 1905 invitation letter appealed to Twain's warm memories of the early years in Nevada.

Mr. Samuel M. (sic) Clemens

Elmira, N.Y.

I have a delicate yet pleasing task; the attempt to honor one of America's citizens, whom I have never seen and who has never heard of me.

Your recollections doubtless turn to Nevada at times for I have never known a man to quite forget her sunny skies, her wide expanse of bold landscapes, her fine sunsets and her hospitable people. She certainly reciprocates any kindly sentiments you may entertain, for she never has given up her claim as one of the scenes of your early life and beginnings of your fame. ...

By order of our citizens I am a committee of one to invite Mark Twain to attend and deliver the oration. The suggestion has created a great deal of enthusiasm here and the whole people of Nevada, and I believe of California as well, would delight in the opportunity to make your visit to the West one which you would remember with pleasure as long as you live.

...

You will find some old friends and many new ones. No doubt most of those you knew have made new homes in other lands, some are dead but the Pioneers of the early '60s are by no means rare and they as well as later comers unite to make you welcome.

...

Robert Larden Fulton

Apparently, Fulton's insightful mention of "'60s Pioneers" captured Twain's interest, though it was not enough to entice him back to

Nevada. On May 24, 1905, Twain responded to Fulton's invitation, interspersed with sentimental reminisces.

> *I remember, as if it were yesterday, that when I disembarked from the overland stage in front of the Ormsby in Carson City in August, 1861, I was not expecting to be asked to come again. I was tired, discouraged, white with alkali dust, and did not know anybody; and if you had said then, "Cheer up, desolate stranger, don't be down-hearted— pass on, and come again in 1905," you cannot think how grateful I would have been and how gladly I would have closed the contract. Although I was not expecting to be invited, I was watching out for it, and was hurt and disappointed when you started to ask me and changed it to, "How soon are you going away?"*
>
> *But you have made it all right, now, the wound is closed. And so I thank you sincerely for the invitation; and with you, all Reno, and if I were a few years younger I would accept it, and promptly. I would go. I would let somebody else do the oration, but, as for me, I would talk— just talk. I would renew my youth; and talk--and talk--and talk --and have the time of my life! I would march the unforgotten and unforgettable antiques by, and name their names, and give them reverent Hailand-farewell as they passed...*
>
> *Those were the days! —those old ones. They will come no more. Youth will come no more. They were so full to the brim with the wine of life; there have been no others like them. It chokes me up to think of them. Would you like me to come out there and cry? It would not beseem my white head.*
>
> *Good-bye. I drink to you all. Have a good time— and take an old man's blessing.*
>
> *Mark Twain*

Friends in Carson City had hoped to see him once more to relive old times and invited him out for a visit. From New York on December 6, 1905, he sent a final two-part message expressing gratitude using the dual personas of Mark Twain and Samuel L. Clemens.

> *To you, & to all my known & unknown friends who have light and the weight of my seventieth birthday with kind words and good wishes. I offer my most grateful thanks & beg leave to sign myself*
>
> *Your and their obliged friend*
>
> *Mark Twain*
>
> *...*
>
> *Oh, no, bless you I love them well, but I am very old & twice as lazy & shall never do any work again except under compulsion of hunger & cold.*
>
> *Truly Yours,*
>
> *SLC*

As he had anticipated, Mark Twain's passing on April 21, 1910 coincided with the return of Halley's Comet; an apt bookend to the birth of Samuel L. Clemens on the previous return cycle of Halley's Comet in 1835.

Appendix I

Selections from the Literature of Mark Twain

In this chapter we have excerpted and abridged the most prominent writings and lecture remarks by Samuel L. Clemens and Mark Twain relevant to Lake Tahoe. Omitted is offensive pejorative and racist language; it is substituted with the book author's replacement terms.

Excerpt of letter to Jane Clemens, undated, probably September 20-23, 1861:

[First part missing]

...The level ranks of flame were relieved at intervals by the standard-bearers, as we called the tall dead trees, wrapped in fire, and waving their blazing banners a hundred feet in the air. Then we could turn from this scene to the Lake, and see every branch, and leaf, and cataract of flame upon its bank perfectly reflected as in a gleaming, fiery mirror. The mighty roaring of the conflagration, together with our solitary and somewhat unsafe position (for there was no one within six miles of us,) rendered the scene very impressive. Occasionally, one of us would remove his pipe from his mouth and say, "Superb! magnificent! Beautiful! but-by the Lord God Almighty, if we attempt to sleep in this little patch tonight, we'll never live till morning! for if we don't burn up, we'll certainly suffocate." But he was persuaded to sit up until we felt pretty safe as far as the fire was concerned, and then we turned in, with many misgivings. When we got up in the morning, we found that the fire had burned small pieces of drift wood within six feet of our boat, and had made its way to within 4 or 5 steps of us on the South side. We looked like lava men, covered as we were with ashes, and begrimed with smoke. We were very black in the face, but we soon washed ourselves white again.

John D. Kinney, a Cincinnati boy, and a first-rate fellow, too, who came out with Judge Turner, was my comrade. We staid at the Lake four days--I had plenty of fun, for John constantly reminded me of Sam Bowen when we were on our campaign in Missouri. But first and foremost, for Annie's, Mollies, and Pamela's comfort, be it known that I have never been guilty of profane language since I have been in this Territory, and Kinney hardly ever swears.--But sometimes human nature gets the better of him. On the second day we started to go by land to the lower camp, a distance of three miles, over the mountains, each carrying an axe. I don't think we got lost exactly, but we wandered four hours over the steepest, rockiest and most dangerous piece of country in the world. I couldn't keep from laughing at Kinney's distress, so I kept behind, so that he could not see me. After he would get over a dangerous place, within finite labor and constant apprehension, he would stop, lean on his axe, and look around, then behind, then ahead, and then drop his head and ruminate awhile.--Then he would draw a long sigh, and say: "Well— could any Billygoat have scaled that place without breaking his --- -- ---- neck?" And I would reply, "No,--I don't think he could." "No-- you don't think he could--" (mimicking me,) "Why don't you curse the infernal place? You know you want to.--I do, and will curse the --- ------ thieving country as long as I live." Then we would toil on in silence for awhile. Finally I told him--"Well, John, what if we don't find our way out of this today--we'll know all about the country when we do get out." "Oh stuff--I know enough--and too much about the d---d villainous locality already." Finally, we reached the camp. But as we brought no provisions with us, the first subject that presented itself to us was, how to get back. John swore he wouldn't walk back, so we rolled a drift log apiece into the Lake, and set about making paddles, intending to straddle the logs and paddle ourselves back home sometime or other. But the Lake objected--got stormy, and we had to give it up. So we set out for the only house on this side of the Lake--three miles from there, down the shore. We found the way without any trouble, reached there before sundown, played three games of cribbage, borrowed a dug-out and pulled back six miles to the upper camp. As we had eaten nothing since sunrise, we did not waste time in cooking our supper or in eating it, either.

After supper we got out our pipes--built a rousing camp fire in the open air-established a faro bank (an institution of this country,) on our huge flat granite dining table, and bet white beans till one o'clock, when John went to bed. We were up before the sun the next morning, went out on the Lake and caught a fine trout for breakfast. But unfortunately, I spoilt part of the breakfast. We had coffee and tea boiling on the fire, in coffee-pots and fearing they might not be strong enough, I added more ground coffee, and more tea, but--you know mistakes will happen.--I put the tea in the coffee-pot, and the coffee in the teapot--and if you imagine that they were not villainous mixtures, just try the effect once.

...

In a day or two we shall probably go to the Lake and build another cabin and fence, and get everything into satisfactory trim before our trip to Esmeralda about the first of November.

...

Love to the young folks,

Sam.

Excerpt from Chapter 20 of Innocents Abroad, published in 1869:

...

Breakfast in the morning, and then the lake [Como].

I did not like it yesterday. I thought Lake Tahoe was much finer. I have to confess now, however, that my judgment erred somewhat, though not extravagantly. I always had an idea that Como was a vast basin of water, like Tahoe, shut in by great mountains. Well, the border of huge mountains is here, but the lake itself is not a basin. It is as crooked as any brook, and only from one-quarter to two-thirds as wide as the Mississippi. There is not a yard of low ground on either side of it-- nothing but endless chains of mountains that spring abruptly from the water's edge and tower to altitudes varying from a thousand to two thousand feet. Their craggy sides are clothed with vegetation, and white specks of houses peep out from the luxuriant foliage everywhere; they are even perched upon jutting and picturesque pinnacles a thousand feet above your head.

Again, for miles along the shores, handsome country seats, surrounded by gardens and groves, sit fairly in the water, sometimes in nooks carved by Nature out of the vine-hung precipices, and with no ingress or egress save by boats. Some have great broad stone staircases leading down to the water, with heavy stone balustrades ornamented with statuary and fancifully adorned with creeping vines and bright-colored flowers--for all the world like a drop curtain in a theatre, and lacking nothing but long-waisted, high-heeled women and plumed gallants in silken tights coming down to go serenading in the splendid gondola in waiting.

A great feature of Como's attractiveness is the multitude of pretty houses and gardens that cluster upon its shores and on its mountain sides. They look so snug and so homelike, and at eventide when every thing seems to slumber, and the music of the vesper bells comes stealing over the water, one almost believes that nowhere else than on the lake of Como can there be found such a paradise of tranquil repose.

From my window here in Bellaggio, I have a view of the other side of the lake now, which is as beautiful as a picture. A scarred and wrinkled precipice rises to a height of eighteen hundred feet; on a tiny bench half way up its vast wall, sits a little snowflake of a church, no bigger than a martin-box, apparently; skirting the base of the cliff are a hundred orange groves and gardens, flecked with glimpses of the white dwellings that are buried in them; in front, three or four gondolas lie idle upon the water--and in the burnished mirror of the lake, mountain, chapel, houses, groves and boats are counterfeited so brightly and so clearly that one scarce knows where the reality leaves off and the reflection begins!

The surroundings of this picture are fine. A mile away, a grove-plumed promontory juts far into the lake and glasses its palace in the blue depths; in midstream a boat is cutting the shining surface and leaving a long track behind, like a ray of light; the mountains beyond are veiled in a dreamy purple haze; far in the opposite direction a tumbled mass of domes and verdant slopes and valleys bars the lake, and here indeed does distance lend enchantment to the view--for on this broad canvas, sun and clouds and the richest of atmospheres have blended a thousand tints together, and over its surface the filmy lights and shadows drift, hour after hour, and glorify it with a beauty that seems reflected out of Heaven itself. Beyond all question, this is the most voluptuous scene we have yet looked upon.

Last night the scenery was striking and picturesque. On the other side crags and trees and snowy houses were reflected in the lake with a wonderful distinctness, and streams of light from many a distant window shot far abroad over the still waters. On this side, near at hand, great mansions, white with moonlight, glared out from the midst of masses of foliage that lay black and shapeless in the shadows that fell from the cliff above--and down in the margin of the lake every feature of the weird vision was faithfully repeated.

Today we have idled through a wonder of a garden attached to a ducal estate--but enough of description is enough, I judge.

I suspect that this was the same place the gardener's son deceived the Lady of Lyons with, but I do not know. You may have heard of the passage somewhere:

"A deep vale,

Shut out by Alpine hills from the rude world,

Near a clear lake margined by fruits of gold

And whispering myrtles:

Glassing softest skies, cloudless,

Save with rare and roseate shadows;

A palace, lifting to eternal heaven its marbled walls,

From out a glossy bower of coolest foliage musical with birds."

That is all very well, except the "clear" part of the lake. It certainly is clearer than a great many lakes, but how dull its waters are compared with the wonderful transparence of Lake Tahoe! I speak of the north shore of Tahoe, where one can count the scales on a trout at a depth of a hundred and eighty feet. I have tried to get this statement off at par here, but with no success; so I have been obliged to negotiate it at fifty percent discount. At this rate I find some takers; perhaps the reader will receive it on the same terms--ninety feet instead of one hundred and eighty. But let it be remembered that those are forced terms--Sheriff's sale prices. As far as I am privately concerned, I abate not a jot of the original assertion that in those strangely magnifying waters one may count the scales on a trout (a trout of the large kind,) at a depth of a hundred and eighty feet--may see every pebble on the bottom--might even count a paper of dray-pins. People talk of the transparent waters of the Mexican Bay of Acapulco, but in my own experience I know they cannot compare with those I am speaking of. I have fished for trout, in Tahoe, and at a measured depth of eighty-four feet I have seen them put their noses to the bait and I could see their gills open and shut. I could hardly have seen the trout themselves at that distance in the open air.

As I go back in spirit and recall that noble sea, reposing among the snow-peaks six thousand feet above the ocean, the conviction comes strong upon me again that Como would only seem a bedizened little courtier in that august presence.

Sorrow and misfortune overtake the legislature that still from year to year permits Tahoe to retain its unmusical cognomen! Tahoe! It suggests no crystal waters, no picturesque shores, no sublimity. Tahoe for a sea in the clouds: a sea that has character and asserts it in solemn calms at times, at times in savage storms; a sea whose royal seclusion is guarded by a cordon of sentinel peaks that lift their frosty fronts nine thousand feet above the level world; a sea whose every aspect is impressive, whose belongings are all beautiful, whose lonely majesty types the Deity!

Tahoe means grasshoppers. It means grasshopper soup. It is Indian, and suggestive of Indians. They say it is Pi-ute [Paiute]--possibly it is [derogatory name for a California or Nevada Native American]. I am satisfied it was named by the [derogatory name for a California or Nevada Native American]--those degraded savages who roast their dead relatives, then mix the human grease and ashes of bones with tar, and "gaum" it thick all over their heads and foreheads and ears, and go caterwauling about the hills and call it mourning. These are the gentry that named the Lake.

People say that Tahoe means "Silver Lake"--"Limpid Water"--"Falling Leaf." Bosh. It means grasshopper soup, the favorite dish of the [derogatory name for a California or Nevada Native American tribe],--and of the Pi-utes [Paiutes] as well. It isn't worth while, in these practical times, for people to talk about Indian poetry--there never was any in them--except in the Fenimore Cooper Indians. But they are an extinct tribe that never existed. I know the Noble Red Man. I have camped with the Indians; I have been on the warpath with them, taken part in the chase with them--for grasshoppers; helped them steal cattle; I have roamed with them, scalped them, had them for breakfast. I would gladly eat the whole race if I had a chance.

But I am growing unreliable. I will return to my comparison of the lakes. Como is a little deeper than Tahoe, if people here tell the truth. They say it is eighteen hundred feet deep at this point, but it does not look a dead enough blue for that. Tahoe is one thousand five hundred and twenty-five feet deep in the centre, by the state geologist's measurement. They say the great peak opposite this town is five thousand feet high: but I feel sure that three thousand feet of that statement is a good honest lie. The lake is a mile wide, here, and maintains about that width from this point to its northern extremity-- which is distant sixteen miles: from here to its southern extremity-- say fifteen miles--it is not over half a mile wide in any place, I should think. Its snow-clad mountains one hears so much about are only seen occasionally, and then in the distance, the Alps. Tahoe is from ten to eighteen miles wide, and its mountains shut it in like a wall. Their summits are never free from snow the year round. One thing about it is very strange: it never has even a skim of ice upon its surface, although lakes in the same range of mountains, lying in a lower and warmer temperature, freeze over in winter.

...

Excerpt from Chapter 48 of Innocents Abroad, published in 1869:

...

The celebrated Sea of Galilee is not so large a sea as Lake Tahoe by a good deal -- it is just about two-thirds as large. And when we come to speak of beauty, this sea is no more to be compared to Tahoe than a meridian of longitude is to a rainbow. The dim waters of this pool can not suggest the limpid brilliancy of Tahoe; these low, shaven, yellow hillocks of rocks and sand, so devoid of perspective, can not suggest the grand peaks that compass Tahoe like a wall, and whose ribbed and chasmed fronts are clad with stately pines that seem to grow small and smaller as they climb, till one might fancy them reduced to weeds and shrubs far upward, where they join the everlasting snows. Silence and solitude brood over Tahoe; and silence and solitude brood also over this lake of Genessaret. But the solitude of the one is as cheerful and fascinating as the solitude of the other is dismal and repellant.

In the early morning one watches the silent battle of dawn and darkness upon the waters of Tahoe with a placid interest; but when the shadows sulk away and one by one the hidden beauties of the shore unfold themselves in the full splendor of noon; when the still surface is belted like a rainbow with broad bars of blue and green and white, half the distance from circumference to centre; when, in the lazy summer afternoon, he lies in a boat, far out to where the dead blue of the deep water begins, and smokes the pipe of peace and idly winks at the distant crags and patches of snow from under his cap-brim; when the boat drifts shoreward to the white water, and he lolls over the gunwale and gazes by the hour down through the crystal depths and notes the colors of the pebbles and reviews the finny armies gliding in procession a hundred feet below; when at night he sees moon and stars, mountain ridges feathered with pines, jutting white capes, bold promontories, grand sweeps of rugged scenery topped with bald, glimmering peaks, all magnificently pictured in the polished mirror of the lake, in richest, softest detail, the tranquil interest that was born with the morning deepens and deepens, by sure degrees, till it culminates at last in resistless fascination!

It is solitude, for birds and squirrels on the shore and fishes in the water are all the creatures that are near to make it otherwise, but it is not the sort of solitude to make one dreary. Come to Galilee for that. If these unpeopled deserts, these rusty mounds of barrenness, that never, never, never do shake the glare from their harsh outlines, and fade and faint into vague perspective; that melancholy ruin of Capernaum; this stupid village of Tiberias, slumbering under its six funereal plumes of palms; yonder desolate declivity where the swine of the miracle ran down into the sea, and doubtless thought it was better to swallow a devil or two and get drowned into the bargain than have to live longer in such a place; this cloudless, blistering sky; this solemn, sailless, tintless lake, reposing within its rim of yellow hills and low, steep banks, and looking just as expressionless and unpoetical (when we leave its sublime history out of the question,) as any metropolitan reservoir in christendom -- if these things are not food for rock me to sleep, mother, none exist, I think.

Chapters 22 and 23 of Roughing It, published in 1872:
Chapter XXII.

It was the end of August, and the skies were cloudless and the weather superb. In two or three weeks I had grown wonderfully fascinated with the curious new country and concluded to put off my return to "the States" awhile. I had grown well accustomed to wearing a damaged slouch hat, blue woolen shirt, and pants crammed into boot-tops, and gloried in the absence of coat, vest and braces. I felt rowdyish and "bully," (as the historian Josephus phrases it, in his fine chapter upon the destruction of the Temple). It seemed to me that nothing could be so fine and so romantic. I had become an officer of the government, but that was for mere sublimity. The office was an unique sinecure. I had nothing to do and no salary. I was private Secretary to his majesty the Secretary

and there was not yet writing enough for two of us. So Johnny K----
and I devoted our time to amusement. He was the young son of an
Ohio nabob and was out there for recreation. He got it.

We had heard a world of talk about the marvelous beauty of Lake
Tahoe, and finally curiosity drove us thither to see it. Three or four
members of the Brigade had been there and located some timber
lands on its shores and stored up a quantity of provisions in their
camp. We strapped a couple of blankets on our shoulders and took
an axe apiece and started--for we intended to take up a wood ranch
or so ourselves and become wealthy. We were on foot. The reader
will find it advantageous to go horseback. We were told that the
distance was eleven miles. We tramped a long time on level ground,
and then toiled laboriously up a mountain about a thousand miles
high and looked over. No lake there. We descended on the other
side, crossed the valley and toiled up another mountain three or four
thousand miles high, apparently, and looked over again. No lake yet.
We sat down tired and perspiring, and hired a couple of [Chinese
men] to curse those people who had beguiled us. Thus refreshed, we
presently resumed the march with renewed vigor and determination.
We plodded on, two or three hours longer, and at last the Lake burst
upon us--a noble sheet of blue water lifted six thousand three
hundred feet above the level of the sea, and walled in by a rim of
snow-clad mountain peaks that towered aloft full three thousand feet
higher still! It was a vast oval, and one would have to use up eighty
or a hundred good miles in traveling around it. As it lay there with
the shadows of the mountains brilliantly photographed upon its still
surface I thought it must surely be the fairest picture the whole earth
affords.

We found the small skiff belonging to the Brigade boys, and without
loss of time set out across a deep bend of the lake toward the
landmarks that signified the locality of the camp. I got Johnny to
row--not because I mind exertion myself, but because it makes me
sick to ride backwards when I am at work. But I steered. [See Figure

52] A three-mile pull brought us to the camp just as the night fell, and we stepped ashore very tired and wolfishly hungry. In a "cache" among the rocks we found the provisions and the cooking utensils, and then, all fatigued as I was, I sat down on a boulder and superintended while Johnny gathered wood and cooked supper. Many a man who had gone through what I had, would have wanted to rest.

It was a delicious supper--hot bread, fried bacon, and black coffee. It was a delicious solitude we were in, too. Three miles away was a saw-mill and some workmen, but there were not fifteen other human beings throughout the wide circumference of the lake. As the darkness closed down and the stars came out and spangled the great mirror with jewels, we smoked meditatively in the solemn hush and forgot our troubles and our pains. In due time we spread our blankets in the warm sand between two large boulders and soon feel asleep, careless of the procession of ants that passed in through rents in our clothing and explored our persons. Nothing could disturb the sleep that fettered us, for it had been fairly earned, and if our consciences had any sins on them they had to adjourn court for that night, any way. The wind rose just as we were losing consciousness, and we were lulled to sleep by the beating of the surf upon the shore.

It is always very cold on that lake shore in the night, but we had plenty of blankets and were warm enough. We never moved a muscle all night, but waked at early dawn in the original positions, and got up at once, thoroughly refreshed, free from soreness, and brim full of friskiness. There is no end of wholesome medicine in such an experience. That morning we could have whipped ten such people as we were the day before-- sick ones at any rate. But the world is slow, and people will go to "water cures" and "movement cures" and to foreign lands for health. Three months of camp life on Lake Tahoe would restore an Egyptian mummy to his pristine vigor, and give him an appetite like an alligator. [See Figure 86] I do not mean the oldest and driest mummies, of course, but the fresher ones.

The air up there in the clouds is very pure and fine, bracing and delicious. And why shouldn't it be?--it is the same the angels breathe. I think that hardly any amount of fatigue can be gathered together that a man cannot sleep off in one night on the sand by its side. Not under a roof, but under the sky; it seldom or never rains there in the summer time. I know a man who went there to die. But he made a failure of it. He was a skeleton when he came, and could barely stand. He had no appetite, and did nothing but read tracts and reflect on the future. Three months later he was sleeping out of doors regularly, eating all he could hold, three times a day, and chasing game over mountains three thousand feet high for recreation. And he was a skeleton no longer, but weighed part of a ton. This is no fancy sketch, but the truth. His disease was consumption. I confidently commend his experience to other skeletons.

I superintended again, and as soon as we had eaten breakfast we got in the boat and skirted along the lake shore about three miles and disembarked. We liked the appearance of the place, and so we claimed some three hundred acres of it and stuck our "notices" on a tree. It was yellow pine timber land--a dense forest of trees a hundred feet high and from one to five feet through at the butt. It was necessary to fence our property or we could not hold it. That is to say, it was necessary to cut down trees here and there and make them fall in such a way as to form a sort of enclosure (with pretty wide gaps in it). [See Figure 63] We cut down three trees apiece, and found it such heart-breaking work that we decided to "rest our case" on those; if they held the property, well and good; if they didn't, let the property spill out through the gaps and go; it was no use to work ourselves to death merely to save a few acres of land. Next day we came back to build a house--for a house was also necessary, in order to hold the property. We decided to build a substantial log-house and excite the envy of the Brigade boys; but by the time we had cut and trimmed the first log it seemed unnecessary to be so elaborate, and so we concluded to build it of saplings. However, two saplings, duly cut and trimmed, compelled recognition of the fact that a still modester architecture would satisfy the law, and so we concluded to build a "brush" house. We devoted the next day to this work, but we did so much "sitting around" and discussing, that by the middle of the afternoon we had achieved only a half-way sort of affair which one of us had to watch while the other cut brush, lest if both turned our backs we might not be able to find it again, it had such a strong family resemblance to the surrounding vegetation. But we were satisfied with it.

We were land owners now, duly seized and possessed, and within the protection of the law. Therefore we decided to take up our residence on our own domain and enjoy that large sense of independence which only such an experience can bring. Late the next afternoon, after a good long rest, we sailed away from the Brigade camp with all the provisions and cooking utensils we could carry off--borrow is the more accurate word-- and just as the night was falling we beached the boat at our own landing.

Chapter XXIII.

If there is any life that is happier than the life we led on our timber ranch for the next two or three weeks, it must be a sort of life which I have not read of in books or experienced in person. We did not see a human being but ourselves during the time, or hear any sounds but those that were made by the wind and the waves, the sighing of the pines, and now and then the far-off thunder of an avalanche. The forest about us was dense and cool, the sky above us was cloudless and brilliant with sunshine, the broad lake before us was glassy and clear, or rippled and breezy, or black and storm-tossed, according to Nature's mood; and its circling border of mountain domes, clothed with forests, scarred with land-slides, cloven by canons and valleys, and helmeted with glittering snow, fitly framed and finished the noble picture. The view was always fascinating, bewitching, entrancing. The eye was never tired of gazing, night or day, in calm or storm; it suffered but one grief, and that was that it could not look always, but must close sometimes in sleep.

We slept in the sand close to the water's edge, between two protecting boulders, which took care of the stormy night-winds for us. We never took any paregoric to make us sleep. At the first break of dawn we were always up and running foot-races to tone down excess of physical vigor and exuberance of spirits. That is, Johnny was--but I held his hat. While smoking the pipe of peace after breakfast we watched the sentinel peaks put on the glory of the sun, and followed the conquering light as it swept down among the shadows, and set the captive crags and forests free. We watched the tinted pictures grow and brighten upon the water till every little detail of forest, precipice and pinnacle was wrought in and finished, and the miracle of the enchanter complete. Then to "business." [See Figure 70]

That is, drifting around in the boat. We were on the north shore. There, the rocks on the bottom are sometimes gray, sometimes white. This gives the marvelous transparency of the water a fuller advantage than it has elsewhere on the lake. We usually pushed out a hundred yards or so from shore, and then lay down on the thwarts, in the sun, and let the boat drift by the hour whither it would. We seldom talked. It interrupted the Sabbath stillness, and marred the dreams the luxurious rest and indolence brought. The shore all along was indented with deep, curved bays and coves, bordered by narrow sand-beaches; and where the sand ended, the steep mountain-sides rose right up aloft into space--rose up like a vast wall a little out of the perpendicular, and thickly wooded with tall pines.

So singularly clear was the water, that where it was only twenty or thirty feet deep the bottom was so perfectly distinct that the boat seemed floating in the air! Yes, where it was even eighty feet deep. Every little pebble was distinct, every speckled trout, every hand's-breadth of sand. Often, as we lay on our faces, a granite boulder, as large as a village church, would start out of the bottom apparently, and seem climbing up rapidly to the surface, till presently it threatened to touch our faces, and we could not resist the impulse to seize an oar and avert the danger. But the boat would float on, and the boulder descend again, and then we could see that when we had been exactly above it, it must still have been twenty or thirty feet below the surface. Down through the transparency of these great depths, the water was not merely transparent, but dazzlingly, brilliantly so. All objects seen through it had a bright, strong vividness, not only of outline, but of every minute detail, which they would not have had when seen simply through the same depth of atmosphere. So empty and airy did all spaces seem below us, and so strong was the sense of floating high aloft in mid-nothingness, that we called these boat-excursions "balloon-voyages."

We fished a good deal, but we did not average one fish a week. We could see trout by the thousand winging about in the emptiness under us, or sleeping in shoals on the bottom, but they would not bite--they could see the line too plainly, perhaps. We frequently selected the trout we wanted, and rested the bait patiently and persistently on the end of his nose at a depth of eighty feet, but he would only shake it off with an annoyed manner, and shift his position.

We bathed occasionally, but the water was rather chilly, for all it looked so sunny. Sometimes we rowed out to the "blue water," a mile or two from shore. It was as dead blue as indigo there, because of the immense depth. By official measurement the lake in its centre is one thousand five hundred and twenty-five feet deep!

Sometimes, on lazy afternoons, we lolled on the sand in camp, and smoked pipes and read some old well-worn novels. At night, by the camp-fire, we played euchre and seven-up to strengthen the mind-- and played them with cards so greasy and defaced that only a whole summer's acquaintance with them could enable the student to tell the ace of clubs from the jack of diamonds.

We never slept in our "house." It never recurred to us, for one thing; and besides, it was built to hold the ground, and that was enough. We did not wish to strain it.

By and by our provisions began to run short, and we went back to the old camp and laid in a new supply. We were gone all day, and reached home again about night-fall, pretty tired and hungry. While Johnny was carrying the main bulk of the provisions up to our "house" for future use, I took the loaf of bread, some slices of bacon, and the coffee-pot, ashore, set them down by a tree, lit a fire, and went back to the boat to get the frying-pan. While I was at this, I heard a shout from Johnny, and looking up I saw that my fire was galloping all over the premises! Johnny was on the other side of it. He had to run through the flames to get to the lake shore, and then we stood helpless and watched the devastation.

The ground was deeply carpeted with dry pine-needles, and the fire touched them off as if they were gunpowder. It was wonderful to see with what fierce speed the tall sheet of flame traveled! My coffee-pot was gone, and everything with it. [See Figure 65] In a minute and a half the fire seized upon a dense growth of dry manzanita chapparal six or eight feet high, and then the roaring and popping and crackling was something terrific. We were driven to the boat by the intense heat, and there we remained, spell-bound.

Within half an hour all before us was a tossing, blinding tempest of flame! It went surging up adjacent ridges--surmounted them and disappeared in the canons beyond--burst into view upon higher and farther ridges, presently--shed a grander illumination abroad, and dove again-- flamed out again, directly, higher and still higher up the mountain-side- -threw out skirmishing parties of fire here and there, and sent them trailing their crimson spirals away among remote ramparts and ribs and gorges, till as far as the eye could reach the lofty mountain-fronts were webbed as it were with a tangled network of red lava streams. Away across the water the crags and domes were lit with a ruddy glare, and the firmament above was a reflected hell!

Every feature of the spectacle was repeated in the glowing mirror of the lake! Both pictures were sublime, both were beautiful; but that in the lake had a bewildering richness about it that enchanted the eye and held it with the stronger fascination.

We sat absorbed and motionless through four long hours. We never thought of supper, and never felt fatigue. But at eleven o'clock the conflagration had traveled beyond our range of vision, and then darkness stole down upon the landscape again.

Hunger asserted itself now, but there was nothing to eat. The provisions were all cooked, no doubt, but we did not go to see. We were homeless wanderers again, without any property. Our fence was gone, our house burned down; no insurance. Our pine forest was well scorched, the dead trees all burned up, and our broad acres of manzanita swept away. Our blankets were on our usual sand-bed, however, and so we lay down and went to sleep. The next morning we started back to the old camp, but while out a long way from shore, so great a storm came up that we dared not try to land. So I baled out the seas we shipped, and Johnny pulled heavily through the billows till we had reached a point three or four miles beyond the camp. The storm was increasing, and it became evident that it was better to take the hazard of beaching the boat than go down in a hundred fathoms of water; so we ran in, with tall white-caps following, and I sat down in the stern-sheets and pointed her head-on to the shore. The instant the bow struck, a wave came over the stern that washed crew and cargo ashore, and saved a deal of trouble. We shivered in the lee of a boulder all the rest of the day, and froze all the night through. In the morning the tempest had gone down, and we paddled down to the camp without any unnecessary delay. We were so starved that we ate up the rest of the Brigade's provisions, and then set out to Carson to tell them about it and ask their forgiveness. It was accorded, upon payment of damages.

We made many trips to the lake after that, and had many a hair-breadth escape and blood-curdling adventure which will never be recorded in any history.

Excerpt from a lecture given on December 14, 1871 in Lansing, Mich.:

...

Now if you would see the noblest, loveliest inland lake in the world, you should go to Lake Tahoe. It is just on the boundary line between California and Nevada. I have seen some of the world's celebrated lakes and they bear no comparison with Tahoe. There it is, a sheet of perfectly pure, limpid water, lifted up 6,300 feet above the sea -- a vast oval mirror framed in a wall of snowclad mountain peaks above the common world. Solitude is king, and in that realm calm silence is brooding always. It is the home of rest and tranquility and gives emancipation and relief from the griefs and plodding cares of life. Could you but see the morning breaking there, gilding those snowy summits and then creeping gradually along the slopes until it sets, the lake and woodlands, free from mist, all agleam, you would see old Nature, the master artist, painting these dissolving views on the still water and finally grouping all these features into a complete picture. Every little dell, the mountains with their dome-turned pinnacles, the cataracts and drifting clouds, are all exquisitely photographed on the burnished surface of the lake, suffused with the softest and richest color. This lake is ten miles from Carson City, and in company with a friend we used to foot it out there, taking along provisions and blankets -- camp out on the lake shore two or three weeks at a time; not another human being within miles of us. We used to loaf about in the boat, smoke and read, sometimes play seven-up to strengthen the mind. It's a sinful game, but it's mighty nice. We'd just let the boat drift and drift wherever it wanted to. I can stand a deal of such hardship and suffering when I'm healthy. And the water was so wonderfully clear. Where it was 80 feet deep the pebbles on the bottom were just as distinct as if you held them in your hand; and in that clear white atmosphere it seemed as if the boat was drifting through the air. Out in the middle it was a deep dark indigo blue, and the official measurement made by the State Geologist of California shows it to be 1,525 feet deep in the center. You can imagine that it would take a great many churches and steeples piled one upon another before they would be perceptible above its surface. You might use up a great deal of ecclesiastical architecture in that way. Now, notwithstanding that lake is lifted so high up among the clouds, surrounded by the everlasting snowcapped mountain-peaks, with its surface higher than Mt. Washington in the East, and notwithstanding the water is pretty shallow around the edges, yet the coldest winter day in the recollection of humanity was never known to form ice upon its surface. It has no feeders but the little mountain rills, yet it never rises nor falls. Donar [Donner] Lake, close by, freezes hard every winter. Why Lake Tahoe does not is a question which no scientist has ever been able to explain.

If there are any consumptives here I urge them to go out there, renew their age, make their bodies hale and hearty, in the pure, magnificent air of Lake Tahoe. If it don't cure you I'll bury you at my own expense. It will cure you. I met a man there -- he had been a man once, but now he was only a shadow, and a very poor sort of shadow at that. That man took the thing very deliberately. He had fixed up things comfortable while he did stay, but he was in dead earnest. Thought he was going to die sure, but he made a sickly failure of it. He had brought along a plan of his private graveyard, some drawings of different kinds of coffins, and he never did anything but sit around all day and cipher over these plans, to get things to suit him, and try to find out which coffin would be the most becoming. Well, I met that man three months afterward. He was chasing mountain sheep over mountains seven miles high with a Sharp's rifle. He didn't get them, but he was chasing them just the same. He had used up his graveyard plans for wadding and had sent home for some more. Such a cure as that was! Why, when I first saw that man his clothes fitted him about as a circus tent fits the tentpole; now they were snug to him; they stuck to him like postage stamps, and he weighed a ton. Yes, he weighed more than a ton, but I will throw in the odd ounces, I'm not particular about that, eleven I think it was. I know what I am talking about, for I took him to the hay scales and weighed him myself. A lot of us stood on there with him. But I hope you won't mind my nonsense about it. It was really a wonderful cure, and if I can persuade any consumptive to go out there I shall feel at any rate that I have done one thing worth having lived to accomplish. And if there is a consumptive in this house I want to say to him: Shoulder your gun, go out there and hunt. It's the noblest hunting ground on earth. You can hunt there a year and never find anything -- except mountain sheep; but you can't get near enough to them to shoot one. You can see plenty of them with a spyglass. Of course you can't shoot mountain sheep with a spyglass. It is our American Shamwah [Chamois] (I believe that is the way that word is pronounced -- I don't know), with enormous horns, inhabiting the roughest mountain fastnesses, so exceedingly wild that it is impossible to get within rifleshot of it. There was no other game in that country when I was there -- except seven-up; though one can see a California quail now and then -- a proud, stately, beautiful bird, with a curved and graceful plume on top of its head. But you can't shoot one. You might as well try to kill a cast-iron dog. They don't mind a mortal wound any more than a man would mind a scratch.

...

Appendix II

Lake Tahoe Campsites Sequence and Identification

Reconstructing the sequence of campsites requires semantic analysis of Twain's previous writings and logical reasoning together with knowledge of the setting. These are applied to the basic hierarchical rules used in this book for interpretation of Twain's writings, i.e., the letters take precedence as the most credible source, followed by the narrative in *Roughing It*, amplified by lecture remarks. In this analysis, we present relevant passages from the 1861 letters for comparison to Twain's nearly 10-year old recollection and fictional embellishments added for humor and entertainment in *Roughing It*. We follow with our interpretation of the more credible of the passages to support a conclusion for that chronological point. The chronological sequence begins with Sam Clemens and friend John Kinney leaving Carson City on the first day.

Day 1

Roughing It – "We strapped a couple of blankets on our shoulders and took an axe apiece and started--for we intended to take up a wood ranch or so ourselves and become wealthy. We were on foot. The reader will find it advantageous to go horseback. We were told that the distance was eleven miles."

Letter – Any relevant text was either lost or not mentioned.

Lectures – Twice mentioned 10 miles as the distance.

Interpretation – Both men walked 11 miles from Carson City to Lake Tahoe.

Day 1, Continued

Roughing It – 'We found the small skiff belonging to the Brigade boys, and without loss of time set out across a deep bend of the lake toward the landmarks that signified the locality of the camp. A three-mile pull brought us to the camp just as the night fell … In a "cache" among the rocks we found the provisions and the cooking utensils…'

Letter – Any relevant text was either lost or not mentioned.

Interpretation – Both men are at the Brigade cache site at the end of the first day.

Day 1, Continued

Roughing It – "In due time we spread our blankets in the warm sand between two large boulders and soon feel asleep…"

Letter – Any relevant text was either lost or not mentioned.

Interpretation – Both men camped overnight at the Brigade cache site.

Day 2

Roughing It - "I superintended again, and as soon as we had eaten breakfast we got in the boat and skirted along the lake shore about three miles and disembarked. We liked the appearance of the place, and so we claimed some three hundred acres of it and stuck our "notices" on a tree."

Letter - *"On the second day we started to go by land to the lower camp, a distance of three miles, over the mountains, each carrying an axe."*

Interpretation - Both traveled on foot from the Brigade cache site to the lower camp that is the same as the timber claim site.

Day 2, Continued

Roughing It - No relevant text appears.

Letter - *"So we set out for the only house on this side of the Lake--three miles from there, down the shore. We found the way without any trouble, reached there before sundown, played three games of cribbage, borrowed a dug-out and pulled back six miles to the upper camp."*

Interpretation - Both men continued travel on foot for another three miles, found an empty cabin, played card games, and paddled a dugout canoe six miles back to Brigade cache site (upper camp).

Day 2, Continued

Roughing It – No relevant text appears.

Letter – *"After supper we got out our pipes--built a rousing camp fire in the open air--established a faro bank (an institution of this country,) on our huge flat granite dining table, and bet white beans till one o'clock, when John went to bed."*

Interpretation – At the Brigade cache site (upper camp), both men dined, played a card game on a flat granite rock and slept overnight.

Day 3

Roughing It – 'I superintended again, and as soon as we had eaten breakfast we got in the boat and skirted along the lake shore about three miles and disembarked. We liked the appearance of the place, and so we claimed some three hundred acres of it and stuck our "notices" on a tree. It was necessary to fence our property or we could not hold it. That is to say, it was necessary to cut down trees here and there and make them fall in such a way as to form a sort of enclosure (with pretty wide gaps in it). We cut down three trees apiece…'

Letter – *"We were up before the sun the next morning, went out on the Lake and caught a fine trout for breakfast. But unfortunately, I spoilt part of the breakfast. We had coffee and tea boiling on the fire, in coffee-pots and fearing they might not be strong enough, I added more ground coffee, and more tea, but--you know mistakes will happen.--I put the tea in the coffee-pot, and the coffee in the teapot-- and if you imagine that they were not villainous mixtures, just try the effect once."*

Interpretation – In the morning, they caught a Lahontan cutthroat trout for breakfast and Clemens accidently mixes the coffee and tea. Both men then traveled by boat back to the timber claim site (lower camp) and began the process to claim the land by posting notices and attempting to construct a rudimentary fence.

Day 3, Continued

Roughing It – "Next day [Day 4] we came back to build a house -- for a house was also necessary, in order to hold the property."

Letter – Any relevant text was either lost or not mentioned.

Interpretation – Although the passage is speaking about fourth day's activities, it strongly implies that both men returned to the Brigade cache site (upper camp) and camped there on the third night.

Day 4

Roughing It – "Next day we came back to build a house – for a house was also necessary, in order to hold the property."

Letter – Any relevant text was either lost or not mentioned.

Interpretation – Both men travel by boat to the timber claim site (lower camp).

Day 4, Continued

Roughing It – 'We decided to build a substantial log-house ... we concluded to build a "brush" house. We devoted the next day to this work, but we did so much "sitting around" and discussing, that by the middle of the afternoon we had achieved only a half-way sort of affair ...'

Letter – Any relevant text was either lost or not mentioned.

Interpretation – The *Roughing It* passage seems to cover two days of work on the house, but an earlier segment from the letter is clear that they spent only four days (and nights) at the lake. Both men worked on the brush house and both return to Brigade cache site (upper camp) that night.

Day 5

Roughing It – "Late the next afternoon, after a good long rest, we sailed away from the Brigade camp with all the provisions and cooking utensils we could carry off…"

Letter – Any relevant text was either lost or not mentioned.

Interpretation – Late in the afternoon, both men traveled by skiff to timber claim site (lower camp) with supplies.

Day 5, Continued

Roughing It – "... I took the loaf of bread, some slices of bacon, and the coffee-pot, ashore, set them down by a tree, lit a fire, and went back to the boat to get the frying-pan. While I was at this, I heard a shout from Johnny, and looking up I saw that my fire was galloping all over the premises ..."

Letter – The letter contains a description of the fire but any reference to the day was either omitted or missing.

Interpretation – The wildfire occurred on the evening of the fifth day at the lake.

Day 6

Roughing It – "We were so starved that we ate up the rest of the Brigade's provisions, and then set out to Carson to tell them about it..."

Letter – Any relevant text was either lost or not mentioned.

Interpretation – Both men traveled by skiff and foot back to Carson City.

Day 6, Continued

Roughing It – "The next morning we started back to the old camp, but while out a long way from shore, so great a storm came up that we dared not try to land. So I baled out the seas we shipped, and Johnny pulled heavily through the billows till we had reached a point three or four miles beyond the camp. The storm was increasing, and it became evident that it was better to take the hazard of beaching the boat than go down in a hundred fathoms of water; so we ran in, with tall white-caps following, and I sat down in the stern-sheets and pointed her head-on to the shore. The instant the bow struck, a wave came over the stern that washed crew and cargo ashore, and saved a deal of trouble. We shivered in the lee of a boulder all the rest of the day, and froze all the night through."

Letter – Any relevant text was either lost or not mentioned.

Interpretation – It seems plausible the boat-swamping incident occurred but it is not clear if this happened on the first or second timber scouting effort. The latter element of spending yet another night at the lake seems improbable for the first trip since Clemens was clear in his letter that they were at the lake only four days.

Use of "Upper Camp" and "Lower Camp" to Identify Campsites

Key to the understanding of the campsite sequence is decoding Clemens' use of "upper" and "lower" as identifying labels for each of the two campsites. In this context, the paired words can have a geographical, topographical or hierarchical connotation. If geographical, upper could mean north and lower could mean south. If topographical, upper could refer to a place of greater elevation and lower to a place of lesser elevation. If hierarchical, upper could mean superior or primary, and lower could mean subordinate or secondary. For the real answer to Twain's use of upper and lower, we look to how he used the terms elsewhere in his travel writings.

While in Kona, Hawaii in 1866, he wrote a dispatch to the *Sacramento Daily Union* on his visit to Kealakekua Bay. Twain gave us the clearest indication of use of the terms in his description the bay's shoreline, "… a steep wall of lava, a thousand feet high at the upper end and three or four hundred at the lower, comes down from the mountain and bounds the inner extremity of it."

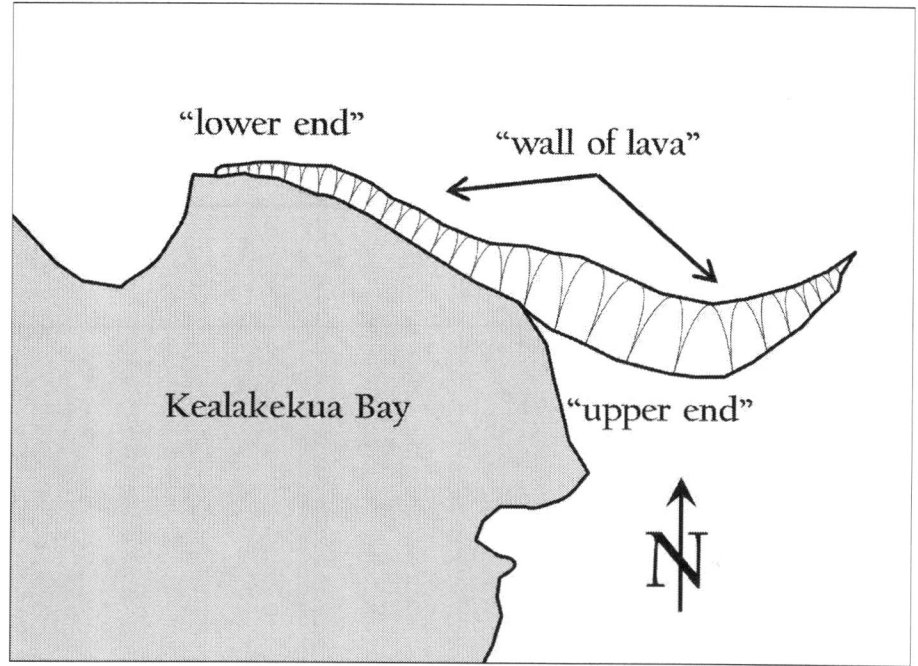

Figure 123. Map of Kealakekua Bay showing Mark Twain's use of the terms "upper" and "lower" to denote the height of adjoining terrain

Here, the "upper" location is the higher in elevation but southwest of the "lower" in elevation location. Figure 123 illustrates Twain's use of terminology in the description.

In *Life on the Mississippi*, Twain used the two words in different contexts; but he always used them to denote height or elevation differences, e.g., upper and lower decks of a steamboat, upper and lower parts of a flooded plantation, and upper and lower sections of a river.

Another way to identify the campsites is to match quotes from Clemens' letter to the respective site.

- *"On the second day we started to go by land to the lower camp ..."* This means they had to be at upper camp on the morning of the second day when they started out for lower camp.

- Continuing on the second day, *"Finally, we reached the camp. But as we brought no provisions with us, the first subject that presented itself to us was, how to get back."* This means they were now at the timber claim site where there was no food or supplies stored.

- After hiking another three miles to the vacant cabin, they then *"...pulled back six miles to the upper camp."* This means they paddled back past the timber claim to the food and supplies cache site at upper camp.

- Once they paddled over the six miles to upper camp, they *"...established a faro bank (an institution of this country,) on our huge flat granite dining table."* This means they were at the food and supplies cache site where they found a flat granite rock.

Sources

Alpine County Historical Society. (2005). *Images of America: Alpine County, Bear Valley, Kirkwood and Markleeville.* Charleston: Arcadia Publishing.

Anonymous. (1860, April). Notes and Sketches of the Washoe Country. *Hutching's California Magazine.*

Anonymous. (1860, May 19). The Wonders of Washoe. *New York Times.*

Anonymous. (1863, September 5). Mark Twain. *Evening Bulletin.*

Anonymous. (1863, December 17). Mark Twain. *Virginia Evening bulletin.*

Anonymous. (1864, August 21). San Francisco to Virginia City in Twenty-four Hours. *Daily Alta California*, p. 1.

Anonymous. (1868, April 22, 23, 24, 27). Mark Twain. *The Virginia City (Nevada) Daily Trespass.*

Anonymous. (1871, December 21). [Transcription of Lecture by Mark Twain]. *The (Lansing, Mich.) State Republican .*

Anonymous. (1871, December 16). Lecture by Mark Twain. *The (Grand Rapids) Daily Morning Democrat.*

Anonymous. (n.d.). *September 2010 Calendar.* Retrieved May 8, 2011, from Calendar-365.com: http://www.calendar-365.com/

Antonucci, D. C. (2010). *The Natural World of Lake Tahoe.* Homewood: Art of Learning.

Antonucci, D. C., & Layne, M. (2005, August 4). Mark Twain's Route to Lake Tahoe. *Fifth International Conference on the State of Mark Twain Studies.* Elmira: Elmira College.

Bancroft, H. H. (1890). *History of Nevada 1540-1888.* San Francisco: The History Company.

Basso, D. (1986). *Nevada Historical Marker Guidebook.* Las Vegas: Nevada Publications.

Bender, H. J. (2011). The Southern Pacific Lines and Truckee. *The Ferroequinologist*, 1-6.

Bohren, C. F. (1987). *Clouds in a Glass of Beer.* Mineola: Dover Publications, Inc.

Branch, E. M., & Hirst, R. H. (1979). *The Works of Mark Twain - Early Tales & Sketches: 1851-1864, Volume I.* Berkeley: University of California Press.

Browne, J. R. (1959). *A Peep at Washoe (1860-61).* Balboa Island: Paisano Press.

Browne, J. R. (1959). *Washoe Revisited (1863).* Balboa Island: Paisano Press.

Bucke, R. M. (1883, June). The Development of the Country - Twenty Five Years Ago. *Overland Monthly.*

Carson City, Nevada . (2010). *City Facts.* Retrieved October 22, 2010, from Carson City, Nevada : http://www.carson.org/

Carson Valley Historical Society. (1991). *Snowshoe Thompson.* Gardnerville: Carson Valley Historical Society.

Coates, G. (2011, July 2). *History of the Truckee Area.* Retrieved July 4, 2011, from Truckee Donner: http://truckeehistory.org/

Copp, H. N. (1884). *The American Settlers Guide.* Inquirer P. & P. Co.: Lancaster.

DeQuille, D. (1864, April). Mark Twain Takes a Lesson in the Manly Art. *Territorial Enterprise.*

DeQuille, D. (1885, March 29). Comstock Reminiscences. A Thrilling Romance That Was Never Written. *Daily Alta California.*

Division of Many Circles Foundation. (2007, August 21). *Washoe.* Retrieved October 13, 2010, from Four Directions Institute: fourdir.com/washoe.htm

Duane, T. P. (1999). *Shaping the Sierra: nature, culture and conflict in the changing west.* Berkeley: University of California Press.

Duncan, J. E. (2004). *To Donner Pass from the Pacific.* Newcastle: Jack E. Duncan.

Duryea, C. K. (2003). *Fire in the Wildland-Urban Interface: Understanding Fire Behavior.* Gainesville: University of Florida.

Elliott-Fisk, Deborah; et al. (1996). *Lake Tahoe Case Study.* Davis: University of California, Centers for Water and Wildland Resources.

Espenak, F. (2010, May 23). *Phases of the Moon: 1861 to 1870.* Retrieved May 8, 2011, from Moon Phases & Eclipses: http://www.life-cycles-destiny.com/

Evans, R. M. (1860). Official Map of the Washoe Mining Region. San Francisco, California: Britton & Co.

Farquhar, F. P., & Brewer, W. H. (1930). *Up and Down California in 1860-1864; The Journal of William H. Brewer.* New Haven: Yale University Press.

fish4travel. (2010). *Virginia City.* Retrieved July 1, 2011, from Virginia City - The Old Washoe Club: http://www.visitvirginiacity.org/saloons/old_washoe_club.html

Fitzgerald, O. (n.d.). *Indians of California.* Retrieved July 14, 2011, from Native American Nations: http://www.nanations.com/

General Land Office. (1861-65). Public Land Survey Plats. California and Nevada Territory.

Godfrey, A. (1994). *Pony Express National Historic Trail Historic Resource Study.* Washington: U.S. Department of the Interior, National Park Service.

Greuner, L. (1971). *Lake Valley's Past.* South Lake Tahoe: The Lake Tahoe Historical Society.

Hastings, J. M. (1862). *Scenes of Wonder and Curiosity in California.* San Francisco: J.M. Hastings Co.

Hayes, C. (2006). *To Truckee's Trail.* San Antonio: Booklocker.com, Inc.

Hinkle, G., & Hinkle, B. (1949). *Sierra Nevada Lakes.* Indianapolis: Bobbs-Merrill Company.

Howard, T. F. (1998). *Sierra Crossing -- First Roads to California.* Los Angeles: University of California Press.

Hymanson, Z. P., & Collopy, M. W. (2010). *An Integrated Science Plan for the Lake Tahoe Basin: Conceptual Framework and Research Strategies.* Albany: U.S. Department of Agriculture, Forest Service, Pacific Southwest Research Station.

James, G. W. (1906). Letter to Mark Twain. New York, New York.

James, G. W. (1914). *California Romantic and Beautiful.* Boston: The Page Company.

James, G. W. (1915). *The Lake of the Sky - Lake Tahoe.* New York: J. F. Tapley Co.

James, G. W. (1919, May). Mark Twain: An Appreciation of His Pioneer Writings on Fasting and Health. *Physical Culture.*

Jordan, D. S. (1922). *Days of a Man, Volume I, 1851-1899.* Yonkers: World Book Company.

King, M. (1891). *King's Handbook of the United States.* New York: Moses King Corporation.

Landauer, L. B. (1996). *The Mountain Sea, A History of Tahoe, 2nd Ed.* Honolulu: Flying Cloud Press.

Lankford, S. (2010). *Tahoe Beneath the Surface.* Berkeley: Heyday Books.

Lekisch, B. (1988). *Tahoe Place Names.* Lafayette: Great West Books.

Lekisch, B. (2003). *Embracing Scenes About Lakes Tahoe & Donner.* Lafayette: Great West Books.

Lillard, R. (1942, May). Hank Monk and Horace Greeley. *American Literature.*

Lindstrom, S., & Wechter, S. (1996). *North Shore Ecosystems Project Heritage Resources Inventory - California Area.* South Lake Tahoe: Lake Tahoe Basin Management Unit.

Lyman, F. (2011, January 15). Truth in the Rough. *SEJournal.*

Mack, E. M. (1947). *Mark Twain in Nevada.* New York: Charles Scribner's Sons.

Mark Twain Project. (2007-11). *Letters.* Retrieved 2011, from Mark Twain Project Online: http://www.marktwainproject.org/homepage.html

McGauhey, P., Eliassen, R., Rohlich, G., Ludwig, H. F., Pearson, E. A., & Engineering-Science. (1963). *Comprehensive Study on Protection of Water Resources of the Lake Tahoe Basin.* South Lake Tahoe: Lake Tahoe Area Council.

Muir, J., & Gifford, T. (1996). *John Muir: His Life and letters and Other Writings.* Seattle: The Mountaineers.

Murphy, D. D., & Knopp, C. M. (2000). *Lake Tahoe Watershed Assessment: Volumes I & II.* Albany: United States Department of Agriculture, Forest Service.

National Geographic Holdings. (2009). Trails Illustrated Explorer 3D Version 4.3.7. *Trails Illustrated Sierra.* Evergreen, Colorado, United States: National Geographic Maps.

Nevada Department of Transportation. (2010, September 14). *Mark Twain in Tahoe 1861: Which Way Did He Go?* Carson City: Nevada Department of Transportation.

Nevada Historical Society. (1917). *Nevada Historical Society Papers 1913-1916.* Carson City: State of Nevada.

Nevers, J. A. (1976). *Wa She Shu: a Washo Tribal History.* Reno: Inter-Tribal Council of Nevada.

Obermayr, E. (2005). *Footpath to Four Lane.* Carson City: Nevada Department of Transportation.

Paine, A. B. (1912). *Mark Twain, A Biography.* New York: Harper & Brothers.

Pitter, R. (1995). *Hank Monk: He'll Get You There on time.* Honolulu: Flying Cloud.

Poppoff, L. (2006, August 18). Science Raises Hope for Basin-wide Restoration. *North Lake Tahoe Bonanza.*

Powell, M. (2003). *Donner Summit -- A Brief History.* Grass Valley: Cottage Hill Publishing.

Project Gutenberg Australia eBook. (2009, October). *Mark Twain Newspaper Articles 1862-1881*. Australia.

Railton, S. (2011). *Roughing It Selected Illustrations.* Retrieved May 24, 2011, from Mark Twain: His Times: http://etext.virginia.edu/railton/index2.html

Rasmussen, R. K. (2008). *Bloom's How to Write about Mark Twain.* New York: Infobase Publishing.

Richards, G. (2006, May 5). Emigrants and extinction: Wildlife impacted by settlement. *Sierra Sun.*

Richards, G. (2006, July 11). Tahoe City in 1873: not quite a booming metropolis. *Sierra Sun.*

Robert H. Osborne, M. C. (1985). *Sedimentology of the Littoral Zone in Lake Tahoe, California-Nevada.* Sacramento: California State Lands Commission.

Salamo, L., Smith, H. E., & Browning, R. P. (2001, August 9). *Mark Twain at Large: His Travels Here and Abroad.* Retrieved January 27, 2011, from UC Berkeley Library: http://bancroft.berkeley.edu/Exhibits/MTP/

Sanborn, M. (1990). *Mark Twain: The Bachelor Years.* New York: Doubleday.

Schmidt, B. (n.d.). *Cases of Mistaken Identity: Mark Twain and His Lookalikes; Same Hair, Different Brains.* Retrieved January 2011, from twainquotes: http://www.twainquotes.com/

Schmidt, L. J. (2009, Fall). Locating Mark Twain's 1861 Timber Camp at Lake Tahoe. *Nevada Historical Society Quarterly*, pp. 213-232.

Schneider, S. J. (2010). Space Observations of Inland Water Bodies Show Rapid Surface Warming Since 1985. *Geophysical Research Letters.*

Schultz, K. (2011). *Cutthroat Trout Fishing*. Retrieved May 24, 2011, from GoFISHn - Tell Your Story: www.gofishn.com

Scott, E. B. (1957). *Saga of Lake Tahoe, Volumes I & II*. Crystal Bay: Sierra-Tahoe Publishing.

Shuck, O. T. (1869). *California Scrap-Book: A Repository of Useful Reading*. New York: H. H. Bancroft & Company.

Stangroom, M. (1860, August 8). Placer County and Washoe Wagon Road. *Sacramento Daily Union*.

State Water Resources Control Board. (1980). *Lake Tahoe Basin Water Quality Plan*. Sacramento: State Water Resources Control Board.

Stewart, G. R. (1962). *The California Trail*. Lincoln: University of Nebraska Press.

Supernowicz, D. E. (1995-96). Surmounting the Sierra: The Opening of the Johnson Cutoff Route, 1850-55. *Overland Journal*, 11-20.

Tahoe Regional Planning Agency. (1998). *Water Quality Management Plan for the Lake Tahoe Region*. Zephyr Cove: Tahoe Regional Planning Agency.

Tahoe Regional Planning Agency. (2010). *Code of Ordinances*. Stateline: Tahoe Regional Planning Agency.

Taylor, A. H. (2004, December). Identifying Forest Reference Conditions on Early Cut-over Lands, Lake Tahoe Basin, USA. *Ecological Applications Journal*, pp. 1903-1920.

Thompson & West. (1881). *History of Nevada*. Oakland: Thompson & West.

Traveler. (1864, May 30). Letter from Silver Mountain District. *Daily Alta California*.

Twain, M. (1863, December 12). Letter from Mark Twain. *Territorial Enterprise*.

Twain, M. (1863, August 19). Letter from Mark Twain. *Virginia City Territorial Enterprise.*

Twain, M. (1863, December 12). Letter from Mark Twain -- The Logan Hotel. *Virginia City Territorial Enterprise.*

Twain, M. (1863, January 6). Local Column - Free Fight. *Virginia City Territorial Enterprise.*

Twain, M. (1863, August 13). Mark Twain's Letter. *Daily Morning Call.*

Twain, M. (1864, April 30). Dan Reassembled. *Territorial Enterprise.*

Twain, M. (1864, February). Legislative Proceedings. *Virginia City Territorial Enterprise.*

Twain, M. (1864, April 28). Letter from Mark Twain. *Territorial Enterprise.*

Twain, M. (1864, September 4). The Californian. *Daily Morning Call.*

Twain, M. (1866, August 24). Still in Kona -- Concerning Matters and Things, Captain Cook's Death Place. *Sacramento Daily Union.*

Twain, M. (1867, June 16). Jeff. Davis. *San Francisco Alta California.*

Twain, M. (1868, January 19). Letter from Mark Twain. The Holy Land Excursion. *Daily Alta.*

Twain, M. (1868, May 31). The Summit of the Sierras—From Flowers to Snow Drifts - Up Among the Clouds. *The Chicago Republican.*

Twain, M. (1869). *Innocents Abroad, or The New Pilgrims' Progress.* Hartford: American Publishing Company.

Twain, M. (1880). *A Tramp Abroad.* Hartford: American Publishing Company.

Twain, M. (1906). *Life on the Mississippi.* New York: Harper and Brothers Publishers.

Twain, M. (1993). *Roughing It (Mark Twain Project version)*. Berkeley: University of California Press.

U.S. Fish and Wildlife Service . (2010, September 14). *Lahontan cutthroat trout*. Retrieved October 22, 2010, from Nevada Fish & Wildlife Office: http://www.fws.gov/nevada/protected_species/fish/species/lct.html

University of California, Davis. (2000). *Annual Progress Report - Water Quality, Air Quality and Forest Health; Research, Monitoring and Modeling*. Davis: University of California.

Volunteers in Technical Assistance. (1980). *Overshot Waterwheel: A Design and Construction Manual*. Arlington: VITA.

Washoe Cultural Resources Office. (2009). *Wa She Shu: "The Washoe People" Past and Present*. Gardnerville: Washoe Tribe of Nevada and California.

Wild, P. (1990). *George Wharton James*. Boise: Boise State University.

Williams, G. J. (1994). *On the Road with Mark Twain in California and Nevada*. Dayton: Tree by the River Publishing.

Wilson, D. (1992). *Sawdust Trails in the Truckee Basin*. Nevada City: Nevada County Historical Society.

About the Author

David C. Antonucci has resided in the Lake Tahoe area for over 35 years. He holds bachelor and master degrees in civil and environmental engineering from California State Polytechnic University and Oregon State University, respectively. He is a licensed professional civil engineer in California. He has pursued a successful professional career at the senior manager and policy level positions in the public sector since 1973. He currently serves on the boards of several not-for-profit organizations and a public agency. He additionally operates a part-time consulting practice in civil and environmental engineering and presentation development.

David's interest in Mark Twain's adventures at Lake Tahoe began when he enrolled in a community college class on Lake Tahoe history. For a term paper assignment, he chose to analyze Mark Twain's route and locations of his encampments at Lake Tahoe based on the *Roughing It* account. This led to rediscovery of Mark Twain's Ash Canyon-Washoe Trail route to Lake Tahoe and campsite locations on the North Shore. With co-author and noted Mark Twain impressionist McAvoy Layne, they presented their findings to an appreciative audience of respected scholars at the 2005 Conference on Mark Twain Studies at Elmira College, Elmira, New York.

In 2010, David published *Snowball's Chance – The Story of the 1960 Olympic Winter Games, Squaw Valley and Lake Tahoe*. The book won the Ullr Award from the International Skiing History Association for its substantial contribution in book form to skiing history. It is the primary source and only book devoted solely to the history of the VIII Olympic Winter Games.

David enjoys studying the science and environmental issues and natural history of Lake Tahoe. He is currently working on his next book, *The Natural World of Lake Tahoe*. He frequently gives multimedia presentations to visitors and conference groups on Lake Tahoe natural history interpretation, Mark Twain at Lake Tahoe, and the 1960 Olympic Winter Games. He also does presentation development consulting using the PowerPoint multimedia platform. To arrange speaking engagements, book signings or presentation development consulting, please visit his web site www.TahoeFacts.com or contact him at (530) 525-5410.

The author enjoys cross-country and alpine skiing, snowshoeing, mountain and road biking, flat water kayaking, hiking and camping. He resides in Tahoma, California with his wife and son.

Acknowledgements

Jeff Kintop of the Nevada State Archive provided help in locating historical maps. Brian Barton of California State Parks kindly reviewed parts of the chapter on Mark Twain's Lake Tahoe. Jeff Cowen and Jason Ramos of the Tahoe Regional Planning Agency retrieved scientific reports for reference. Chad Blanchard of the Federal Watermaster's office helped with historical hydrology of the Tahoe area. David Borges, D.C. carefully reviewed the historical elements for factual accuracy. United States Geological Survey geologist Jim Howle collaborated on the writing of the geologic formation description of Lake Tahoe and the explanation of flat-surface granite rocks along the shore. *Sacramento Bee* writer Tom Knudson provided insight and encouragement to endure this writing project. Susan Lindstrom provided original research on pre-contact forest conditions on the North Shore. Ann Lindemann edited certain chapters and Kelly McElravey proofread the manuscript. Bob and Nancy Maddox made available their boat on Lake Tahoe for offshore photography. McAvoy Layne of the Mark Twain Cultural Center in Incline Village, Nev. read and commented on certain chapters. Liz Posas of the Braun Library at the Autry National Center of the American West assisted in retrieving and researching documents within the George Wharton James collection. Jenny Antonucci patiently and carefully reviewed the manuscript and provided constructive comments. And a world of thanks to all who have encouraged the author to bring truth of Mark Twain's experiences at Lake Tahoe to a greater audience.

Index

19th century beliefs on health, 142
Antonucci, David C., 287
Ash Canyon, directions to, 184
Atmospheric conditions: Reduced visibility in 19th century, 14
Barter, Dick, 72
Bigler-Tahoe name change, 165; Closet Confederate theory, 166; DeGroot changes name, 166; Letter to Grub, 166; Naming history, 165; Tahoe means grasshopper, 168
Blackwood, Hampton. See Settlements and resorts: Blackwood's cabin
Brewer, William H.: Impression of Lake Tahoe, 11
Browne, J. Ross: Impression of Lake Tahoe, 12
Cabin with dugout canoe location, directions to, *190*
Campsites at Lake Tahoe: Chronology, 268; Use of upper and lower as names, 274
Carson City: Description in letter from Sam Clemens, 92; Founding of, 91; Location of, 91; Naming of, 91
Clemens, Orion: Secretary of the Territory, 89; Trip to West, 90
Clemens, Sam: Hears about Lake Tahoe, 95; Helping Orion Clemens, 94; Impression of Lake Tahoe, 10; Meets John Kinney, 95; Ormsby House residence, 94; Partnership with Kinney, 95; Reason for traveling to Nevada, 89; Trip to West, 90
Climatic conditions: 19th century, 13; Mid-19th century changes, 13; Perennial snowcap, 13
Creation of Nevada Territory, 89
DeQuille, Dan, *159*; Twain nose parody, *160*
Discovery of silver, 4
Donner Summit train trip, 151; Central Pacific Railroad history, 152; Chicago Republican article, 153; Dutch Flat-Donner Lake Toll Road, 154; Mark twain passes by Donner Lake, 154; Sends telegram from Truckee, 155; Transfer to sleigh, 154; Transfer to stagecoach, 154; Twain confuses Cisco and Donner Summit, 154; Virginia City lecture, 152
Dutch Flat-Donner Lake Toll Road, directions to, 198
East Shore timber claim myth: Cabin not vacant, 221; Campsite chronology, 218; Campsites description, 216; Color of submerged boulders, 228; Confusion over cache and Nye timber claim, 209; Cove misnamed and rejected, 241; Distance to blue water, 232; Forest size, 224; Glenbrook Bay, 213; Glenbrook sawmill not operating, 215; Illogical approaches, 208; Initial view restricted by terrain, 226; Kings Canyon-Clear Creek

route, 210; Mentioned in Saga of Lake Tahoe, 208; No beach existed, 234; No cabin found, 221; North Shore location statement, 228; Population estimate conflict, 214; Preponderance of evidence comparison, 240; Started by tour boat captains, 208; Submerged boulders of insufficient size, 238; Synopsis, 206; Twain biographical writer disputes, 238; Wildfire advancement description, 236; Wildfire scars absent, 236

Fairest picture vista point, directions to, 185

Fisheries and fishing: Abundance of fish, 25; Fish species occurrence, 26; Lahontan cutthroat extinction, *27*

Forests and logging: Destruction by logging companies, 24; Early logging history, 20; Long-term consequences, 25; Onset of industrial logging, 21; Pre-contact forest conditions, 19

Fremont, John: Discovery of Lake Tahoe, 3; Impression of Lake Tahoe, 4

Fulton, Robert, 243

Hidden Beach. *See* Timber claim travel: Hidden Beach

Hidden Beach, directions to, *186*

Holladay, Ben Jr.. *See* Settlements and resorts: The Cottage

Interpreting the writings of Mark Twain: Accuracy of *Roughing It* illustrations, 86; Accuracy of *Roughing It* lectures, 87; Comparison of multiple sources, 80; *Innocents Abroad* exaggerations and inaccuracies, 87; Mark Twain or Samuel L. Clemens speaking, 80; Multidisciplinary approach, 79; News articles accuracy, 87; *Roughing It* as creative nonfiction, 81; *Roughing It* avalanche error, 84; *Roughing It* Lake Tahoe circumference error, 83; *Roughing It* Lake Tahoe depth error, 84; *Roughing It* Lake Tahoe population error, 83; *Roughing It* many trips to Lake Tahoe error, 86; *Roughing It* number of timber claim trips, 83; *Roughing It* sawmill location error, 85; *Roughing It* timber claim time frame error, 81; *Roughing It* wildfire exaggeration, 85

Invitation to come to Carson City, 246

Invitation to come to Reno, 241

Irish Brigade, 94; Timber claim, 23

James, George Wharton: Lectures in Nevada, *139*; Mark Twain sources, *139*, *140*; Names location of timber claim. *See* Timber claim: Location

Kinney, John. *See* Clemens, Sam: Meets John Kinney; Civil War record, *139*

Lake House: Amenities, 143; Guests, 145; Hank Monk stage driver, 144; J. Ross Browne

description, 143; Location, 143; Mark Twain activities, 145; Suffering with cold, 142; Unsuccessful cure to cold, 146; William Brewer description, 144
Lake House location: Directions to, *192*
Lake Tahoe as standard of measurement, 169
Lake Tahoe Basin Statistics and Facts, 6
Lake Tahoe clarity, 178
Lake Tahoe described in Twain lecture, 178
Lake Tahoe first sight by Clemens, 176
Lake Tahoe fish not troublesome, 169
Lake Tahoe forest, 177
Lake Tahoe means grasshopper soup, 174
Lake Tahoe name, 8
Lake Tahoe restores a mummy, 177
Lake Tahoe-Lake Como compared, 172
Lamson, Joseph: Impression of Lake Tahoe, 10
Lincoln, President Abraham. *See* Creation of the Nevada Territory
Logan Hotel: Kings Canyon Road, 149; Mark Twain article, 148; Mark Twain description, 149; Mark Twain visit, 148; Owners, 149
Maritime activities: Beginning of steamboat era, 38; Early history, 37; Sail-powered craft, 37

Mark Twain-Lake Tahoe myths. *See* East Shore timber claim myth; Cascade Lake, 204; East Shore timber claim and fire, 206; Jewel of the Sierra quote, 205; Lake House at Hobart, 204; Lake Shore House, 203; Reasons for, 202; Repetition on Internet, 202; Where encountered, 201; Wrote book at Friday's, 205
Marklee, Jacob, *159*
Masterpiece of the Creator: Supernatural beauty, 165
Meadowlands and agriculture: Impact of Euro-Americans, 36; Pre-contact natural conditions, 35; Use for grazing and animal feed, 36
Monk, Hank. *See* Lake House
Movement of people, goods and information: Bonanza Road traffic, 45; Comstock-bound travelers, 46; Freight and livestock, 50; Pony Express, 52; Snowshoe Thompson, 54; Stagecoach service, 48; Washoe wagons, 50; Winter road conditions, 53
Native American presence and use: Campsite locations, 16; Campsites on the North Shore, 58; Euro-American encroachment, 17; Glenbrook Meadow campsite, 63; Madden Creek campsite, 77; Meeks Bay campsite, 73; Range of foods, 16; Residence of Washoe Tribe, 14; South Shore campsites, 71; Truckee River Outlet campsite, 58; Washoe adaptation to Euro-

American occupation, 17;
Washoe campsites, 16;
Washoe culture, 17; Washoe
fishing, 26; Washoe hunting,
29; Washoe population, 16;
Washoe territory, 15; Washoe
Tribe today, 19
Nose injury, *159*
Nye's horse, *136*; Zephyr Cove
area, *137*
Saxton, Augustus H.. *See*
Settlements and resorts:
Saxton's Sawmill
Sea in the clouds, 181
Settlements and resorts:
Blackwood's cabin, 77;
Friday's Station, 64; Gilmore
Mineral Springs at Glen
Alpine, 72; Glen Brook
House, 63; Glenbrook, 61;
James Nye & Co. cabin, 59;
Knoxville and Claraville
(Squaw Valley), 56; Lake
(Bigler) House, 71; Lake
Valley House, 69; McKinney
Station, 75; Meeks Bay cabin,
72; North Shore cabins, 58;
Pine Grove Station, 58;
Roadhouses and inns on
wagon road, 66; Saxton's
Sawmill, 77; Squaw Valley
and Truckee River Outlet, 56;
Tahoe City, 56; The Cottage
(Emerald Bay), 72; Walton's
cabin, 61; Yank's Station, 67;
Zephyr Cove House, 63
Silver Mountain, 159;
Abandoned, *162*; Esmeralda
stage, *159*; Traveler's article,
162
Silver Mountain City, directions
to, 200

Speedboat Beach (cache site),
direction to, *187*
Steamboat Springs, 146
Stephens-Townsend-Murphy
Party, 8; Angeline Morrison, 8
Submerged boulders drifting
over location, *188*
Tahoe and Sea of Galilee
compared, 170
Timber claim: Bathed in cold
lake water, *136*; Bighorn
sheep, 136; Blue water
location, 134; Boat drifting
"balloon voyages", 131; Boat
swamped, 127; Brush house,
118; Cache site description,
110; Caught trout, 116;
Description, 113; Failed to
complete preemption process,
137; Fence, 116; Fifth day
move camp, 121; Fifth day
relaxation, 119; Flat granite
rock, 115; Fourth day, 116;
Hike to cabin, 115; Located in
California, *138*; Location, 114;
Names of claimants, 127;
Needed sawmill, 130; North
Shore location clues, 131;
Paddle back to cache site, 115;
Sam Clemens Bay theory, 129;
Sawmill misrembered, 110,
See Interpreting the writings of
Mark Twain; Second day, 110;
Second trip, 130; Sixth day
departure, 127; Size of claim,
129; Third day, 116;
Unproductive fishing, 136
Timber claim travel. *See*
Transportation routes: Washoe
Trail; Deep bend of lake, 104;
Determination of true dates,
96; Encounter with Chinese

Index 293

workers, 100; Find skiff and row to campsite, 104; Franktown Creek, 100; Hidden Beach, 104; Initial view of Lake Tahoe, 103; Route to Lake Tahoe, 96; Time frame and possible travel by moonlight, 103; Washoe Trail, 99

Timber claim, directions to, *189*

Transportation routes: Georgetown to Lake Bigler (McKinney Station) Road, 38; Kings Canyon road, 45; Kings Canyon Road and Mark Twain, 45; Kingsbury Grade, 42; Lake Tahoe Wagon Road, 40; Rufus Walton Toll road, 44; Tahoe as passage to Mother Lode, 38; Walton's Landing, 39; Washoe Trail, 39

Trout from Lake Tahoe, 179

Upper camp, 107

von Schmidt, Alexis. *See* Water resources and shorezone, export schemes

Wagon Road, Lam Watah, directions to, 195

Wagon Road, Logan Shoals location, directions to, *194*

Washoe: Mining region, 13

Washoe Tribe. *See* Native American presence and use

Water resources and shorezone: 19th century water temperature, 34; Beach development, 31; Effects of damming of outlet, 32; Growth of attached algae, 34; Precipitation and flooding in early 1860s, 32; Pre-dam conditions, 30; Water clarity, 32; Water export schemes, 29; Watershed disturbance and erosion, 35

Wildfire at timber claim: Burned debris and ash, 125; Campfire starts, 122; Clue to location, 125; Description of fire, 123; Embellishment of description, 126; Observed from beach, 125

Wildlife and hunting: Hunting by emigrants and market hunters, 29; Pre-contact species and distribution, 28; Species loss and recovery, 29; Washoe hunting, 29

Wright, D. H. *See* Settlements and resorts: Pine Grove Station